Th Eyemouth Branch

by
Roger Jermy

THE OAKWOOD PRESS

© Oakwood Press & Roger Jermy 2018

Published by Oakwood Press, an imprint of Stenlake Publishing Ltd, 2018

British Library Cataloguing in Publication Data
A Record for this book is available from the British Library
ISBN 978 0 85361 364 0

Printed by Claro Print, Unit 2, Kirkhill House, 81 Broom Road East, Glasgow,
G77 5LL

This book is dedicated to Jonah and Oscar, my two youngest grandsons

From the same author:
Northern Northumberland's Minor Railways:
Volume One: Brickworks, Forestry, Contractors, Military Target railways
and various other lines (ISBN 978 0 85361 703 7)

Northern Northumberland's Minor Railways:
Volume Two: Colliery & Associated Lines
(ISBN 978 0 85361 704 4)

Northern Northumberland's Minor Railways:
Volume Three: Sandstone, Whinstone & Gravel Lines
(ISBN 978 0 85361 705 1)

Northern Northumberland's Minor Railways:
Volume Four: Limestone Industry Lines
(ISBN 978 0 85361 706 8)

Front cover: 'J39' class 0-6-0 No. 64813 stands at the platform at Eyemouth awaiting departure for Burnmouth with a mixed train in June 1956. *J.G. Wallace/Colour-Rail SC274*

Rear cover, top: The 1 inch to 1 mile Ordnance Survey map of 1955 showing the Eyemouth branch (reproduced to scale). *Crown Copyright*

Rear cover, bottom: Railway Clearing House map showing the Eyemouth branch and surrounding area. *Stenlake Publishing Collection*

Title page: The month is August 1958 as No. 64843, a Tweedmouth 'J39/3' class 0-6-0 hauls its single BCK coach up the steep gradient away from Eyemouth passing Netherbyres (or Eyemouth) Mill in the background. The rails on this section were often made greasy with the fish oils leaking from wagons and wheel-slip could be quite common.
W.J.Verden Anderson/Rail Archive Stephenson

Oakwood Press, 54-58 Mill Square, Catrine, KA5 6RD,
Tel: 01290 551122 *Website:* www.stenlake.co.uk

Contents

This is a delightful study of the station staff at Eyemouth. Depending on the date when this photograph was taken, the gentleman in the hat in the foreground may well be either Mr Mundell or George Miller, both station masters at the start of the 20th century.

Stenlake Publishing Collection

Right: This view of Lower Burnmouth shows part of the local fishing fleet inside the harbour.
Author's Collection

Below: A North British Railway postcard extolled the attractions of the Scottish East Coast as tourist destinations.
Author's Collection

Chapter One

Introduction

Border branches from the East Coast main line

Although the main railway route from London to Edinburgh is known as the East Coast main line, passengers heading northwards from Kings Cross towards the Scottish capital city don't get a glimpse of the North Sea until they approach Alnmouth in Northumberland. From there to Edinburgh the main line is never more than a few miles from the sea, yet despite this, several short branch lines were constructed to create links to locations on the coast. On the English side of the border an independent company constructed and operated the North Sunderland Railway to the fishing port of Seahouses (opened in 1898), whilst south and east of Edinburgh several branches were built from the main line, including what became the North British Railway's (NBR) lines to Gullane (opened in 1898) and North Berwick (opened in 1850). In addition the Eyemouth Railway Company (ERC) created the branch linking Burnmouth to Eyemouth which was opened in 1891, though it, too, was soon absorbed by the North British Railway.

The Gullane branch was closed to passengers in 1932 and to goods traffic in 1964. The North Sunderland Railway (which had 'escaped' the Grouping and later the nationalization of the railways) ceased its operations in entirety in 1951, whilst the Eyemouth branch closed to passenger and goods traffic in early 1962, leaving the North Berwick branch as the single survivor in the 21st century.

Berwickshire

Berwickshire was formerly the most south-easterly county in Scotland. It was named after the town, Berwick-upon-Tweed, which was its historical seat of local government. Later, as Berwick became part of Northumberland, this seat passed to Greenlaw (1596-1890) and then to Duns. Prior to 1975 both Duns and Eyemouth were Scottish Burghs with a certain amount of autonomy in local government terms. In 1973 the management of the area passed to the Borders Regional Council and in 1996 the area became governed by a new unitary authority, the Scottish Borders Council, with its headquarters based in Newtown St Boswells, near Melrose.

For just over 70 years the small branch line linked the coastal port of Eyemouth in Berwickshire with the Berwick-upon-Tweed to Edinburgh main line at Burnmouth. It opened on the 13th April, 1891 and after passing from the Eyemouth Railway to the North British Railway and thence to the London & North Eastern Railway (LNER), it was finally closed by British Railways (BR) on the 5th February, 1962.

The main line northwards to connect Berwick-upon-Tweed with Edinburgh had opened in 1846. Just to the north of Berwick the first branch line to be

1. At the Pier Head : Fishermen Directing Eyemouth Fishing Boats into Harbour.—2. An Eyemouth Fishing Boat Entering the Harbour.—3. Fishing Boats Driven Ashore : The Life Brigade at Work.

THE RECENT GREAT GALES—SKETCHES FROM BURNMOUTH, BERWICKSHIRE

A contemporary engraving illustrated the 1881 storm disaster which devastated Eyemouth and nearby Burnmouth.   *Author's Collection*

A postcard showing a large part of Eyemouth's fishing fleet at the start of the 20th century. The parish church, located near to the station, dominates the skyline.   *Author's Collection*

Eyemouth from the Golf Course

Brown's Series.

opened was that heading inland from Reston to the county town, Dunse, (opened in November 1863) and later through to St Boswells (opened in October 1865); the change of spelling from Dunse to Duns was effected in 1883. The Eyemouth branch was thus a much later arrival on the railway network, though it survived the Duns branch by over 10 years. The Reston to Duns line closed to all services on 10th September, 1951.

Eyemouth

'... dark and cunning of aspect, full of curious alleys, blind and otherwise,
and having no single house of any standing but what could unfold its tale of wonders ...'
(Chambers' Pictures of Scotland)

In *The Post Office Directory* for 1884-85 the River Eye was described as 'falling into the 'German Ocean' (the former name of the North Sea) at a semi-circular bay in which ships could anchor, secure from all winds except those from the north and north-east'. On each side of the bay are whinstone and sandstone rocks forming steep cliffs of over 300 ft in height. The *Directory* refers to Eyemouth, in the 18th century, as being known as a place of 'free trade', in other words, smuggling! This illicit trade is described and illustrated in both the local Eyemouth Museum and at Gunsgreen House by the harbour. By the end of the 19th century the trade had been turned 'into more honourable and less hazardous channels'!

The first harbour was constructed in 1768 under the design of John Smeaton who was an eminent civil engineer responsible for the design of many harbours, canals and lighthouses, including the Coldstream Bridge over the River Tweed and the third Eddystone lighthouse. Smeaton's harbour involved a stone pier on the eastern side and a short jetty on the west. The entrance between these was 154 ft wide. However it was to prove inadequate and enlargement works were completed between 1885 and 1887 by Meik of Edinburgh. The new harbour, which cost over £82,000, involved the creation of a new eastern pier (440 ft long), a west pier (1,050 ft), a middle pier (680 ft) and a harbour quay (500 ft). Much concrete was used in the construction of the walls and the completion of the works created a new basin of 9½ acres in area. The need for such a secure and safe harbour was illustrated dramatically by the huge storm of 14th October, 1881. The effects of this storm are described in detail in Peter Aitchison's book: *Black Friday – The Eyemouth Fishing Disaster of 1881*. This storm was responsible for a huge loss of life, 129 line fishermen from Eyemouth were lost along with 15 vessels of the 41 that had set out earlier.

The fishing industry of Eyemouth took a long time to recover. Before the disaster there were up to 48 boats at Eyemouth setting out to fish for haddock; this was reduced to 28 afterwards. Nearly 100 boats were formerly involved in the herring fishing industry; this reduced to just 70. The number of barrels of herring cured at Eyemouth in 1880 was 58,639, whilst in 1890 the figure reduced to 49,096.

The population in 1890 was nearly 2,700 of whom over 2,500 lived in the town itself. The town had its own gasworks, bank branch, post office and coastguard

The road from the former Burnmouth station leads down 'The Glen' towards the harbour at Lower Burnmouth. In former years fish from the harbour was carted up this very steep slope to the station.   *Author's Collection*

Partanhall is one of the small settlements that makes up part of Lower Burnmouth. This was the location of a group of fishermen's cottages.   *Author's Collection*

station. There were numerous fish curers, coal dealers, a boatbuilder, a sail maker and even a cod liver oil manufacturer! In addition there were all the retail trades one might expect in a town of this size: bakers, butchers, drapers, tailors, a blacksmith, and boot and shoe makers. Today its population is nearer to 3,500. In ecclesiastical terms the town of Eyemouth is part of a Parish of the same name whilst Burnmouth is tied into the Parish of Ayton.

Burnmouth

> *'Burnmouth … a place formerly celebrated for smugglers, and near which are some large stone quarries…'* (Bradshaw's Handbook. 1863)

In fact, Burnmouth is a village divided into several parts. It is located where a small stream or burn carves its way through 300 foot cliffs. There may have been a mill here in the middle ages but no settlement of any size. Upper Burnmouth is a settlement which developed after the construction of the Great North Road, now the A1, and the main line railway, on the section linking Berwick-upon-Tweed and Edinburgh. Burnmouth's station opened in 1846. There were just a few houses located nearby with the Flemington Inn at the side of the main road. This popular establishment burned down in 2006. Burnmouth now houses the aptly-named First and Last Inn close by the site of the former Flemington Inn.

Lower Burnmouth, approached via a very steep road, now consists of three separate groups of cottages, those at Partanhall, the Harbour and Cowdrait. Back in the 1850s the harbour consisted of a just a single pier with its adjacent cottages and a lifeboat station nearby. Today it consists of outer and inner basins, but very much smaller than that at Eyemouth. The first jetty was originally built in the 1830s and extended in 1879. Fishing was always the main occupation at Lower Burnmouth. Five of its vessels were lost, and about 25 Burnmouth men drowned, in the tragic disaster of 1881, though some boats from both Eyemouth and Burnmouth managed to reach the shelter of Burnmouth Harbour.

The other nearby villages

Other small villages will be mentioned in the story of the Eyemouth branch and so it is convenient to mention a little about them for the sake of completeness.

Ayton parish encompassed Burnmouth and its surrounding area. Ayton ('town on the Eye') is an old village through which, until the 1980s, passed the Great North Road. It developed as a settlement with a coaching inn, the Red Lion. Nearby is Ayton Castle, an edifice described by Michael Hall in an edition of *Country Life* magazine as 'a masterly composition, built of red sandstone'. In the 1850s Ayton was already a substantial place with its station (opened in 1846), shops, a school and a 'lock–up' for those who had committed minor misdemeanours! Today its population is around 500.

In the 1880s, Reston was discussed as a possible branch station for the Eyemouth branch. It was already the junction for the line to Duns and St Boswells.   *Author's Collection*

If the Eyemouth branch had commenced at Reston, then Coldingham would have been an intermediate station on the line, offering the possibilities of holiday traffic to the hotel and beach.
                    Author's Collection

Reston, a short distance to the north-west was the next station north from Ayton on the line to Edinburgh and was sometimes referred to as Reston Junction. Like Berwick it had a telegraph station. The station was opened, as at Ayton, in 1846, with the junction for the line to Duns increasing its importance some three years later. At this time the village was a small linear affair located just off the Great North Road on the west side of the Eyewater. This stream provided the power for a couple of water mills and the village was large enough to support its own school. The area around both Ayton and Reston has always been primarily agricultural, with mixed farming involving the rearing of cattle and growing of some grain and turnips. The population of Reston and its surroundings currently numbers about 750. Moves are afoot to reopen Reston station with a train service to Edinburgh and Berwick.

Coldingham, in its own large Parish, was established around an ancient monastery dating back to the seventh century. It is located several miles to the east of the Great North Road and the main line railway. In the 19th century it suffered from a small decline in size and population but it was the centre of a largely farming community, with some fishing boats being based on the coast at St Abbs. Indeed one Coldingham boat and three men were lost in the 1881 storm. In the mid-19th century it possessed a school, two smithies, a post office and a brewery. Today its population is a thriving community of around 600 with tourism playing an increasing part in the local economy. Coldingham has never had a station although some early promoters favoured a route from the main line to Eyemouth via this village. It was linked to the main line station at Reston by horse-drawn conveyances and, later, motor coaches.

The local influence and role of the North British Railway

Although the Eyemouth Railway started out as an independent organization within 10 years it became absorbed by the North British Railway. Indeed the North British Railway provided the line's early locomotives and rolling stock, and operated the Eyemouth Railway's trains from its opening day. Tables detailing these services appeared in NBR timetables, albeit appearing under the heading of the 'Eyemouth Railway'. Some senior officers of the NBR, especially G.B. Wieland, were intimately linked with the early years of the Eyemouth line.

The North British Railway was based at Waterloo Place in Edinburgh. It was established in 1844 and its first main line of railway linked Edinburgh with the English border town of Berwick-upon-Tweed, where, after the completion of the Royal Border Bridge, it made an end-on connection with the North Eastern Railway (NER), whose line approached Berwick from Newcastle-upon-Tyne. It also built branch lines, the first of which linked Haddington to the main line. Later it built a line to Hawick which eventually allowed direct running over the line between Edinburgh and Carlisle. As well as building its own lines the North British absorbed a large number of small independent companies, its network eventually extending into the north of Northumberland and Cumbria as well as southern Scotland. The North British Railway became part of the London and North Eastern Railway at Grouping.

It is low tide as a former North British Railway 0-6-0, now LNER class 'J21', makes its way southwards across the Royal Border Bridge towards its 'new' home, the former North Eastern Railway depot at Tweedmouth. *Author's Collection*

The Anglo-Scottish border

Of course the Royal Border Bridge, spanning the Tweed, does not mark the line of the border between England and Scotland! The site of the border is actually located between the Scottish hamlet of Lamberton and Marshall Meadows in England. It is marked by a prominent sign at the side of the main line rail tracks, visible from passing trains. The sports grounds of the football team, Berwick Rangers, and Berwick's rugby union team are both located south of the Tweed. However, both play all of their matches in Scotland's leagues, perhaps confusing the visitor! Finally the accent and dialect speech of many Berwick residents relates more strongly to those of their cousins over the border to the north rather than to rural Northumberland to the south!

The 'Across the Border' sign was located at the side of the East Coast main line between Lamberton and Marshall Meadows just to the south of Burnmouth station.
Armstrong Railway Photographic Trust

Chapter Two

Possibilities, plans and proposals

The background to the coming of the railway

Eyemouth had had a harbour trust from the end of the 18th century. With ambition, but little in the way of direction, it had failed, in comparison with similar bodies at other east coast ports, to obtain Government cash and develop facilities for fishing. The quays were inadequate and the depth of water in the harbour was poor in comparison to Eyemouth's competitors. Despite this the fishing industry had enjoyed some boom years in the 1860s and 1870s and Eyemouth's population, most of whom were directly or indirectly associated with the fishing trade, reached its maximum.

The North British Railway's Berwick to Edinburgh main line was opened in 1846 but Eyemouth was located several miles to the east of the stations at Burnmouth and Ayton. Other East Coast Scottish fishing ports had much closer rail links. For example, in 1838 the rail line was opened between Forfar and the port of Arbroath and in 1858 the Formartine and Buchan Railway provided a direct link between the ports of Fraserburgh and Peterhead with Aberdeen. Ironically materials, including railway sleepers, metal and plant for the building of the Berwickshire section of the main line railway were unloaded from vessels at Eyemouth!

It is not surprising therefore that the merchants and elders of Eyemouth developed the twin aims of transforming Eyemouth into a premier fishing port with improved quayside facilities, and building a branch railway to facilitate linking their own port with the inland markets, an idea which had been in the backs of local people's minds since August 1846 when a petition was forwarded to the Board of the North British Railway. Then in August 1864 the promoters of a proposed Eyemouth Railway again approached the North British Railway which agreed to work the line if built. However, this proposal also foundered. Later, in early 1872 meetings were held between various interested parties. The local correspondent of *The Scotsman* produced an article which appeared in the newspaper on 22nd February of that year. He referred to applications having been made by the merchants and traders of Eyemouth to the North British Railway Company which expressed their desires to have a line constructed between Eyemouth and Burnmouth. This was important considering the extensive and growing importance of the local fisheries and the need to compete with other fishing stations which had the benefit of direct rail communication to their markets. They suggested that the costs of the line would not exceed £15,000 and that the expected traffic would result in the line paying its way, with dividends payable from the profits. Apart from the fishing industry, mention was made of the chemical manure works in the town and other branches of trade that could benefit from the development.

This article appeared just two days before a public meeting was held in the town on Saturday 24th February, 1872. It was chaired by Major John L'Amy of

Netherbyres, who was an officer in the 1st Berwick Artillery Volunteers. Correspondence had been received from the North British Railway indicating that they were not in a financial position to construct the line. However, if the promoters were to raise the necessary funds to build the line then the NBR was prepared to work it at cost price. A committee was then appointed by the meeting which had been unanimous in its desire to secure the advantages of railway communication for the town. The committee was to form a deputation to meet with local landowner Col Milne Home, to explain their wishes and solicit his aid together with the other landed proprietors of the county. (Milne Home was the landowner of the estates at Wedderburn, Billie and Paxton.) His son, also David Milne Home, who was elected MP for Berwick in 1874 and who would inherit the estates on his father's death, will appear later in the Eyemouth Railway story.

In December 1873 a memo was submitted to the NBR urging their company to construct a branch to Eyemouth but the Board said that such a project could not be entertained on the grounds that the line would not be remunerative. However, Eyemouth was soon to experience a period of extreme bad luck and fortune.

In particular the spring of 1881 was marked by frequent bad storms and consequently the haddock fishery produced low fish catches. Money became short and food kitchens to feed the poor became a necessity. The herring fishery also had a poor summer season. The gales persisted into October until, on 14th of that month, a clear day arrived. The prospect of making a good catch and supplying a market crying out for fish encouraged the Eyemouth fleet to set sail despite the warning of another imminent storm indicated by the falling barometer. The fishermen were not foolhardy, merely desperate.

What followed is considered to be the greatest disaster in the history of the British fishing industry. Of some 45 boats that had left the harbour that morning only 26 returned. A total of 189 men perished in the storm, 129 of these were from Eyemouth. In Eyemouth, 14th October, 1881 is referred to as 'Black Friday'; it became a town of despair with 93 women becoming widows and 267 children becoming deprived of their father. The devastating, chilling and moving story is detailed by Peter Aitchison in his book *'Black Friday'* (*see Bibliography*).

From tragedy arose determination. Earlier in 1881 the harbour trust and the fishermen's own committee, for some time at loggerheads, got together and with the support of the newly elected Liberal Member of Parliament, Edward Marjoribanks, engaged engineer Thomas Meik to produce a new plan for the development of the harbour. Meik's plan which involved extending the harbour into the mouth of the Eye and also out into the bay, was well received as it would provide Eyemouth with a harbour of refuge from storms and also vastly improved facilities for the fishing trade. In addition contacts with the North British Railway identified that this company was prepared to build a line to Eyemouth provided that the new harbour was built and in operation.

Meik's ambitious harbour plans were sent off to London, and sympathetic consideration, especially after 'Black Friday', was hoped for. The cost of the new harbour, following Meik's plans, would be £82,000 (as reported in the *Edinburgh Evening News*, though figures of up to £200,000 have been quoted elsewhere).

The Trust hoped to receive the sum from state funds rather than as a public works loan. The local MP backed the scheme fully. Meanwhile a consortium involving local dignitaries and businessmen was established to act as a provisional committee for steering the creation of the railway branch line through contacts with the North British Railway. However, the news that emanated from London in March 1883 was bleak. There would be no grant of public money.

Despite this the Trust was determined to press on with developing the harbour and further negotiations with the Public Works Loans Commissioners resulted in the granting of a loan of £25,000 secured against the rates of the town as the port revenues were insufficient. This would at least allow the implementation of a small part of Meik's scheme, specifically the dredging of the harbour and the extension of quays into the mouth of the Eye, together with the provision of space for the rail line. Work commenced in late 1884. The *Edinburgh Evening News* of Thursday 22nd October, 1884 contained a report headed *'OPENING OF NEW HARBOUR AT EYEMOUTH'*. The occasion was the laying of a memorial stone by Lady Fanny Marjoribanks. The day had been declared a holiday in the port and the event was well attended. The principal buildings were decked in bunting. A procession, starting in front of the town hall, marched down to the new works. A new boat was launched from Weatherhead's yard but not without incident! A bottle of wine was knocked from Miss Home's hands by a jerking cable from a donkey engine assisting in the launch! A bottle of unfermented wine was substituted! After the National Anthem the procession continued to Saltgreens Quay where the memorial stone was laid. The Eyemouth lifeboat then entered the harbour and broke a blue ribbon in front of the estimated 2,000-3,000 crowd. Proceedings ended with a banquet and dinner in the town hall.

The newspaper referred to the harbour works as being a more limited scheme than described in Meik's Plans, being confined to widening, deepening and extending inwards of the present harbour, thus considerably adding to the quayage. The harbour area would be increased from 1½ acres to about 4¼ acres. The water depth at high tide would be 18 ft and 2 ft at low tide, rather than being dry at ebb tide as formerly. The water channel width would become 60 ft and the River Eye would be carried past the harbour by means of a long 900 ft jetty and the cutting back of the rock on the Gunsgreen side. The total quay space was to become two and a half times the previous size with berthage provided for up to 90 vessels. There followed a reference to the future railway: '… the railway scheme includes the construction of lines of rails along the quays, so that the fish can at once be trained and despatched to the markets.'

The work was carried out by the contractor, George Lawson of Glasgow and the resident engineer was William Kidd.

All of this took place against a background of some concern in the local fishing business. The haddock fishing was collapsing and even the earnings from the herring industry slumped as a result of enormous landings in the more northern ports causing a depression in the fish price. The boats could not afford to go to sea and the local shipbuilding yard was mothballed. The coopers, the carpenters and other tradesmen lost their jobs. Money became desperately short

THE EYEMOUTH RAILWAY COMPANY.

CAPITAL, £30,000,
In 3,000 Shares of £10 each.

Provisional Committee.

*Colonel DAVID MILNE HOME of Wedderburn, M.P., Paxton House, Berwick.
*The Honourable EDWARD MARJORIBANKS, M.P., Ninewells, Chirnside.
*ALEXANDER GIBSON, Esq., of Netherbyres, 10 Belgrave Crescent, Edinburgh.
*JAMES GIBSON, Esq., of Gunsgreen, Eyemouth.
*ROBERT A. ALLAN, Esq., Chief Magistrate of Eyemouth.
*JAMES S. MACK, Esq., of Hillend. Coveyheugh House, Reston.
*JAMES F. GILLIE, Esq., Clareknowe, Berwick-upon-Tweed.
JAMES FORSYTH, Esq., M.D., Eyemouth.
CHARLES MUIRHEAD, Esq., Fish Merchant, Edinburgh.
W. S. SCOTT, Esq., Fish Merchant, Birmingham.
JOHN FORD, Esq., Junior Magistrate, Eyemouth.
JOHN M'GALL, Esq., Farmer, Hallydown, Eyemouth.
JOHN JOHNSTON, Esq., Farmer and Brick Manufacturer, Linthill, Junior Magistrate of Eyemouth.
ROBERT DICKSON, Esq., Fishcurer, Eyemouth.
ALEXANDER ROBERTSON, Esq., Grocer and Wine Merchant, Eyemouth.

Those marked [*] have qualified as Directors.

Bankers.

The COMMERCIAL BANK OF SCOTLAND LIMITED, Edinburgh and Branches.

Solicitors.

Messrs BOWHILL & DOUGHTY, Writers, Ayton.

Engineers.

Messrs THOMAS MEIK & SONS, MM.I.C.E., 6 York Place, Edinburgh.

Secretary (pro tem.)

JAMES L. RAE, Esq., Eyemouth.

Offices.

EYEMOUTH.

Applications for shares should be made to the Interim Secretary or to the Bankers.

The shares will be payable as follows :—£1 on application, £1 on allotment, and the remainder by calls of not more than £2 at intervals of not less than three months. In cases where no allotment is made, the Deposit will be returned.

and Eyemouth became the blackspot for crime in the Borders. Poorhouse accommodation was organized and many moved away from the town to seek a future elsewhere. A further Public Works Loans Board sum of £10,000 facilitated the completion of the moderate harbour development started in 1884. But at least the hoped-for railway line was on the way!

Preparations for the branch railway

On 11th October, 1883 a meeting of the provisional committee appointed Messrs Cope & Co., of Great George Street, London SW, as their 'Parliamentary Solicitors', to deal with the application for a Board of Trade Certificate. They were experts in such matters.

A brief statement in the *Edinburgh Evening News* of Saturday 3rd November, 1883 read:

THE EYEMOUTH RAILWAY SCHEME – At a meeting in the Town Hall, Eyemouth, last night, Mr R.A. Allan, chief magistrate presiding, a committee was appointed to take active measures in support of the proposed branch railway.

Mr Allan was accompanied to the platform by Colonel Milne Home of Wedderburn, the local Member of Parliament. The Chairman briefly stated the object of the meeting. Colonel Milne Home then spoke at length of the great advantages which would accrue to the community if Eyemouth became connected to the main line of the North British Railway. Referring to the new harbour work he said that it was of the utmost importance that the railway scheme be promoted at the same time. The meeting, which was largely represented by the various industries of the burgh, unanimously passed resolutions approving the scheme and pledged assistance in carrying it through. The meeting then appointed a committee. The meeting closed with a vote of thanks to the Chairman and Colonel Milne Home.

A letter of 5th November, 1883 from Mr J. Walker of the North British Railway and received by Messrs Bowhill & Doughty, the railway's solicitors in Ayton, said that the NBR Directors were willing to enter an agreement to work the proposed line for 50 per cent of the gross receipts subject to the 'usual' conditions regarding the construction and maintenance for the first six months.

After the formal meeting the local committee met with Colonel Milne Home, the Chairman of the newly-formed working committee of the Eyemouth Railway, Mr Whittle, who had been appointed as the Interim Secretary, and the Chief Magistrate, Mr Allan. Arrangements were made for the issue of a Prospectus for the company.

The list of the members of the provisional committee is shown on the front of the share application Prospectus.

James Rae was identified as the *pro tem* Secretary of the company replacing Mr Whittle who had formerly acted as interim Secretary.

The Directors of the company were identified with an asterisk (*) on the Prospectus. However, Robert A. Allan, whose name appeared with an asterisk, was not elected at the first general meeting. T.J. Gordon of Edinburgh was proposed as a provisional addition to 'strengthen' the Board but didn't, in fact, become a Board member. However, an application was made to the Board of Trade for a certificate in connection with the building of the Eyemouth Railway, under the terms of the Railways Construction Facilities Act of 1864. The submission included the plans which had been drawn up by Thomas Meik & Sons, the appointed Engineers. Messrs Cope & Sons [sic] of Great George Street, London SW were appointed as Parliamentary solicitors to look after the process (2, Great George Street happened to be the London office of the North British Railway.) After due process and consideration, the Certificate was granted and signed by T.H. Farrer, Secretary to the Board of Trade, on 18th August, 1884. It was duly published by the *Edinburgh Gazette*, under the heading 'The Eyemouth Railway Certificate 1884' in its edition of 22nd August, 1884, No. 9551.

This document, in a standard format, contained 34 clauses, identifying, amongst other matters, the name of the Company and its Incorporation, powers to make the railway, matters concerning capital, shares and borrowing powers, Meetings, Directors, powers of leasing and selling the railway, the gauge of the line, road crossings and tolls. The time for the building of the railway was set as five years from the publication of the certificate in the *Edinburgh Gazette*. One amusing clause was clause 31 which stated that it was not compulsory for the Railway to carry any night soil, dung, manure, compost or other offensive matter! The certificate also contained several tables relating to the maximum charges which could be made for the use and supply of carriages, wagons and trucks (with various specified commodities), also for the supply of motive power on the line and charges for the transport of small packages and items of 'great weight'. An attached schedule referred to the agreement with the North British Railway concerning the use of the junction station at Burnmouth, the granting of running powers to the NBR over the line, and permission for the Eyemouth company to use part of NBR sidings at Burnmouth whilst the line was being constructed.

The company was required to hold six-monthly general meetings, the first of which was required to take place within six months of the publication of the certificate. A quorum was set for both these and for Directors' meetings, which were to be held in Eyemouth or other suitable place as determined by the Directors themselves. Accordingly the first general meeting was fixed for the afternoon of 23rd February, 1885. Subsequent meetings would be held in March/April and September/October as specified in the certificate.

Before the first general meeting the Directors held several meetings to deal with matters which had arisen. On 9th November, 1883 they received a letter from John Walker, the General Manager of the North British Railway. The letter said that the NBR agreed to work the Eyemouth line for 50 per cent of the gross receipts. The plans and sections for the line would have to be agreed by the NBR Engineer and that the line was to be constructed to the Engineer's satisfaction. Also the line was to be maintained by the NBR for six months after the opening had been sanctioned by the Board of Trade. Some adjustment to the Plans for the Burnmouth station layout would be needed.

A further meeting took place on 9th January, 1884 at which the engineers were present. A Mr Audison resigned as a provisional committee member, and various documents from the solicitors in Ayton, and also the proposed working agreement with the NBR, were studied. It was reported that copies of the Prospectus had been distributed to all of the wholesale warehousemen, fish salesmen and other persons in centres such as Edinburgh, Glasgow, Leith, London, Birmingham and Manchester.

The venue for the first general meeting was the town hall in Eyemouth and was fully reported in *The Scotsman* newspaper. Colonel Milne Home MP presided at the meeting which was well-attended. He invited the Secretary to read the report which explained that the purpose of the company would be to construct a railway between the North British Railway's Burnmouth station and the town and harbour of Eyemouth. One of the first steps that the provisional committee had carried out was to issue a Prospectus which invited the public to purchase shares in the concern. A canvass had been made throughout the town and by that date applications had been received for between £5,000 and £6,000 of shares.

He continued by saying that the Engineers, Messrs Thomas Meik & Sons of Edinburgh, had been instructed to make careful surveys of the intended route of the railway and to prepare detailed estimates of the expense of making a continuous line from Burnmouth station to the harbour quay, near the footbridge, there to have a station for passengers and goods. The connections at Burnmouth had been arranged to suit the traffic requirements of the North British Railway as set forth in the agreement forming part of the Board of Trade Certificate. The company also intended to enter into negotiations with the NBR to work the line for 50 per cent of the gross receipts. While the plans were being prepared the company had entered into negotiations with Messrs Scott & Lawson, contractors, of Leith. The committee had received an offer from this firm to construct the line at a fixed schedule of prices. The Secretary stated that the committee would recommend acceptance of the offer provided that the contractors would accept one-third of the amount of their contract in ordinary shares. The total estimate of the prices referred to amounted to about £25,000 which was slightly below the Parliamentary estimate for the work.

The Chairman moved the adoption of the report. He congratulated the company and the town of Eyemouth on the progress which had already been made on the scheme. He said that the report stated that Meik's had been requested to make a continuous line from Burnmouth to Eyemouth Quay. There had been a great deal of discussion about where the end of the Eyemouth Railway was to be located. It was to have been in two sections: one ending at the toll house, and one at the harbour quay. (These were called Railway No. 1 and Railway No. 2 on Meik's plan.) The committee had ultimately decided that the cheapest way would be to make one line only from Burnmouth direct to the harbour quay. Had they come to the toll house, they would have had to have a station there and a 'shoot' or branch between the toll house and Netherbyres Gate down to the quay. This would have added greatly to the expense. The working agreement with the North British Railway was practically decided and the committee also thought it desirable that the agreement with the contractors, Messrs Scott & Lawson, be closed. Whilst this last matter could be discussed by any persons present, the committee felt that the agreement with the contractors

EYEMOUTH RAILWAY COMPANY

FORM OF APPLICATION.

To the Directors of the Eyemouth Railway Company.
(JAMES L. RAE, Banker, Eyemouth, Interim Secretary.)

Gentlemen,

Having paid to your Bankers, The Commercial Bank of Scotland Limited,

the sum of £ : : , being the amount of deposit of £1 per Share on ....

Shares in the "EYEMOUTH RAILWAY COMPANY," I request you to allot me that number of Shares,

and I agree to accept such Shares, or any smaller number that may be allotted to me, and to pay

the further amounts due thereon according to the terms of the Prospectus of the Company; and I

authorise you to place my name upon the Register of Shareholders in the "Eyemouth Railway

Company," in respect of the Shares to be so allotted.

Signature ....

Name in full ....

Application form for shares. *Eyemouth Museum Collection*

was highly satisfactory, in that eight or nine thousand pounds of share capital was passed to the contractors. Although a sum of £2,400 had been deposited in London (in connection with the certificate application) this would be returned once the sum of £14,000 had been raised. To applause he stated that this would be done in the autumn!

The Chairman proposed the adoption and Mr Gibson of Gunsgreen, another Director, seconded. It was unanimously adopted. A list of the Directors of the company was submitted to the meeting and this was unanimously approved also. One of the company's solicitors, James Doughty, explained that the North British Railway would run not less than four trains each day, and, of course, it was in their interests to develop traffic on the new railway as much as possible. With the proposal of the usual votes of thanks the meeting was brought to a conclusion.

On 9th July the Directors received the information that the Eyemouth Railway certificate had been laid before both Houses of Parliament. On 19th November the Clerk to the Directors reported that only 563 shares had been taken up and regret was expressed that the public of Eyemouth had not shown a greater interest in the scheme. (With the depressed economic climate in Eyemouth this was, surely, no surprise!) In addition the Directors were informed that Meik's estimate for the railway was £20,000 plus £3,000 for the purchase of land and sundries. This was less than expected as modifications had been made to the Eye viaduct plans. Mr Whittle offered his resignation as Secretary as he had been appointed to the Inspectorship of the head office of the Commercial Bank of Scotland based in George Street, Edinburgh; his resignation was accepted at the next meeting.

On 5th December, 1884 the Directors were informed that George Lawson, the contractor, had indicated that he would introduce £6,000 of share capital provided that he was awarded the construction contract and agreed to accept £3,000 of his payment in the form of shares. This was approved by the committee.

The next meeting of the provisional committee was held at Meik's office in Edinburgh on 10th December, 1884. James Gibson on behalf of the Eyemouth members proposed that costs could be saved if an alternative route for the line into Eyemouth could be chosen, avoiding the need for the costly viaduct. He suggested that the line could pass to the south side of Netherbyres to a station on the south side of the river. Alternatively the line could pass through Netherbyres with a terminus in the same location. This suggestion was considered to be impractical as it was outside the powers of the Board of Trade Certificate. At the same meeting the contractors, Mr Lawson and Mr Scott, discussed the contract of works with the committee and the decision was made that Scott alone would fulfil the contract.

A further meeting took place on 29th December, on this occasion reverting to Eyemouth as the venue. Three of the committee were present plus Meik's representatives. It was concluded that the railway should consist of the length of line known as Railway No. 1 plus Railway No. 2 with the terminal section beyond the junction, i.e. the line to a toll house station, being abandoned (*see sketch overleaf*). The meeting felt that the sum of £24,000 was rather too much for the contract but stated that the aim was to start work 'in February next', that is, February 1885. Once again they were clearly in optimistic mood!

At the next meeting held at Ayton on 7th January, 1885 the suggestion was made for the laying of a line of rails along the quay. The Secretary was asked to approach the harbour trustees to endeavour to work with them on this matter.

Those at the first general meeting of the railway (held in Eyemouth town hall on 23rd February, 1885) were told 'officially' of the aim of the railway, the names of the Directors and committee members and what had been achieved so far, including the publication of the Board of Trade certificate. Details of the canvass in the town, the Prospectus, the consultations with the contractors and with the North British Railway as regards the Burnmouth link and the working of the line, were all mentioned. The total cost of £25,000 was £2,000 below the Parliamentary estimates. 'In the meantime the contractors are desirous of taking

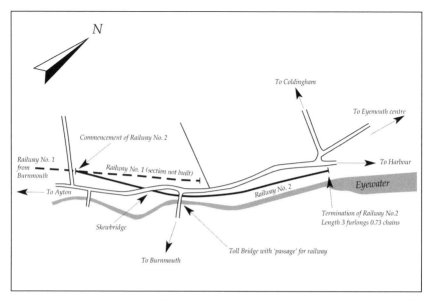

advantage of the spring weather to commence their operations' so as to get the line open before the end of 1885. The optimism continued!

On 9th April Mr Gillies said that he could not take up his Directorate as he was suffering from loss of sight. Alexander Gibson was elected as Vice-Chairman. It was agreed that the Chairman should meet Mr G.B. Wieland, Secretary of the North British Railway, to see if that company could offer assistance.

The second general meeting was held on 22nd October. The meeting was told that the agreement with the North British Railway was ready to be signed. The Chair passed on the disappointing information that the share applications had been insufficient to warrant the start of construction. The need for further advertising was made clear. The question of making other arrangements was discussed and the changing of the route to that via Netherbyres was raised by a John Dickson. He was told that this was impracticable.

Following the meeting between the Chair and George Wieland the latter said to the Directors that he would be prepared to take a considerable interest in the Eyemouth company provided certain conditions were complied with. This 'interest' was at first in a personal capacity. However, Wieland's somewhat forceful character resulted in his quickly exercising considerable influence at Eyemouth despite his employers at the North British Railway remaining somewhat at 'arm's length'. However, Wieland clearly did not want to be associated with an abortive scheme and it is recorded that the Eyemouth Railway would need to complete land purchase and the raising of capital before Wieland's formal and active assistance would take place.

The next general meeting took place on 29th April, 1886. It was reported to those present that the current low prices for materials and labour would help reduce construction costs, the engineers estimating that the cost of the work could be reduced by about one quarter. It was felt that this news would encourage shareholders to introduce more capital. The Directors were to carry through the negotiations regarding land purchase. The meeting ended on an optimistic note, once again: '[There is] great reason to hope that the Railway works will be commenced at an early date.'

The 7th October general meeting was held at Bowhill & Doughty's offices at Ayton. Wieland had obtained a tender from the contractors Brand & Co. to do the construction work for £14,630, to which the committee suggested should be added the sum of £4,000 for items not included in the tender such as legal and engineering fees. The Chairman replied to the suggestion by committee member Alexander Robson that £6,000-7,000 could be saved by terminating the line at a station at Brownbank by Mr Gibson's mill. Such a terminus would require 'two backshunts' to get the line to the harbour quays, would involve an increased distance of the station from the town, would require the cost of extra compensation to Mr Gibson and therefore there would be little in the way of savings. Meik suggested that the savings be as little as £1,600 without taking into consideration land and building costs. Wieland had declared against the alternative route and his relationship with the company was clearly one involving much influence! It was decided that Mr Doughty should continue as interim Secretary.

Time continued to pass and there was no sign of the start being made on construction. Another meeting was held in the Town Hall at Eyemouth on 28th October when it was revealed that an engineer of standing had submitted a tender, the result of which might be to reduce the share capital by £8,000. The Directors expressed their pleasure that the people of Eyemouth were alive to the great importance of the railway for the prosperity of the town and urged them to increase their own shareholdings. In addition they should get their friends and business associates interested in the scheme to increase the share capital! Continued questions regarding the route to a station at Gunsgreen were dealt with!

On 28th April, 1887 a Director's meeting was held at 2 pm prior to the general meeting in Eyemouth. Only Milne Home, Alexander and James Gibson, plus Meik and Mr Doughty were present. The Gibsons stated that they would be prepared to reduce their compensation claim if it would make the building of a station on Gibson land easier. A letter had been received from a Mr Usher, of Northfield, proposing that the line to the town should be constructed, not from Burnmouth, but from Reston Junction, via Coldingham to Eyemouth. Meik was asked to look at the costs of the line again.

The half-yearly general meeting, starting at 2.30 pm, was well attended. It received the Report which said that little progress had been made in the matter of share capital. It was accepted that the depressed agricultural and trade conditions were responsible. The report asked the Directors and people of Eyemouth to make a special effort to help by taking up shares.

By now the Directors must have been feeling somewhat desperate for at their meeting on 13th October, with Alexander Gibson in the Chair, the question of alternative routes for the line was discussed. In particular the Directors would feel warranted, if sufficient funds can be found to abandon the present route, to

Above: Colonel David Milne Home of
Wedderburn, MP, the Eyemouth Railway's
Chairman in the 1890s.   *Berwickshire News*

Right: The 10th Marquis of Tweeddale, the
North British Railway Chairman and Eyemouth
Railway Director.   *Author's Collection*

Below: A view of Manderston House which was
the country seat of James (later Sir James) Miller
the Eyemouth Railway's Chairman in the 1890s.
   Author's Collection

Manderston, Duns

Published by James Swan & Co., Duns.

favour a new route via Coldingham! It was obvious that opening of the line to Eyemouth (by whichever route) would develop the fishing industry and improve the lot of the fishermen, would enhance the value of property in the town and produce a return on capital of more than originally predicted. However, it was considered that the Coldingham route would have little or no chance of becoming a reality and staying with the present route was the best course of action, whilst impressing on the Eyemouth public the absolute necessity to make an effort to get the required capital. Mr Gillie suggested that costs might be saved if the Eye viaduct were to be made of wood, rather than masonry. This was the last to be heard of this suggestion! The meeting was told of the continued support for the scheme from Mr Walker, the Chairman of the NBR.

The year 1887 saw very little progress with the railway scheme, the depressed state of trade no doubt continuing to be an important contributory factor.

On 26th April, 1888 a report was presented to the half-yearly general meeting which stated that the possibility of a route via Coldingham had been abandoned. It was pointed out that the need for the railway was more urgent than ever. They regretted, though, that despite their endeavours their efforts had been unavailing owing to the want of sufficient local financial support. There was a need for a final effort to secure some more capital! This was repeated at the Directors' meeting which took place on 30th October just before the general meeting when it was stated that there was a continued need for approaches to likely parties to take shares in the project.

The general meeting was told that there was some cause for optimism as the number of shares applied for in the previous six months had doubled from the previous period. However, further applications would be welcomed.

Of course the Board of Trade certificate, requiring the railway to be complete within five years, ran out on 30th April, 1889. This meant that the required Parliamentary deposit of £2,400 was forfeit. This financial penalty placed the railway in difficulty but fortunately Sir James Miller of Manderston House bought £500 shares and a large number were bought by the 10th Marquis of Tweeddale who had become Chairman of the North British Railway. (Tweeddale was formerly William Montagu Hay.)

On the same day, 30th April, 1889, what was to be the final meeting of the provisional committee was held before the start of the general meeting. Plans for the station arrangements were submitted by Mr Urquhart of Thomas Meik & Sons. The scheme was to involve the creation of branches to the quays, one branch onto the middle jetty (which separated the harbour and the River Eye), and one branch to the Salt Green quay. The committee favoured a branch to the former, leaving Salt Green quay for local traffic only. A recommendation from Wieland was considered in which he proposed the reduction in the number of Directors to just three, namely the Marquis of Tweeddale, Sir James Miller (Bart) and Colonel Milne Home. The following general meeting ratified this proposal and passed on the good news that the sum required for the line's construction was practically assured and that work may be expected to commence in the coming summer. Details of the planned construction were conveyed to the meeting. This time the confidence was to be realized, as detailed later.

Subsequently a Directors' meeting took place at 2 Great College Street in Westminster on 22nd June. This was the London office of the North British Railway! All three Directors attended. James Miller was the nomination as Chairman with Colonel Milne Home as Vice Chairman. Mr Wieland was officially appointed as Secretary to the company at a salary of £300 per annum and he would provide, free of charge, secretarial staff and support. He was thus in a position of considerable influence and authority. In addition to this new post he was still the Secretary of the North British Railway but earned an additional salary from the Edinburgh Suburban & Southside Railway, a subsidiary of the NBR, and was running the Ayrshire & Wigtownshire Railway for its owner James Renton. On resigning the NBR Secretary position in March 1892 he was presented with a sum equivalent to three years' salary and he was made a Director of the company, becoming its Chairman in 1901 until his death in 1905. (In reality, according to the accounts, Wieland was paid £125 per half-year for his role as the Eyemouth Railway Company Secretary.)

The appointment of Wieland as Company Secretary and the reduction in the number of Directors to just three meant that the conduct and administration of affairs became more streamlined. His strong personality and experience resulted in a more businesslike approach to Eyemouth Railway matters. Venues for meetings could be arranged to fit in with the business and availability of a smaller number of persons and the likelihood of rambling and recurring discussions (such as those associated with the route from the East Coast line to Eyemouth and the location of Eyemouth station in the town) would be minimized. Of course it was the case that with just three Directors, once a person had been nominated, for example to the Chair and duly seconded, then there was no other Director present to oppose the nomination! Directors' meetings were often held prior to general meetings and policy matters were decided at these. Finally any 'local control' from the businessmen and merchants of Eyemouth had disappeared completely.

It must have been with great relief and satisfaction on the part of the Directors that the report to the half-yearly meeting, held at 4 Princes Street, Edinburgh, on 18th October, 1889, stated that since the last shareholders' meeting the contract had been let to Messrs William Beattie & Sons of Edinburgh who had commenced work in July. The balance sheet and statement of accounts were received and adopted. Colonel Milne Home and Wieland were the only two persons present; the former proposed and the latter seconded these adoptions. The appointed auditors were recorded as Messrs James Howden, a chartered accountant, and George Simpson (the latter on the staff of the North British Railway's accountant's office).

At long last, entering into a new decade and after years of hope, struggle and frustration, the Eyemouth Railway was becoming a reality!

Chapter Three

Building the line

Fulfilling the contract: the construction of the permanent way and bridges

As mentioned earlier, the Eyemouth Railway Company had held its half-yearly meeting on 30th April, 1889 in Eyemouth town hall. Colonel David Milne Home, the Chairman of the provisional committee, was in the Chair. He spoke at great length.

He informed the meeting that all of the land proprietors had agreed to grant ground for the railway and that agreement had been reached with all of the occupying tenants. As a result the railway had invited four or five contractors ('men of high respectability in their line of business and of substantial working capabilities') to tender and they had responded readily. As a result, and subject to the approval of the first Board of Directors, 'arrangements had been made with a contractor of high standing who would undertake the work'. The appointed contractor was required to complete the work (including the harbour branch) within 16 months of the contract being signed. In addition there was a stipulation that the work would be maintained in good order by the contractor for a period of six months after completion, after which time the company would assume the responsibility. The supervising engineers, referred to by the Chairman as 'Messrs Meik and Company', had expressed their approval of the contractor and expressed their satisfaction with the arrangements.

Later in the meeting, after the adoption of the half-yearly report, Montague Urquhart, representing Meik, answered questions concerning details of the contract which related, mainly, to the Eyemouth end of the line. He referred to the station facilities and to the amount of land at the company's disposal at the terminus. Where the station was to be located there was a breadth of 120 ft. One third of an acre would be taken from the river, but the cost estimates provided for the provision of a stone wall so that 'no muck would be washed into the harbour or river'.

The route and plans of the line had been selected and designed by Messrs Thomas Meik & Sons, Civil Engineers of Edinburgh and London, to quote their proper title. They were approved by the Eyemouth Railway and by the North British Railway, which latter company was described as their 'coadjutors'. The construction work was let to Messrs W. Beattie & Sons, contractors, of Edinburgh. Beattie started work on the contract in July 1889, establishing a working base, with stables and stores, at Hillburn (sometimes referred to as 'Hill Burn' in contemporary documents), close to the Great North Road and the main line railway. The resident engineer was Mr A.K. Mackay, later replaced by Mr F. Wrench, and a certain Mr W. Inglis was the contractor's agent.

The formation of the railway was to be 15 ft wide throughout, sufficient for the laying of a single line of track. The permanent way would be of the same description as that currently used by the North British Railway. The deepest cutting was to have a depth of 37 ft and the highest embankment 40 ft. The whole line would fall by some 250 ft between Burnmouth and Eyemouth and the steepest gradient would be 1 in 50. The line would involve the construction of both over- and under-bridges plus the viaduct over the Eye Water, about one mile from the Eyemouth terminus.

A local newspaper report, dated 4th July, 1889, reported that the work on the railway was 'on a fair way to being commenced', the contractors were arranging to have the necessary plant brought forward immediately. One or two men had already been engaged to work the line and it was understood that when construction operations actually commenced that special attention would be given to the unemployed of Eyemouth. The Berwick Commissioners of Supply were perhaps prudent in deciding that, in view of the contractor 'having employed a number of labourers ... that it may become necessary to re-appoint an extra constable', there having been an extra constable employed after the earlier harbour works were completed.

Work by the contractor actually commenced in mid-July, the start being reported in the *Southern Reporter* of 18th July: 'Eyemouth railway works are now under way, and the contractor expects to finish the making of the line in about a year. Plant and material for bridging the river Eye are being rapidly collected, while part of the route has been cleared of trees etc.'

By mid-August other newspapers were reporting that considerable progress had been made with more than 100 men already working along the line. Reports contained the estimation that the line would be completed and opened within a year, that is, within the specified limit of 16 months.

On 10th October the Engineer's report to the Board of Directors stated that about 2,200 cubic yards of rock and 4,300 cubic yards of earth had been excavated and tipped into bank and that work was completed on two of the cuttings. Blasting had taken place to loosen the whinstone at the site of Burnmouth station to create space for the additional tracks needed. In addition the masonry of the bridges at Fairnieside, alongside the NBR, and at Hillside Farm, had been completed and the girders would soon be in place. The foundations at Hillburn public road bridge were in, and the abutments were being built. The excavations for public road bridges at Biglawburn and Eyemouth Toll were proceeding and rolled iron beams for the latter were on the ground at the site. All of the work associated with drains and culverts (except for one near to the viaduct) had been completed. The foundations for the retaining wall at Crooked Haugh were built and the upper part of the wall was progressing. The engineers also reported that the permanent fencing in the ground occupied by the works was practically completed. The only exceptions were at places where it had been necessary to make diversions of the local roads. At these locations temporary fencing was in place. They stated that their supplies of plant and materials at the site were good and that the works could carry on apace.

However, an accident took place on Thursday 24th October at Burnmouth which could have had disastrous consequences. It was reported in the *Berwickshire News and General Advertiser* on the following Tuesday and involved the passing 'Flying Scotsman' train being hit by materials thrown up by a blast close to the main line at Burnmouth. Fortunately there appears to have been no human casualties as a result of the incident and work on the Eyemouth line carried on. Further details are described in Chapter Thirteen.

The weather during the winter of 1889-1890 must have been relatively kind for by early February, and despite the local influenza epidemic, it was reported that the contractors were pushing on rapidly. The view was expressed that the line would be open for traffic before the end of summer. Blasting was being employed for making the cuttings through the solid rock encountered and horse-drawn wagonways with tipper wagons were being used to move the spoil from the cuttings, and to build embankments.

The Berwickshire News (30th April) and the *Berwick Journal* (1st May) contained identical articles referring to the resolution of the Eyemouth Railway Company Directors not to extend the lines of rails to the piers in the harbour. 'Clearly a blunder, and a serious one, has been made.'

On the 30th April the line's Engineer reported that the totals of soft material and rock excavated had reached 27,395 and 15,767 tons respectively. These materials had been tipped to bank. However, until the viaduct was completed the material from one of the cuttings (the 36 ft one at Ballabraes) could not be finally dealt with as it had to be taken over the viaduct for tipping. Some 1,479 yards of rail were in place ready for ballasting. These had been obtained from the Moss Bay Haematite Iron & Steel Co. of Workington, which company was experienced having rolled steel rails since 1877. The rails had cost £4 17s. 6d. per ton delivered to the contractors at Burnmouth.

At the half-yearly meeting of the Eyemouth Railway Co. held on Thursday 1st May at the offices of the North British Railway on Princes Street, Edinburgh, the Chairman mentioned that 'the railway was going on satisfactorily as far as they knew.' Surprising vagueness!

This plaque, photographed in 1954 by C.J.B. Sanderson was to be found on the road overbridge at Burnmouth station.   *Armstrong Railway Photographic Trust*

By late June 1890 rapid progress was still being reported but forecasts for its date of completion were being revised to early September. For about half of the way from Burnmouth the work was almost complete. This section had included a 250 yard cutting involving blasting through solid rock. The permanent way had been laid on this section. At the Eyemouth end the work was in a similarly advanced state. Operations were being concentrated at a point mid-way along the line. Here was to be the heaviest cutting on the railway. It was about ¾ mile in length and varying from 10 to 40 ft in depth. Operations were proceeding slowly, with a great deal of rock boring and blasting being necessary. Work was taking place in both day and night shifts to speed up the work, with spoil being taken across the completed viaduct to form an embankment.

As the construction work approached the Eyemouth terminus an obstruction lay in the path of the workmen, namely the ancient Toll Bridge over the Eye. It was with reluctance that the engineers had to design and construct a tunnel through this ancient structure. However, on examination, it was discovered to be in very poor condition and the works, when carefully planned and completed to a high standard, probably resulted in a bridge that was stronger than before! The tunnel itself consisted of an arch above the line with an inverted arch spring underneath the trackbed to give extra stability. At this point the rails were laid on a 1 in 50 gradient on a 'shelf' above the river.

The Engineer reported, on the 3rd September, that all of the permanent way was laid except for the section in 'Redhall Cutting' and that most of it had been ballasted.

By December the railway was still not complete! Revised opening dates of October 1890 and then New Year 1891 had been quoted. The cutting at Millbank was described as having been a very heavy job with difficulties in connection with the 'wings' which were not over stable rock. There had been landslips in this vicinity. It was considered that more work would have to be done before the Board of Trade inspector would be satisfied.

The first Board of Trade inspection, by Major Marindin RE, took place on Monday 16th February. His inspection report is dated 18th February and the inspection was reported in the *Berwick Journal* of Thursday 19th February. Accompanying Major Marindin were Mr James McLaren, the passenger superintendent of the North British Railway, Mr Beattie of Beattie & Sons, the contractors, Mr Urquhart, representing Messrs Meik & Son, the engineers of the railway (of which he was a partner), and Mr Wrench, the firm's resident engineer. Two heavy engines and a carriage were used in the testing of the line and its viaduct.

At the start of his report Major Marindin, as was customary, listed some facts and figures regarding the line. It was a single line of 2 miles 70.55 chains in length. The railway was of standard gauge with a width of 15 ft at foundation level. The permanent way had been laid to the North British pattern with 75 lb. per yard rails in lengths of 24 ft. The rail joints were attached by means of fishplates weighing 20 lb. per pair, cast-iron chairs each weighing 34 lb. and fixed by iron spikes. The transverse sleepers were made of Scotch fir. Each was 9 ft long and 10 inches by 5 inches in section with eight of these supporting each rail length. The rails were fixed in position with outside keys made of oak. The ballast was described as broken stone and gravel. The fencing for the line was post and wire. Agreements with the local estates required these fences to be maintained by the railway. In addition the agreements required the railway to make good and preserve the drainage of the adjoining lands as well as the water supply, in so far as they had been interfered with by the line's construction.

He described the works as light but he specifically identified one cutting which was 36 ft deep, mainly through rock, and one 37 ft high embankment.

There were two underbridges on the line, one with abutments made of concrete and steel girders of 16 ft span, the other with 15 ft girders on masonry abutments. He referred to the seven overbridges, two being cattle bridges made entirely of timber, three with wrought-iron tops on masonry abutments and the final two as having masonry arches. The widest girder bridge had a span of 31 ft 6 in.

He noted that all of these works were standing well and appeared to be substantially built. (The detailed plans for all of the bridges, showing the materials for construction and full engineering details, are today kept in the Scottish Archives in Edinburgh.)

In his requirements before the line could be opened he noted that the fencing at the wing wall at the bridge located 35 chains from Burnmouth, and the bridge at 1 mile and 30 chains, should be made good. He also required that the wooden floors of the underbridges be covered with ballast as a protection against fire. He required the rails at many places to be bent to create smoother curves and asked for check rails on all the 10 chain radius curves to be provided. He also required that some of the top ballast needed to be broken into smaller pieces. Finally, in connection with the general works, he required that the approach to another of the bridges, that at 1 mile and 53 chains from Burnmouth, be made good.

The report of the Engineer to the Board written on 16th March and received on 26th March stated that all of the work was completed with the exception of a few small items (not specified in the report), but that these would be finished by the end of the current week. 'The line will be ready for the Board of Trade Inspector early next week.'

In his report after his second inspection on 1st April, Marindin noted, separately from his remarks on the station facilities, that 'the other minor requirements noted at my previous inspection have been satisfied'.

The total cost of the line's construction, nearly three miles in length and with difficult works involved in its construction, was reported in the July 1894 edition of The Engineer as being £21,000, with the additional comment that 'The railway is already a paying concern and when the present works on the harbour are completed, there is no doubt that the capital expended on them will also bring good returns.'

The final report of the Engineer was dated 24th September, 1891. It stated that the construction of the line was completed and that it was being worked by the North British Railway.

Some years after the line's opening an edition of The Engineer, dated 6th July 1894, reported that, from the quay level at Eyemouth to the junction with the main line at Burnmouth, there was a rise of some 250 ft, the whole length of the line being on an 'up grade'.

On the Eye Eyemouth   Brown's Series.

This is an early picture postcard which shows the new-looking Linthill viaduct crossing the River Eye upstream from Eyemouth. It was taken when the water level in the river was very low.   *Author's Collection*

This postcard depicts the former Toll Bridge at Eyemouth near the start of the 20th century. The main span crosses the Eye whilst the small arch on the left accommodates the railway line leaving Eyemouth and running on the ledge above the river.   *Author's Collection*

Toll Bridge, Eyemouth.   53444

Fulfilling the contract: the Linthill viaduct over the Eye Water

> *'Spanning a picturesque dean, within 200 yards of the public road between*
> *Ayton and Eyemouth, the viaduct will be well seen from the road, and will add to,*
> *rather than detract from, the beauty of the locality.'*

This was part of the description of the Linthill viaduct, over the Eye Water, which appeared in *The Berwick Journal* dated 22nd August, 1889.

The railway had considered three ways of approaching Eyemouth. The first, approaching from the Coldingham direction, was rejected early in the planning stage, leaving two other alternatives.

The first of these, would have involved the line remaining to the south-east of the Eye, with a terminus near Eyecliffe Mill, being approached via Netherbyres and Gunsgreen crossing land owned by one of the company's Directors, James Gibson. It may have appeared to be the cheaper of the two choices but would have created a terminus in an inconvenient position, being on the opposite side of the river from the town, well away from the harbour. Rail traffic would, from this terminus, have required the laying of additional track so as to reach the harbour and wagon movements would have required two reversals. The reconstruction of the road toll-bridge could have been needed to allow increased number and size of vehicles crossing between the town and harbour and the station.

The second possible choice was to bridge the river, thus switching the line of railway from the south-east to the north bank of the river. This would necessitate the construction of a tall viaduct of several spans, but would bring the railway station much closer to the town centre with a terminus between Victoria Road and the river. In addition it would facilitate any future extension of the rails into the harbour and dock area. It was this latter choice that was proceeded with.

From both directions the approach to the viaduct was on a left-hand curve. The viaduct was built so as to cross not only the River Eye but also the 'lade' or leat of the Eyemouth Mill. As recorded in the *Berwick Journal* it was to have six spans, 'each of 55 feet, with a height of about 50 feet and a total length of 350 feet.' Some of the piers of the viaduct were founded upon river gravel whilst others were built upon solid rock. The five piers were to have brick walls and a concrete filling, resting upon foundations of concrete. The superstructure was to consist of lattice-girder spans and cross girders, both made of wrought iron. The flooring was to be of timber and outside guard rails were to be provided for the single line of track. According to drawings in *The Engineer*, the tops of the piers measured 5 ft 3 in. in length by 12 ft wide, with the lattice girders adding another 7 ft to the viaduct's height, the girders being 8 ft apart. The rails rested upon longitudinal timbers of 16 in. cross-section supported by cross-timber joists measuring 10 in. by 5 in. The guard rails were 5 ft in height and positioned 3 ft 10 in. to each side of the viaduct's central line.

Progress on the construction of the viaduct was rapid. By 10th October, 1889 the Engineer was able to report that three of the piers were up to full height and the work of erecting the intermediate girders was shortly to be started.

By 6th February, 1890 the *Berwick Journal* was able to publish:

> The girders of the Linthill viaduct are now all placed, and the work of completing the bridge is being vigorously pushed on. It is expected that waggons will run over it in the course of a week. The Secretary of the N.B. Railway went over the line last week, and it is understood he was satisfied with the progress of the work.

However the author of the same article considered that there was no doubt that the line would be open 'before the summer is gone'. This would prove to be unrealistic!

The Engineer's report, dated 10th April, 1890, reported that the viaduct (and all of the bridges) had been completed and on the 3rd July, 1890 the *Berwick Journal* was able to report:

> A handsome viaduct of 6 spans of 55 feet, a height of 50 feet, and a length of 350 feet, over the river Eye and Eyemouth Mill lade, requires only the finishing touches ….

The newspaper further reported that materials, extracted from near the mid-point of the railway, where a substantial cutting was being excavated, were being carried across the viaduct at the rate of some 80 to 100 waggon-loads per day, to form an embankment in the valley of the Eye, connecting with the viaduct. This embankment was described as 'tapering downwards from over 40 feet in height, and extending about a quarter of a mile, near to where the railway passes under the road at Biglaw Burn'. The contractors commented to a reporter from the *Edinburgh Evening News* that the work on the cutting had been as hard as any in Scotland. The rock, described as a 'shaley whinstone', was hard to blast with subsequent slipping and blockage of the cutting.

There were construction problems elsewhere on the line and in December 1890 *The Journal* felt that the opening of the Eyemouth Railway seemed to be 'a little like a "Will o the Wisp"' Despite earlier forecasts of an opening in October 1890 or the New Year (1891) it had been 'extended to the 1st March, and some prophets predict that even that is too early a date'.

Although the viaduct was complete by the autumn of 1890 delays in the completion of the trackbed and rail-laying between the viaduct and Burnmouth meant that it was not possible to run a train along the line to test the viaduct.

Near to the Eyemouth terminus the engineers were 'reluctantly compelled' to pass an archway through the ancient Eyemouth Bridge, more often referred to as 'The Toll Bridge'. It was at the north end of this bridge that the Turnpike Road divided with one branch leading towards Burnmouth, the other towards Ayton. At the time of the building of the Eyemouth Railway the bridge was considered to be in an unsafe condition. The work on the bridge was considered by the reporter in *The Engineer* to have been 'very carefully considered and well carried out, and the bridge is probably stronger than before'. The archway, through which the railway was to pass, had an inverted sprung arch beneath the track foundation to give added stability. The arch was 15 ft wide and 16 ft 6 in. in length. The walls were about 11 ft in height with the arch above giving a maximum height of 14 ft. Substantial additional support work was performed on the banks of the River Eye adjacent to the bridge.

It was thus not until the first week of February 1891, as reported in the *Edinburgh Evening News*, that the first railway engine was to pass from Burnmouth over the entire length of the Eyemouth Railway to test the condition of the line. The engine and tender together were reported as weighing about 94 tons. Special tests were made at certain points and one of these was the viaduct across the Eye. The engine was stopped upon the viaduct and two gentlemen, Messrs Urquhart and Wrench, representing the engineers Messrs Meik & Sons, made various measurements and observations. The first girder tested gave a deflection of $^5/_{16}$ of an inch, the second ¼ of an inch, the third ½ an inch and the others so little that they could not be measured! After the stop on the viaduct the locomotive proceeded to the terminus of the line at Eyemouth. The local newspaper anticipated an early inspection from the Board of Trade.

Major Marindin inspected the viaduct during his inspection of the rest of the line on 16th February, 1891. In his report to the Board of Trade he considered that the viaduct was 'the only work of any importance'. He described it as having concrete abutments, intermediate piers of brick with concrete hearting, and six spans of 50 ft with a wrought girder lattice. He quoted the length of the viaduct as 120 yards with the extreme height being 53 ft 6 in. He noted that rail guards were provided. There are some small discrepancies between these figures and those taken from the engineer's drawings.

He considered that all of these works (i.e. the viaduct) were standing well and appeared to be substantially built. The girders had sufficient theoretical strength and those under the line were stiff under test. However, he noted that some rivets in the bottom flanges of the girders in spans numbered 2, 3, 5 and 6 had to be added. It was his conclusion that, because of other inadequacies and deficiencies, the line could not be opened without danger to the public.

Major Marindin, as mentioned earlier, revisited the railway and conducted a second inspection on the morning of Wednesday 1st April. His second report made no further mention of the viaduct. On this occasion he was generally satisfied with what he saw elsewhere and he therefore sanctioned the start of passenger traffic. The line opened on 15th April for both goods and passenger traffic, and the *Berwick Journal* reported this in their edition of Thursday 16th April.

The viaduct safely carried the railway's traffic, passing successively through the ownership of the Eyemouth Railway, the North British Railway and the London & North Eastern Railway until, on nationalization of the railways in 1948 it became part of the property of the new British Railways. It was in mid-August of that year that huge storms with torrential rain caused the Eye Water to change from a gently flowing small river into a raging torrent. As well as flooding large tracts of countryside, the water caused seven bridges on the Berwick to Edinburgh line to be washed away, whilst on the Eyemouth line the scouring effect of the Eye Water torrent caused the viaduct's central pier, number 3, to collapse, thus necessitating the cessation, for the time being, of all traffic on the branch. As described in a later chapter, it was to be June 1949 before repairs to the viaduct would allow resumption of the Burnmouth to Eyemouth train service.

Fulfilling the contract: the stations and their facilities

> '*It was absolutely necessary in all concerns, especially in that of the Eyemouth Railway Company, that due regard should be had to economy.*'

This extract is taken from the speech made by Col David Milne Home, the Chairman of the railway's provisional committee, when proposing the adoption of the report entitled 'The Proposed Railway to Eyemouth' at one of the half-yearly meetings of the Eyemouth Railway Company referred to earlier. He qualified his statement by mentioning that the materials used should be 'such as would not likely require renewal in a short time'.

As mentioned above, the contractors were represented at this meeting by Mr Urquhart, the junior partner of the firm of Messrs Meik & Sons of Edinburgh, the appointed supervising engineers for the line. Urquhart was described as a person who knew every detail of the plans, and, after the seconding of the adoption of the Report, was asked specific questions relating to certain matters. He said that the station at Eyemouth would be close to the place where the fishing boats would be hauled up. The plans for the proposed station included the provision of a platform, booking office and loading bank. There was no provision for a house for the station master. He referred to the plans which 'also accounted for all the necessary signals, etc. en route', this being an interesting statement as from the start it was planned to operate the line under the 'one engine in steam' principle, thus requiring no signalling except where the branch met the main line at Burnmouth!

What station facilities were initially provided at the ends of the line? At Burnmouth the major part of the station had been constructed in time for its opening in 1846 as a wayside station on the North British Railway's Edinburgh to Berwick line. The construction of the Eyemouth branch necessitated the construction of a single bay platform on the north or 'down' side, thus allowing cross-platform interchange with trains heading for Berwick. No additional buildings were provided on this platform, passengers for the branch being expected to use the existing facilities. When Major Marindin first inspected the new platform at Burnmouth he noted that there was no 'running junction' with the main line. He commented that the accommodation provided for passengers was very poor. In particular the platforms were set far too low and were dangerously narrow beneath a road bridge. This comment was not directly related to the Eyemouth platform as it was only the existing down platform which extended beneath the road bridge, the Eyemouth line bay ending before the station buildings on the north side of the bridge. Marindin commented that the accommodation for passengers was 'scanty'. The new platform was unfinished, was too narrow, there was no nameboard for the station, and no provision had been made for lighting. 'The station is quite unsuitable for an exchange station and it should be improved'.

At Eyemouth a single platform was constructed on the north side of the line, the platform road initially having a run-round loop for the locomotive. A single wooden building was erected on the platform, which, from a contemporary photograph, appeared to have rooms at each end, one presumably housing the booking office. It lacked an awning extending over the platform. The centre of the building was a covered area, presumably a waiting area for passengers. Also on the platform was a coach body, which, it has been suggested, acted as a 'bothy' for the railwaymen and also housed toilet facilities. No separate entrance for passengers was initially provided, and it was planned that intending travellers should share access via the steep station approach road with commercial traffic. As at Burnmouth no station nameboard ('running-in board') and no platform lighting were provided. Shortly after the Railway opened the company applied for permission to obtain a water supply for their engines. Soon, just beyond the Burnmouth end of the platform, a large water tank, for locomotive purposes, was erected on a brick base.

Major Marindin was quite scathing in his report following his initial inspection of Eyemouth station:

> The buildings consist of a small wooden hut, and the accommodation provided is insufficient; the station approach is too narrow and badly metalled, and no provision has been made for lighting the platform. The station is not properly fenced in. A separate approach for foot passengers should be added, and proper station buildings constructed.

To conclude his first report he added, that as a result of the incompleteness of the Works the line could not be opened to passenger traffic without danger to the public. He added that the North British Railway should be contacted as to whether they would give an undertaking to improve the station at Burnmouth. Finally he commented that the existing buildings at Eyemouth could be sanctioned for use as a temporary measure, but only on an undertaking to provide proper buildings within six months.

In his second report, written after a further inspection some six weeks after the first, Major Marindin recognised the improvements that had been made at Burnmouth platform and at Eyemouth Harbour [sic]. He noted that the North British station remained as before, but that the officers of the North British Railway were drawing up plans for considerable amendments, to be carried out without delay. His comments about Eyemouth were brief:

> At Eyemouth the station buildings are poor, but as far as I can ascertain, the passenger traffic will be very small. Under these circumstances I think it will be sufficient if the Eyemouth Railway Company undertake to erect buildings of a more permanent character whenever called upon to do so.

He sanctioned the opening of the line for passenger traffic provided that an undertaking was received from the North British Railway that the improvements, including a ramp at the end of the Eyemouth platform, be carried out within a year. He also required an Annett's Lock to be fitted at a set of points at Eyemouth and that the line should be worked with one engine in steam, carrying a staff as authority to proceed.

Within a short time after opening the Eyemouth Railway provided alternative access to the Eyemouth station platform in the form of a flight of steps leading directly down to the platform from Victoria Road. Documents survive which illustrate this additional work that was required at the Eyemouth end of the line. Works proposed in March 1895, for example, involved the expenditure of over £400 on embankment works, construction of retaining walls, fencing, a gate and metalling of road surfaces. In addition work was necessary on the moving of buffer stops, on some of the permanent way in the sidings and to the office and weighing machine.

Paying the bills

The initial capital authorized for the building of the Eyemouth line was a total of £40,000 made up of a possible £30,000 from the sale of stocks and shares and loans up to the value of £10,000. The majority of the expenditure on 'Construction', some £20,318 16s. 3d., had been spent by the half-year accounts after the opening of the line in April 1891. A further £7,354 2s. 9d. was spent by the end of 1891. Then, between the start of 1892 and the amalgamation with the North British Railway in 1900 the company accounts show that additional construction costs, some referred to above, raised the final sum to £29,915 4s. 11d.

Whilst the length of line appearing in early half-yearly reports was described as being of '2 miles, 7 furlongs and 7 chains' it is interesting to note that from 1894 onwards until 1899 the reports refer to '1 furlong and 8 chains' still to be constructed. This, of course, refers to the possible extension of the line to the quayside, though as early as the 30th April, 1890 it had been decided that any extension of the rails into the harbour, and the associated expenses, should be left to 'those interested'! The costs of the extension would have included the expensive purchase of two properties lying in the line of the proposed route.

Trials and tribulations: the builders of the railway

By the start of the last decade of the 19th century the era of the 'navvy', the hard-working, hard-drinking railway-building labourer was almost over. With the exception of the Great Central Railway's London Extension, all of the great railway works were complete. Those contracts that did remain, and they included the building of the Eyemouth Railway, were generally much smaller and involved the construction of short branch lines, track widening or the shortening of existing routes. Finally, machines were taking over from the manual labour of the navvies.

Nevertheless railway building was still an arduous occupation on these remaining smaller contracts. Health and safety was not of paramount importance as it is in the 21st century and accidents could, and did, take place, often with calamitous results.

At the end of the working day it was traditional for heavy manual workers to replenish their lost body fluids with many pints of the local beverage and, as a consequence, arguments and fighting could break out. Local courts could be kept busy adjudicating on these incidents and it was fortunate that the local police were able to anticipate possible trouble. On Tuesday 8th October, 1889 the *Berwickshire News and General Advertiser* reported:

> The contractor for constructing the Eyemouth Railway having employed a number of labourers it may be necessary to re-appoint an extra constable when the workmen are increased, the Treasury giving one half his pay, the Secretary for Scotland having consented to an extra constable being added to the force for duty on Eyemouth harbour works, and retained as an extra constable after that harbour was completed.

Fortunately the local newspapers reported both the trials and the tribulations! For example, t*he Berwick Journal* of 24th April, 1890 reported that on the night of Saturday the 19th the navvies, engaged on what was described as 'the New Railway Work', were unusually turbulent. A riot took place in a local common lodging house and at about 10.30 pm two of Eyemouth's policemen arrived to apprehend one of the ringleaders. Whilst they were sorting out this problem a message arrived to say that another riot was taking place, this time at the house of widow Collin, near the Salt Greens, where other navvies lodged. A crowd of nearly 2,000 people was collected around the house when the policemen forced their way in accompanied by a coastguard officer and some members of the public who had volunteered to assist! A young lodger named Michael Gallagher was badly cut and bruised whilst all of the inmates were generally smeared with blood. The police enquiries revealed that Gallagher had been attacked by a certain Michael O'Keffe [*sic*] and his son Bernard 'Barney' O'Keffe who used both their hands and their boots in the affray causing their victim to receive injuries of a serious nature. Another lodger, Alexander Cockburn, took part in this assault also, whilst another lodger, James O'Nairn, claimed to have been attacked by the O'Keffes. The O'Keffes and Cockburn were handcuffed and taken away to be locked up awaiting trial.

When brought before the magistrates, charged with committing a disturbance, the accused pleaded not guilty. Following the testimony of witnesses the cases were considered proven with Bernard sentenced to 30 days' imprisonment, and Michael O'Keffe and Alex Cockburn being given the option of 14 days' imprisonment or a 15s. fine. Michael paid his fine whilst the other two were sent to prison. Another navvy, Bernard McGladrigan, attended the same Magistrates' session and was sent to prison for 20 days having committed a breach of the peace on the same evening in Church Street and High Street.

Both the *Berwick Journal* and the *Berwickshire News* reported that on 28th April another labourer on the railway, namely Bernard Gallacher, appeared before the Eyemouth Burgh Court charged with a breach of the peace in the lodging house of David Simpson in Church Street on the previous evening. He pleaded guilty alleging that drink was the cause! He was given the option of seven days in prison or a fine of 7s. The Burgh Court found John Becket, another railway navvy, guilty of a similar offence a week later, and in July the navvy William Winship was found guilty of rioting, being given the option of seven days in prison or a 7s. fine.

Another sitting of the Burgh Court dealt with about 20 cases in August 1890. The cases included:

James Ballantyne, labourer on the railway pleading guilty to being drunk and unable to take care of himself
Dennis Ferry, railway labourer, similar charges; also pleaded guilty
Alexander Simpson, William Crombie Patterson and John Purves, labourers, perhaps working on the railway, charged with breaches of the peace; all three were found guilty.

On 6th October, two railway labourers, Patrick and Bernard Lynch, pleaded guilty to a charge of breach of the public peace and were given the option of imprisonment or fines. On the same day a railway labourer, Thomas Wilson and his wife Mary were charged with stealing a silver watch and chain whilst sleeping in the Yawl Hotel and for stealing a bath towel! Mary received the alternative of 30 days imprisonment (in Edinburgh's Calton jail) or a fine of 21s.; her husband's punishment was half of these amounts.

So much for the 'trials' which revealed a variety of charges which would not be considered 'untypical' of those associated with the navvies on other railway building contracts. During the duration of the Eyemouth works there were several 'tribulations' suffered by members of the navvy community.

On 17th April, 1889 a certain John Gibson, employed as a waggon driver on the Eyemouth railway works met with a serious accident. He needed to tip a loaded waggon and with this in mind he started his horse at a brisk pace aiming to give the waggon some impetus. He was trying to unfasten a tail chain when he lost his footing and fell under the waggon. One of the waggon's wheels ran over his right arm, fracturing bones and causing lacerations. In view of the severity of his injuries he was taken to the Royal Infirmary in Edinburgh, arriving the day after the accident where a portion of the fractured bone was removed from his arm. The *Berwick Journal* described his case as 'an unfortunate one' as Gibson had a wife and a large family.

On 13th June, 1889 another unfortunate and serious accident took place on the railway works, referred to as a *'Blasting Accident'* by the local press. It appears that on an unspecified section of the works the members of the night shift had prepared two blasts. They had, as required, retired to a safe distance and taken shelter. The two blasts duly took place and the men started to return to their place of work when a totally unexpected third blast took place! A labourer, John Brown, resident in nearby Ayton, was knocked to the ground by this blast and was badly injured by flying pieces of rock. His subsequent treatment was not recorded.

A totally different tribulation took place at Eyemouth at about 3.30 on the afternoon of 4th August, 1889 when there was a sad case of drowning. James Hiferty, aged 27, an Irish labourer working on the construction of the Eyemouth Railway, was sea bathing, with two companions, in Killiedraught Bay near Eyemouth Fort. Hilferty claimed to be able to swim and ventured into deeper water whilst his two companions, who could not swim, remained in the shallows. The companions noticed that Hiferty was in difficulty and shouted for assistance. Various people came to help, with a fisherman, David Windram, being the first to approach Hilferty, but his body had already started to sink beneath the surface. Another fisherman, Robert Oliver and his son also approached and made attempts to reach Hilferty by diving. These efforts were unsuccessful and the body of the drowned man was eventually removed from the water 30 minutes later by means of a boathook. A camp meeting was being held on the nearby fort at this time and a huge crowd of people witnessed the event and the recovery of the body. Hilferty was said to be a respectable man who had banked money since working at Eyemouth. It was reported that he had a brother in Scotland whilst his mother was resident in Ireland.

Another incident on the railway's construction was reported in the *Edinburgh Evening News* of Wednesday 18th February, 1891:

> In the Second Division of the Court of Session today, their Lordships ordered issues for trial by jury of an action by Andrew Macfarlane, labourer, Berwick, against William Beattie & Sons, contractors, 29, Fountainbridge, Edinburgh, for £800 as damages. In June last pursuer was working on the Eyemouth Railway, and on the 9th of that month, the day on which he entered their employment, the foreman, without warning, allowed a waggon to run him down, while he was working with his back to it, one of his legs being run over, and requiring to be amputated. Defenders say that pursuer knew the waggon was being fetched, and should have kept clear of it, and they also say that it there was any fault it was that of fellow workmen.

The *Edinburgh Evening News* of 25th August, 1891 reported that after a two-day trial at the Courts of Session that the contractors should pay Macfarlane £800 for damages in respect of his injuries. The jury decided that he should also receive £130 under the Employers' Liability Act. The fault for the accident was attributed to a single, unnamed, fellow workman.

It is unfortunate that the 1891 census took place shortly after the navvies had been laid off from the Eyemouth works. As a result it has not been possible to compile a complete list of those involved. However, a study of the census shows that some of the persons whose names have appeared in this section remained as householders or residents in Eyemouth or nearby. Other individuals, with names of Irish and Scottish origin, appear in the lists of those who suffered 'trials' and 'tribulations' but many of these do not appear in the census, having, perhaps, migrated on to other works in the true navvy tradition!

A turn-of-the-century scene showing part of the Eyemouth fishing fleet in the bay waiting its turn to enter the rather space-restricted Eyemouth Harbour. At this time both sail- and engine-powered vessels operated out of Eyemouth.   *Author's Collection*

CORONATION EXPRESS CROSSING ROYAL BORDER BRIDGE.
BERWICK-ON-TWEED.
45

A Gresley-designed class 'A4' Pacific hauls the northbound 'Coronation Express', which originated at Kings Cross and is heading for Edinburgh (Waverley), crossing the Royal Border Bridge and passing the signal gantry controlling the approaches to Berwick-upon-Tweed station.
Author's Collection

This pre-1920 photograph of Berwick station shows the original platform layout before rebuilding. Platforms lie at the side of each of the running lines. Note the plethora of advertisements decking the walls, including those on boards headed 'East Coast', 'Great Northern' and 'Midland' railways.
Berwick Record Office Collection

Chapter Four

The route described

The main line: Berwick-upon-Tweed to Burnmouth

Although most trains shuttled between Eyemouth and Berwick, some trains on the Eyemouth branch either started or terminated their journey at Berwick-upon-Tweed station. As detailed later, the locomotives operating on the branch were allocated, until 1923, to the North British Railway locomotive shed at Berwick. After this depot closed, they were transferred to the former North Eastern Railway depot at Tweedmouth, south of Berwick beyond the Royal Border Bridge over the River Tweed. At the start and end of many working days the Eyemouth branch locomotive would proceed from or to its depot, using the Burnmouth to Berwick portion of the East Coast main line. Therefore in the interests of 'completeness' it is useful to include a brief historical summary relating to the station at Berwick and the two locomotive depots, plus a brief description of the short section of railway between Berwick and Burnmouth.

The North British Railway's Parliamentary Bill for the building of the line from 'the City of Edinburgh to the town of Berwick-on-Tweed' received the Royal Assent on 4th July, 1844 after a surprisingly straightforward passage through Parliament. Grainger and Miller were appointed engineers for the line and 12 different contractors started work at different places. The line reached Berwick in 1846.

Meanwhile the Newcastle & Berwick Railway was approaching the River Tweed from the south. It arrived at Tweedmouth in March 1847. At first passengers between Tweedmouth and Berwick had to travel via the Tweed road bridge in horse-drawn carriages. However 18 months later, in September 1848, a temporary wooden viaduct across the river was opened to allow through rail travel. The foundation stone for the rail bridge (at first known as the 'Tweed Viaduct') across the Tweed was laid on 15th May, 1847. It was designed by Robert Stephenson and Thomas E. Harrison. The resident engineer was George Barclay Bruce and the contractors were McKay & Blackstock (who had already constructed part of the line northwards from Newcastle). The bridge had 28 arches of which 13 spanned the river and had a total length of 2,160 ft.

Though scheduled for completion in July 1849 it was not ready for traffic until March 1850. The official opening, by Queen Victoria and Prince Albert, took place on 29th August, 1850. The Queen gave her permission for the viaduct to be named 'The Royal Border Bridge'.

Berwick station was initially constructed by the North British Railway as a terminus. The arrival of the line from the south necessitated the provision of a through station. It had two platforms, the up platform being 156 yards in length with the down platform being 153 yards long. The station was on a curve with some 73 yards of the platforms being covered. The main facilities were located on the up platform: booking office, refreshment rooms, waiting rooms, telegraphic office and sales stalls. The down platform was provided with just a small waiting room. The platforms were linked by a narrow footbridge. Two through roads were provided to the west of the passenger station. (Note that in England the 'up' direction was towards London; in Scotland the 'up' platform was for trains heading for Edinburgh.)

By the start of the 20th century this station provided for the main line services as well as the branch line trains to St Boswells (via Tweedmouth), Duns (via Reston) and Eyemouth. The main line trains were becoming longer and the Directors of the North British Railway authorized improvements in November 1914. The provision of an up goods loop was completed in 1916 and a new Castlegate bridge was finished in 1921 but the works for the new station and signal boxes were deferred for war reasons. The works commenced in April 1924 by which time the North British Railway had become part of the LNER. A new island platform was constructed for passenger traffic, with the up platform having a face of 813 feet, whilst the down platform measured 807 feet in length. Some of the station facilities were moved to the new platform: the first and third class refreshment rooms (plus their kitchen), waiting rooms, station master's office, bookstall and telegraph office. Other facilities were located on the site of the old buildings: booking office, a refreshment room and parcel office. A covered footbridge and a luggage bridge linked the main station buildings and the new platforms. The platforms had a 240 ft glazed roof. The work was carried out by the contractors Hugh Symington & Sons with William A. Fraser as the supervising engineer and the work was completed by 1927.

The North British Railway locomotive shed was located on the west side of the main lines just to the north of the 'old' Berwick station and this provided motive power for the Eyemouth branch from its opening until its closure in 1924. Details of the North British Railway depot, and the North Eastern Railway's shed at Tweedmouth which survived it, are described later.

Eyemouth trains left Berwick firstly under the control of Berwick Central signal box (located at the station) and then Berwick North box. The line curved from a north-easterly direction towards the north-west, hugging the East Coast for almost all of the distance towards Burnmouth. On leaving the level track in Berwick station the line commenced an uphill 1 in 190 gradient for almost the entire section to Burnmouth, slackening to 1 in 400 just under a mile before the latter. For much of the Berwick to Burnmouth section the coastline consists of rather friable sandstone cliffs with rocks exposed at low tide. There has never been a station between Berwick and Burnmouth but there was an intermediate railway 'location' namely Marshall Meadows. In the 19th and early 20th century the main line was double tracked at this point, though a North British Railway plan shows a very short siding, of unknown function, on the south side of the down (i.e. from Edinburgh) line. In 1884 the railway published a plan, a copy of which resides in the Berwick Record Office, to create a 'new railway' to the north of the signal box. In reality it was a diversion of the main line inland as a result of the poor condition of the sea cliffs which were very close to the original alignment. The diversion was some 1,390 yards in length. The new line necessitated the steepening of the gradient for a short distance from 1 in 190 to

1 in 150, though a short section followed at 1 in 320 before the 1 in 190 resumed onwards towards Burnmouth. The plan, and accompanying notes, indicated the need to demolish an old farm road bridge at this point and create a new one further inland, though a temporary wooden bridge was to be used whilst the works progressed. The old route and trackbed of the railway was abandoned.

Ready for the 1921 Parliamentary Session the North British Railway published a further plan for the purchase of additional land at the side of the main line, a short distance to the south of the diverted route, near to a coastal feature known as 'Needles Eye'. The land was to provide additional space for the creation of up and down loops. Thus was formed a short length of quadruple track under the control of the Marshall Meadows signal box. This box had a 44-lever frame though some 15 or so of its levers were unused. The track layout here thus consisted of the two main lines, connected at the south end by a trailing crossover. On the outside of each main line was a loop, one loop passing behind the signal box. The two loops were fitted with trap points at both ends. They were used to allow slower trains to be overtaken by expresses. At the turn of the century the Marshall Meadows signal box was closed from 10 pm on Saturdays until 6 am on Monday mornings; otherwise it was open continuously.

There is another interesting feature at Marshall Meadows, namely a tunnel, constructed in the mid-19th century, which connects the rocky beach at Marshall Meadows Bay with the cliff surface. Various suggestions have been proposed over the years for its function. These have including housing a railway for bringing up seaweed (for fertiliser) or fish or even to support smuggling activities! However, it is now known that the tunnel was actually used to convey cut stone from a nearby quarry down to a small loading jetty for onward transport by sea for the building of the Royal Border bridge. The tunnel was fitted at one time with a type of water-powered winch at its upper end. Originally the mouth of this tunnel was on the landward, or west, side of the main line but later, as a result of the new alignment the tunnel mouth could be found to the east of the line. (The former track alignment now forms part of the Berwickshire Coastal Path and also an access road to caravans and holiday lodges.)

North of Marshall Meadows train travellers can enjoy views over the sea as the line continues to hug the coast. Approaching Burnmouth the gradient eases to 1 in 400 and the line starts to turn inland so that the sea disappears from sight until just beyond Cockburnspath. Entering Burnmouth station the route passes beneath the Burnmouth to Eyemouth road. When heading north, Burnmouth was the next signal box, in the 1890s, being 3 miles and 63 chains north of Marshall Meadows.

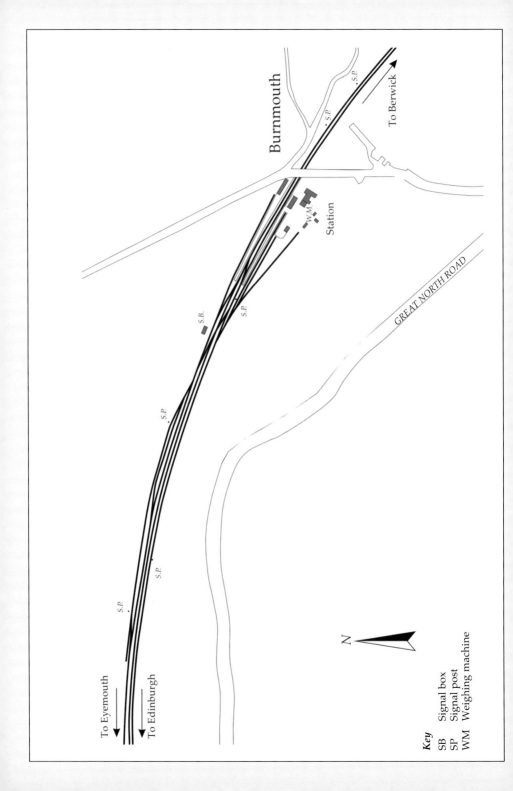

The branch line: a contemporary description

The *Berwick Journal* of 22nd August, 1889 contained a brief description of the line published *well in advance* of its opening, though it was largely written in the present tense! This description is reproduced here with maintenance of the original spellings and punctuation:

> The new line branches off from the 'down' line (that from Edinburgh to Berwick) of the North British Railway at Burnmouth station, runs parallel with it in the direction of Ayton for about half-a-mile on the existing railway embankment, then strikes into Fairneyside Wood, beginning a curve of 25 chains radius, which, after passing through the grounds of Ayton Castle and Lord Brownlow, and crossing underneath the public road near Hillburn Smithy, goes down and along the south bank of the river Eye, until nearly opposite to Linthill Cottages. Here the river and the Eyemouth Mill Lade are crossed by a handsome viaduct of six spans ... Spanning a picturesque dean, within 200 yards of the main road between Ayton and Eyemouth, the viaduct will be well seen from the road, and will add to, rather than detract from, the beauty of the locality. After crossing the Eye, the railway enters the lands of Colonel Mills Home [*sic*], passing underneath the public road near Biglaw-Burn, and thereafter running parallel with the public road, for about half a mile, along its Northside until near to Eyemouth Old Toll, where it recrosses the road to the haugh on the north side of the Eye, continuing along the haugh through a tunnelled way at the north end of Eyemouth Bridge, reaching Mrs. Jardine's garden (opposite to Messrs. Weatherhead's boat building yard) where the Eyemouth Station will be situated. A branch line will be taken down to the harbour, and arrangements made to meet the traffic there.

This 1889 report is somewhat brief and omits both details of the branch stations and details of the severe gradients, the sharp curves and some of the engineering works. Fortunately other sources allow these details to be added.

Burnmouth station

As the above article stated, the Eyemouth branch started at Burnmouth station. The station at Burnmouth first appeared in the North British Railway's timetable dated July 1848. The NBR had decided in September 1845, to build 'permanent' stations which included Ayton and Berwick. Burnmouth thus appears to have been a later addition.

Fortunately large scale maps have survived showing details of Burnmouth station before the branch was constructed. The first large scale (25 in.) Ordnance Survey map shows the up and down main lines passing through the station. To the north of the main lines, adjacent to the down line (i.e. carrying Berwick-bound trains) there was a single siding. A trailing crossover linked the two main lines on the Ayton side of this crossover. A single trailing point left the up line (i.e. carrying Edinburgh-bound trains). After a few yards this connection gave rise, via a possible three-way point, to three sidings: the first, running parallel to the main lines terminated at the side-loading dock, the second led to, and through, the goods shed, whilst the third was the shortest of the three and served the goods yard. The OS map indicates that the platforms were rather

Two postcard views of Burnmouth station. Note the lattice-post signals and the station buildings in the background. The top picture shows the up sidings with both open wagons and a van. The lower picture shows two North British locomotives in the platforms, one hauling a northbound stopping train. Note the fashionably-dressed passengers awaiting the train. The Eyemouth bay platform is visible on the left-hand side of both pictures.

Author's Collection (upper) & R.W. Lynn Collection (lower)

short but were extended on the Berwick side of the road bridge. Writing some 30 years later Major J.A. Marindin, inspecting on behalf of the Board of Trade commented: 'The North British Station at Burnmouth is … dangerously narrow beneath a road bridge'.

The main station building was located adjacent to the up platform and was approached via a driveway from the nearby Eyemouth road. This could be closed off by means of a pair of gates. In the yard was a weighbridge with adjacent weigh-house. The Berwick-bound platform appeared devoid of any buildings, with passengers presumably sheltering from any rain beneath the road overbridge! Various signal posts are shown on the map but curiously the position of the signal box is not indicated.

By the time that the next Ordnance Survey 25 in. maps were surveyed the Eyemouth branch had been open and operating for four years and Burnmouth station had undergone several changes. The track layout had changed to accommodate the Eyemouth traffic. The trailing crossover still linked the up and down main lines but was by this time within the confines of the extended platforms. The goods yard and sidings were substantially the same but with the addition of some small buildings, perhaps sheds. A new facing point, protected by a bracket signal, allowed a direct progression from the up main line, over a diamond crossing on the down main line, to the line of the Eyemouth branch. Another connection allowed Berwick-bound trains from the Eyemouth branch to access the down line. In addition there was a line which ran behind the down line platform providing a bay platform for terminating branch trains. Because of the narrowness of the site no run-round loop was provided in the platform. A train leaving the bay platform would first of all traverse the two points providing the main line links. Then there were two further points creating three parallel loop lines. After a hundred yards or so the left-hand loops joined to form a single track which then progressed further westwards. A short distance further on this line was joined, on its right-hand side, by the third of the original loop lines thus marking the start of the single line heading for Eyemouth. A short trap siding on the third loop prevented unauthorized movements across the link.

The 1890s map appears to indicate a larger signal box superimposed on a smaller building at the same site; certainly a larger lever frame would have been necessary to control the additional pointwork and signals after the opening of the branch. Some changes had taken place at the station itself. Firstly a station master's house had been constructed adjacent to the start of the drive leading to the station. The original goods shed on the middle siding had been demolished. However, a substantial platform building had been erected opposite the extended first siding, quite close to the main station building. A set of steps had been created linking the Eyemouth road to the platform and the station building appears to have a fenced off area between it and the platform. Other buildings had been erected in the yard including the goods shed and station store. On the down platform a building, presumably including a waiting room, was indicated adjacent to the road bridge.

Photographs show that the station now complied with Major Marindin's requirements regarding both station nameboards and lighting being provided on the platform. The upside platform (in 1903) is fenced with wooden palings and both platforms have paraffin lamps. In addition the two platforms have seating for passengers and proper sloping end-ramps. The downside accommodation presumably arose as a result of the Major's comments that 'accommodation for passengers is scanty' and 'the station is quite unsuitable for an Exchange Station' [sic]! A gated path allows access to the Eyemouth road. Post and wire fencing surrounds the station site. The signals are all of standard North British type carried on lattice posts with finials. Some, especially those located close to the Eyemouth road bridge, are very tall to improve visibility.

At the Eyemouth branch platform end a 'Warning' notice was provided for passengers. Some official drawings referred to this platform as the 'Dock Platform'. The platform ramp allowed station staff access to the boarded crossing across the main lines. A raised disc shunt signal, on the platform end, allowed a locomotive or train to reverse from the main line platform towards the Burnmouth loops, while on the east side of the track, on the opposite side to the platform face, was located a water tank with a brick-built base including a store with a centrally placed door and windows on either side. A water crane was placed, off the end of the Eyemouth platform. In the late 1950s the upper quadrant branch starting signal, still mounted on a lattice post, was also located on the side of the track close to the signal box and a further shunting disc signal was mounted on the same post. On the up Edinburgh platform, at the same time, there was an upper quadrant bracket signal with, of course, the arm controlling movements onto the Eyemouth branch being mounted lower than the signal for the main line. Track circuiting signs were mounted on all of these signals. There was no advanced starting signal for the branch despite the existence of connections to the 'branch sidings'. However, a train leaving the easternmost siding had such a signal mounted to the right of the track together with a ground-mounted shunt signal permitting access to the short headshunt. Track circuiting was not associated with this signal. A train approaching Burnmouth from the branch was faced with the Burnmouth distant signal (originally worked from a lever in Burnmouth box, but in the 1950s becoming fixed at caution) followed by the outer home signal. At the station end of the branch sidings there was a bracket signal which extended across the branch sidings. This carried the inner home signals, the last before the platforms. From the right to the left, as seen by the driver of a branch train, there was an upper quadrant arm controlling access to the main line platform, a shunt signal, a second arm for admission to the bay platform, below which was a short-armed calling-on signal for use when the platform was already partly occupied. Finally there was another signal on the bracket carrying a cross to indicate it was out of use. Two ground signals controlled egress of trains from the branch sidings, both of which were fitted with catch points to derail any runaways.

As with much of the Eyemouth line, the fencing at the start of the branch, marking the edge of the railway property was constructed of post and wire. The remains of this are still visible in some places along the line.

Burnmouth to Eyemouth

Fortunately both the large scale Ordnance Survey maps and Meik's amended 1884 plans for the line survive, although in the case of the latter there are some small differences between what was planned and what was actually constructed. A datum point for the measurements of the height of the lines was fixed, by Meik, as the OS mark on the side of Eyemouth church at about 119 ft above the Ordnance Datum. The heights of the Burnmouth station junction is recorded as just over 346 ft, whilst that at Eyemouth station as just over 111 ft. The railway thus fell about 235 ft in its total distance of 2 miles and 7 furlongs.

Note that the distances quoted in the following are taken from Meik's plan and are measured from the start of the new line. The trackside mileposts marked the distance from the connection to the main line at Burnmouth station. There is a difference of about 1 furlong between the two values.

The connection with the Edinburgh to Berwick main line at Burnmouth was on the level. The first furlong of the branch, as far as the Fairnieside bridge, descended on a gradient of 1 in 362, with the main line on the south side side and a steep cutting face on the other. The curve radius at this point was similar to the main line of between five and six furlongs. Fairnieside (to use the present spelling) bridge crossed a small road leading from the Great North Road to the house, farm and smithy at the hamlet of the same name. Its span was 15 ft and the bridge height was 14 ft, though the road had to be lowered by about five feet beneath the bridge to create this clearance.

Beyond the Fairnieside road bridge the down gradient steepened to 1 in 50 as the line switched from a left-hand curve to a curve towards the right, starting to lead it into a northwards direction. A fairly gentle radius of 3 furlongs 5 chains decreased to 1 furlong and 8 chains, then 1 furlong and 5 chains. The Hill Burn crossed the line in a 7-yard arched culvert at this point close to the last viewpoint towards the Great North Road and the main line. After the crossing of the burn the gradient eased slightly to 1 in 75. Five chains further on the railway passed beneath the bridge carrying the Duns to Eyemouth road. The hamlet of Hillburn with its smithy could be seen on the left-hand side. After this Netherbyres Mill, a corn mill powered by the Eyewater, could be glimpsed down in the steep-sided river valley on the left. The line was now becoming straighter as the curve radius increased to 7½ furlongs, the downward gradient steepening to 1 in 50 once more. A small overbridge, which enabled pedestrians or animals to cross the track, spanned the line opposite the house known as Balabraes, located on the opposite bank of the Eyewater.

A short distance after this bridge the line commenced a sharp left-hand curve, originally planned as of 1 furlong and 4 chains radius, but eased to 1 furlong 5 chains when the plans were amended. At 1 mile and 6½ furlongs the falling gradient eased to 1 in 80 as the line approached the brick and concrete abutments of the viaduct over the Eyewater, or River Eye on Meik's plans. The viaduct took the railway across both the river and the mill leat (or lead) taking water to power the mills at Netherbyres. The track over the brick-piered viaduct levelled off but resumed its 1 in 80 gradient immediately afterwards. The alignment of the viaduct was modified slightly from the original plans making

After leaving Burnmouth and crossing the road to Fairnieside Farm trains rounded a curve changing their direction from westwards to a more northerly direction. Here, a tender-first 'J39' class 0-6-0 descends around the curve with its Eyemouth-bound train.

Armstrong Railway Photographic Trust

'J39' class 0-6-0 No. 64843 of Tweedmouth depot hauls the 4.07 pm Burnmouth to Eyemouth train over the viaduct on the afternoon of 4th August, 1953. The train consists of the usual single BCK carriage. The rebuilt central pier still appears in 'pristine' condition.

Armstrong Railway Photographic Trust

the curvature of this section of the line less acute. For example the radius of the curve after the viaduct became 1 furlong and 5 chains rather than the 1 furlong 2 chains originally planned. The line then passed beneath the Ayton to Eyemouth public road at Biglawburn. The road needed to be altered so that the bridge over the railway provided sufficient clearance. Its span was 35 ft and the clearance was 16 ft over the line of rails. At this point the gradient was 1 in 60 downwards towards Eyemouth. The line after the Biglawburn bridge paralleled the road before Netherbyres Mill cottages and the twin mills on the right-hand side. The first mill to come into view from the carriage window was the sawmill and then the corn mill appeared. At different times the mills were known as Gunsgreen Mills or Eyemouth Mills, but were generally referred to in the community as 'Netherbyres Mills', despite there being a mill of the same name near Burnmouth. Before the coming of the railway the corn mill prepared pearl barley and oatmeal for shipping from the harbour to London.

Heading now in a north-easterly direction, and with Netherbyres House on the opposite bank of the Eye, the line passed beneath a small bridge (between Redhall and Hillburn, known as Gilsland or Gillsland bridge) where the road had to be raised by some seven feet to provide sufficient clearance for the railway. This bridge, as shown on Meik's map, was about 2 miles and 3 furlongs from Burnmouth. From 1 in 60 the gradient lessened slightly to 1 in 70 for a further furlong. The Road Trustees expected the road to be 'finished with a good metal surface and properly fenced'!

At this point it is necessary to explain that Meik's original plan had divided the proposed line into two parts, identified as Railway No. 1 and Railway No 2. The majority of the line appeared as part of Railway No. 1 starting at Burnmouth. This was shown as terminating on the north side of the Ayton to Eyemouth road almost opposite the Eyemouth Toll Bridge. This made the railway 2 miles, 4 furlongs and 6 chains in length to this point. As shown on the plan Railway No. 2 was to commence shortly before the bridge located at 2 miles and 3 furlongs. This deviation line was planned originally to descend towards the Eyewater on a short curve of 4 furlongs radius. By creating a skew bridge under the Ayton road this curve ceased to exist and, with both a new arch under the Toll Bridge and a ledge created above the river, it was possible to approach the proposed terminus at Eyemouth on a left-hand, 2 furlong radius curve. The roads mentioned required their surfaces to be raised at the bridges by 3 ft and 2 ft respectively. The length of Railway No. 2 was shown as 3 furlongs and 73 chains with planned gradients of 1 in 50 as far as the Toll Bridge and 1 in 65 onwards to the terminus on the opposite side of the river from Weatherhead's boat yard. The Eyemouth terminus site was rather cramped, squeezed in, as it was, between the river and, what is now, Victoria Road. The town end of the station site was almost level; one old postcard shows a gradient post, marking the start of the gradient up from the station, close to the platform end.

About 1½ furlongs of the planned Railway No. 1 were thus not constructed. The final length of 'new' railway using Meik's distance scale was just over 2 miles and 6 furlongs, in other words 2 miles 7 furlongs and 2 chains (2.9 miles) from the junction with the main line. A small extension into the harbour area, shown on one of Meik's plans with a lack of detail, was also not proceeded with.

Biglawburn bridge carried the Ayton to Eyemouth road over the branch railway on the Eyemouth side of the Linthill viaduct. The siding created at this point, mainly handled fuel oil and agricultural items, such as machinery, which could not be managed at Eyemouth's limited siding space.   *Eyemouth Museum Collection*

Netherbyres (or Eyemouth) Mill was located at the side of the road linking Eyemouth with Ayton. It was visible from trains on the branch. It obtained its power from the Eyewater. Recently the mill has undergone considerable modifications and restoration.   *Berwickshire News*

On the completed railway, using distances measured from the main line junction, Milepost 1 was placed midway between Hill Burn and the Duns road bridge whilst Milepost 2 was located on the embankment on the southern approach to the viaduct over the Eyewater.

Eyemouth station

The gentle curve to the left, over the land known as Crooked Haugh, brought the line into Eyemouth station directly below the large villa named 'Summerhill' still extant on Victoria Road. Another of Meik's plans, dated 4th May, 1891, shows the track plan of the station at Eyemouth, built on the land known as Kiln Haugh, for which a total area of 2.062 acres (2 acres and 10 perches) was needed. A facing point led a track away from the road leading to the platform; there followed a second point allowing access to the single quay siding adjacent to the Eyewater; this was generally used for the storage of fish wagons. Another point gave rise to a second shorter siding which ran parallel to the first; this was used by coal merchants. Both terminated at buffer stops. The platform road itself followed a gentle s-shaped curve alongside the platform on the left towards the buffer stops. Shortly before the buffer stops there was a crossover onto a run-round loop which connected with the second of the two sidings mentioned previously. This crossover allowed the train locomotive to run around onto the other end of its carriages (and wagons) before shunting or returning to Burnmouth. This was the layout when the line opened in the 1890s.

By the time of the next Ordnance Survey in 1906 the station layout had changed. Although the sidings were substantially the same, the crossover, permitting the release of the locomotive from the head of a train, had been removed and so 'running round' was no longer possible. This gave rise to an unusual, though not unique, method of releasing the loco for the rest of the line's existence! (The same method was used, for example, at Killin in Scotland, at Ramsey on the Isle of Man and various branch lines in the English West Country such as Princetown trains at Yelverton.)

On arriving in Eyemouth's platform a passenger or mixed train would discharge its passengers. Under the supervision of the guard and station staff the train would then reverse out of the station with the locomotive propelling its carriages and wagons. Once clear of the first set of station points the locomotive would halt and the train guard would pin down the brakes on the carriages and wagons to hold them on the sharp gradient. Once this was achieved the locomotive would be uncoupled from its train, the points would be changed (having been released by the key on the train staff) and it would run forward into one of the sidings. The points would then be reset for the platform road. On the release of the brakes by the guard the train would then gently roll forward, under the influence of gravity, regaining the station platform road. (Use of a pull cord prevented the vacuum brake operating thus permitting carriage movement.) At this point the locomotive could be freed from the siding for shunting or for heading a train back to Burnmouth. An edition of the *Edinburgh Evening News* referred to the fact that there were no signals apart from 'hand ones for the catch points'.

A crossing of the Ayton to Eyemouth road over the railway was located at Gillsland (or Gilsland) to the south of the Toll Bridge, beneath which the railway also passed. The Gillsland bridge was built on a 'skew'. In this old view, taken well before the advent of recent housing developments, the Ayton road crosses over the line from left to right.

Eyemouth Museum Collection

Pictures of tank locomotives on the Eyemouth branch are rare. No. 828 was recorded by Coldingham photographer Mr J. Wood in the sidings at Eyemouth. The combination of the 1900/01-built locomotive, the post-1900 new station building (with its awning) and the continued existence of the platform run-round loop (removed by 1904) allows the photograph to be dated to about 1902-03. The locomotive became a member of the 'J83' class in LNER days.

Author's Collection

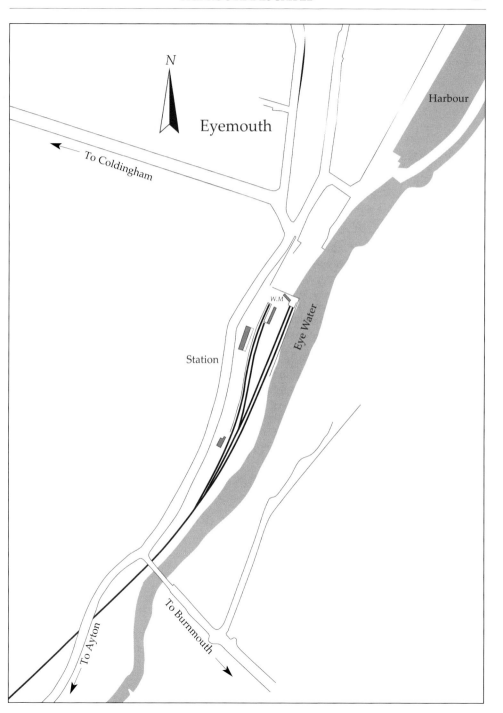

The 1898 map shows that the station was approached via a short driveway down from Victoria Road. This was quite steeply inclined. The small station building was located on the platform. In his inspection at the time of the line's opening, Major Marindin had been most unhappy with the facilities here.

Fortunately picture postcards, published before and around 1900, have survived and show the station and its facilities both before and after improvements. The station approach drive is visible and is gated at the station entrance. Later cards show that an L-shaped staircase was provided for foot passengers leading down from the main road. A stone wall separates the roadway from the steep bank above the station platform. Another short length of retaining wall was built against the steep bank at the base of the slope and fencing was erected beyond this as far as the station building on platform. This building has plain barge boarding but lacks an awning; it is recessed towards its centre. A smoking chimney stack on one end indicates the presence of a fire and posters adorn this left-hand end of the building! Next to the station building is the grounded body of an old coach, perhaps acting as a store or as a waiting room facility for passengers. Another of Marindin's requests was followed in that several lamp standards were erected at this end of the platform though there appears to be none beyond the grounded coach. At the Eyemouth end of the platform was located the water tower for replenishing locomotives. Details of the changes in the water supply are described later. The map indicates the presence of a weighbridge and adjacent weighhouse in the small station yard.

The 1906 survey map indicates some changes apart from the removal of the engine release crossover. In the yard there are a crane and loading dock adjacent to the siding formed from the original run-round loop. A small shed or shelter appears to have been made abutting onto the water tank and a small hut, perhaps for platelayers, has been built adjacent to the track on the Eyemouth side of the Toll Bridge. However by far the most dramatic change on the map is the appearance of a new station building which replaced the original which was destroyed in a fire on 15th February, 1900. The event was reported in both the *Berwick Journal* and the *Sunderland Daily Echo and Shipping Gazette*. The *Journal* article read as follows:

> On Thursday a storm of unusual severity raged here … About midnight while the gale was at its height the booking office and waiting rooms at the station were burned to the ground. These buildings were of wooden construction, and with such a high wind to fan the flames the fabric soon became a wreck, despite the efforts of the fire brigade. The origin of the fire is unknown.

The replacement station building was constructed in the NBR-style with yellowish brick-built gables and rear walls plus a timber framed and lined screen. James Hay, in an article in *Railway Modeller* magazine, stated that the walls were built with 13½ in. brick. The timber screen consisted of $2^7/_8$ in. x $2^7/_8$ in. frames with vertical 3 in. tongued and grooved cladding. The roof was of Ballachulish slate from the west of Scotland capped with a zinc roll. Originally the paintwork was an off-white colour with brown doors but later it was changed, for a few years, to a blue-green shade all over. The final colour scheme, right up to the final closure of the station, was of cream above the level of the sills, with the lower portion being in a dark chocolate shade. The doors and window frames were in the same chocolate shade with cream window sashes. The roof bore three chimney stacks with a small gable and fanlight above the toilets at the right-hand end. The end windows had stone lintels and sills. From the passenger point of view the presence of an awning on the rail side of the building was a marked improvement! Photographs showing the new station building in slightly later years also indicate the extension of the fencing at the rear of the platform and the presence of additional lamps along the platform.

Note that no running signals or signal box were ever provided at Eyemouth station, the points being worked by hand levers released by the Annett's key carried by the guard. The branch was always worked on the 'one engine in steam' principle though two locomotives coupled together could count as a single engine to follow this rule. Evidence of this latter practice arises, for example, from some photographs of special trains on the branch in the 1950s.

Now the character of a railway line derives from its day-to-day happenings, its relationships with the communities that it serves, incidents happening on the line both major and minor, and the various other trivia and minutiae related to the running of the line. Fortunately many official documents relating to the Eyemouth branch have survived and, for the early years at least, the census records can be viewed. Over the years the memories of local residents and handed-down information recall happenings on the line. Finally film-makers, reporters and informants of both local and national newspapers and journals have produced more permanent records of the Eyemouth branch. In the following four chapters, are described some of the details of events, happenings and memories that have survived. The train services, the operations and the various railway accidents on the line are detailed in separate chapters later in this work.

A 1950s view of 'J39' class No. 64843 in Eyemouth station. The usual gravity-shunting of the carriage has allowed the locomotive to be attached to the front of the train which it will shortly haul to Burnmouth. However, it appears to have a red lamp attached to the buffer-beam bracket. The crew relax on the platform awaiting their departure time. The yard, with its goods shed and crane, is littered with crates, barrels and boxes.   *R.M. Casserley*

Victoria Road, Eyemouth

This picture postcard dates from the 1890s and appears to be the only view of the station in Eyemouth Railway days, as it shows the first station which was destroyed by fire in February 1900. The grounded coach body provides the additional passenger accommodation requested by Inspector Marindin, though the platform lighting is still confined to the vicinity of the building. The steps leading up to Victoria Road are, however, in place. The sheeted wagons almost certainly contain fish. Most are of North British origin though at least one is labelled 'G&SW' (Glasgow & South Western Railway). *Author's Collection*

Chapter Five

Eyemouth Railway days: 1891-1900

By 30th April, 1890 the Directors had decided that the extension of the rails from the new Eyemouth station site into the harbour area, and the associated expenses, should be left to 'those interested'. Yet after the line was opened to traffic, half-yearly and annual Reports, throughout the 1890s contained references to 1 furlong and 8 chains of the railway still being constructed, presumably the harbour extension! The *Berwickshire News* reported that this 1890 half-yearly meeting had lasted little more than a minute!

The line was opened in the absence of any opening ceremony or celebrations on Monday 13th April, 1891. Even the local newspapers considered the event to be 'low key'. The *Berwickshire News*, in its edition published the day after the opening, reported as follows: 'Yesterday the branch line between Burnmouth and Eyemouth was opened for passenger and goods traffic'. The edition of 21st April was a little more forthcoming in that it mentioned that the newly opened branch had done a good business in its first week. However, it was somewhat scathing about the station accommodation at Eyemouth it being 'not equal to the amount of goods traffic'. It added that a heavy day's fishing would undoubtedly bring things to a deadlock. 'As it is, a number of fish-carts may be seen daily on the passenger platform, a circumstance which causes much inconvenience'. It commented favourably on the efficient railway station staff who were doing their best to carry out the work as smoothly and efficiently as they could!

During the 1890s various plans were proposed, presumably in the light of both Marindin's Report and operating experience, to modify the station layout at Eyemouth. The *Southern Reporter* of 13th July, 1891 stated:

The work in connection with the Eyemouth railway station improvements has again commenced, and the siding, which was stopped by the Eyemouth Harbour trustees interdicting the railway company, is being proceeded with. The accommodation for traffic is to be greatly augmented, and a new entrance for passenger traffic from the toll road is to be made, at the foot of which a new booking office is to be erected. The platform is to be entirely renewed and greatly enlarged, and the cost is estimated at £1,100.

The article went on to refer to the large amount of fish traffic passing and an incident when the platform edge fell away.

In August 1891 it was agreed that the Eyemouth Railway be leased to the North British Railway for 999 years, the agreement being retrospectively dated to 1st January, 1891. The NBR took a quantity of Debenture stock and would guarantee a temporary loan made to the Eyemouth Railway by the Clydesdale Bank.

Examination of the Eyemouth Railway accounts reported that a total of over £7,350 was spent on 'construction' items in the six-month period leading up to 31st December, 1891. This expenditure, after the line was open to traffic, was almost as much as any 'six-month expenditure' when the line was under construction! The works included the construction of the weigh house, by Beattie, and (in early 1892) the purchase of an old carriage body from the NBR, (for the princely sum of £10), for use on the platform as a store. This carriage appears in some early photographs of the station.

By March 1892 the *Berwickshire News* was able to report that a new siding had been completed, thus affording greater accommodation for wagons. Some slight alterations had been made to the booking office but it was felt that these were only temporary improvements and that in order to secure sufficient railway accommodation at Eyemouth the line should be taken down to the Quay. 'It is understood that this will be done at no distant date.' One major stumbling block to the extension was that it should be done at the expense of those interested! The inflated cost of purchase of a house standing in the way of the proposed extension made the whole scheme prohibitive to both the railway and the harbour company. This issue was raised over many future years and, in the event, the project was never effected.

However, the new railway was clearly having an impact locally. The *Berwickshire News* reported that several visitors had already made their appearance at Eyemouth. The paper even predicted that Eyemouth would become a favourite seaside resort! Notice of the opening of the railway had clearly percolated down the Northumberland coast for in May 1892 the same newspaper referred to North Sunderland, which, having seen that the Eyemouth Railway was established, wanted its own branch railway to run to the North Eastern Railway main line at or near to Chathill. The prospects for the line, estimated to cost about £16,000 were considered to be hopeful with the coastal village of Bamburgh also set to benefit from the line's construction. This independent line was authorized in 1892 with construction starting in 1896 and the opening of the line taking place in 1898. A similar proposal for a line from Goswick to Holy Island came to naught.

Returning to Eyemouth itself the local newspapers contained several more references to potential tourist traffic. So as to popularize Eyemouth some residents were in favour of 'introductions' to meet the wants of visitors (*Berwickshire News* 7th May, 1892). A bathing pond was suggested, for example, with the thought that the local hotel and lodging keepers should contribute to the subscription for its construction as they would ultimately benefit. The *News* also suggested that changes to the NBR's timetable for the line could be adjusted so as to allow Glasgow residents to leave the city at 5.15 pm on Saturday afternoons and reach Eyemouth the same evening. It was suggested that if this arrangement could be extended into the summer season, and linked with trains from Berwick and North Berwick, it would benefit Eyemouth to an enormous extent. 'The little village is becoming more and more popular with western visitors'.

The same month the NBR made itself unpopular with the fishing trade in Eyemouth. The first train of the morning from Eyemouth was the 7.35 am. Until the first days of July 1892 this train had carried fresh fish, particularly herring, for the local markets. These fish were of value when used at once; they were not suitable for kippering. This was a serious matter to the fish-curers and buyers.

On the day after the introduction of a new rule prohibiting fish transport on this train the loss to the buyers was said to be just a little short of £40 whilst the loss to the railway was some £20 in carriage! The *Dundee Courier* reported that as the fleet followed the herring, the number of boats entering Eyemouth could increase tenfold within ten days! Representatives of the local trade were appointed to communicate with the railway managers with a view to having this rule abolished. As the matter received no further reporting it is assumed that the trade presented its case successfully!

The Eyemouth Railway, and the North British Railway that operated the line on its behalf, were still under pressure to improve facilities at Eyemouth. On the 29th November, 1894 a joint deputation of the harbour representatives and the NBR met with the Public Works Loan Commissioners in London. The General Manager, on behalf of the railway interests stated that a submission to the Directors of his company for finance would not take place unless the Commissioners would advance the sum of £30,000 necessary to make the harbour suitable for steam trawlers. However the railway did receive a 'bonus' in that a North British 'omnibus' Act authorized the repayment of the monies that had been forfeited when the railway was late in its completion. The Act is often described as an omnibus Act in that it contained a very wide range of unrelated provisions: extending time limits, authorizing subscription increases and acquisition of additional land as well as the repayment for the Eyemouth company.

In March 1895 successive plans were drawn up for improvements at the station. One proposal was to construct a goods shed adjacent to the sidings adjacent to the Eye, together with a new siding and an extension to the loading bank next to the passenger road. This would have necessitated moving the ground frame which operated the points to allow the locomotive to run-round its train. It would also have involved removal of the weigh house, weighing machine and stores adjacent to the loading bank. The total cost of all of the works would have amounted to £835 including a 10 per cent contingency sum.

Examination of the Eyemouth Railway's accounts indicates that this scheme was not advanced: the railway only spent a total sum of about £130 on 'construction' during the period from July 1895 to the end of 1898.

The second plan, dated 19th March, 1895, suggested some possible intent on the part of the NBR to extend beyond the station site towards the harbour, in that it indicated the 'Land Required' for the development. Immediately beyond the railway's loading bank and buffer stops was ground of 0.198 acre which was the property of a certain Mrs Topping, of 136 Causewayside in Edinburgh. Beyond this was 0.394 acre which was the property of Miss Hay of Bridgend, Eyemouth.

This scheme, after the purchase of the land, would have involved substantial changes to the station layout. The run-round at the end of the platform would have been retained but the loop line onto which the locomotive was released would have been extended to accommodate 10 wagons. A new loading bank would have been provided on the station access road side of this line. Two new stores (purpose unspecified) would be erected on the south side of this new siding, level with the end of the platform. The existing weigh house, weighbridge and store would have been removed, a new store and the 'weighs' to be re-erected adjacent to the end of the new 10-wagon siding. The removal of the original weigh house would permit the extension of the second quayside siding to accommodate seven extra rail wagons. The yard area would be increased and there would be new access from the highway for vehicles via the former land of Miss Hay. The wall adjacent to the quay would be strengthened and a new small slipway provided. Both of these plans showed the new passenger access to the station via steps from Victoria Road. Nothing came of this scheme either in Eyemouth Railway days; however, some changes were to be made when the line became part of the NBR.

In the early 1890s the station master at Eyemouth was John Gordon whilst his counterpart at Burnmouth was Robert Kean. In 1893 Kean was replaced by John Johnston who had been a ticket-clerk at Newtown St Boswells for almost seven years. Others known to have served the branch railway in the 1890s were William Gordon (surfaceman), Andrew Purves, Ninian Black and William Gillespie (porters), James Borthwick and George Miller (railway clerks) whilst David Fairbairn and John Stewart were clerk-apprentices (both aged 14). Other railwaymen, resident in Eyemouth and district served the NBR at, for example, Ayton, Lamberton and Grantshouse.

Throughout the period of the 1890s the Eyemouth company paid an annual dividend of five per cent to its shareholders. Wieland continued to receive his six-monthly salary of £125 though there were other sums paid to him for clerical services. His last salary payment, of £145 16s. 8d., was paid in June 1900 when the Eyemouth Railway was taken over by the North British Railway. The railway's balance of net revenue was between £250 and £350 annually. The Directors continued to re-elect themselves but little changed on this front until in 1899 Henry Grierson was elected to replace the Marquis of Tweeddale who had resigned. Grierson, along with Wieland's clerk, W.F. Jackson, had become shareholders in 1894. Some of the meetings had been attended by the Marquis and Wieland only! For at least one meeting only one Director turned up. As it was thus inquorate the meeting was deemed to be 'informal'. It was in December 1899 that the company Directors received details of the proposed amalgamation with the North British Railway, along with the Aberlady & Gullane and the Newport railways. The date of amalgamation was fixed for 1st August, 1900. £5,000 of North British Railway 3 per cent debenture stock and £24,850 of NBR consolidated lie stock would be allocated to holders of stocks in the Eyemouth Railway Co. The Directors were happy with these terms. At the half-yearly meeting on 7th March, 1900 the above arrangements were formally ratified and allocated a 3 per cent dividend to the ERC shareholders. The local Berwick newspapers duly recorded these events.

The last act of the Eyemouth Railway, on the motion of George Hair (a landowner and farmer of Acredale, Eyemouth) was recorded: 'A vote of thanks was unanimously accorded to the Chairman.' The Eyemouth Railway, as a separate entity, thus passed into history, though, in truth, the NBR (often through G.B. Wieland) had already exerted a very considerable presence for some time!

Chapter Six

NBR days: 1900-1922

The *Dundee Courier* of 23rd February, 1900 reported on the special meeting of the proprietors of the North British Railway, held the previous day, to consider and approve the two Parliamentary Bills securing additional powers for the company. Amongst many other matters one Bill authorized the repayment of the Eyemouth Railway deposit fund whilst the other contained the authority to amalgamate the Aberlady, Gullane & North Berwick Railway, the Newport Railway and the Eyemouth Railway Company with the North British Railway. Around this time the proprietors of the individual companies named had given their own approval, that of the Eyemouth company being ratified at their 7th March meeting. The date for the 'takeover' by the North British Railway was the 31st July, 1900.

However, with this about to take place the Eyemouth Railway lost its station building in unexplained circumstances. The event took place on the evening of Thursday 15th February, 1900. The station buildings were of wooden construction and they were completely destroyed in a large fire. The flames were fanned by the strong gale-force wind blowing at the time and the fabric of the building quickly became a total wreck. The discovery of the fire was made at midnight. The event was first reported in the *Sunderland Daily Echo and Shipping Gazette* of Saturday 17th January but only briefly in the local Berwick newspapers. However, rebuilding of the station would become the responsibility of the NBR.

The dates for the construction of the replacement building also appear not to have been recorded or reported in the press. However, a surviving NBR plan, drawn over 10 years later, shows that its layout provided far superior facilities to the original Eyemouth Railway building. At its western end there was a booking hall with a door opening onto the station platform and three windows to aid illumination. A fireplace was provided. A door led into the booking office with a ticket window between the two rooms and four windows giving a view over the platform. The booking clerk also had the benefit of a fire! Next to this room was the single-windowed 'agent's room', also with a door onto the platform and a fireplace. Next to this was the ladies' room which measured 12 ft square and had two windows. It had a lavatory compartment, a fireplace and a door opening onto the platform. At the eastern end of the building were the gentlemen's facilities. Approached via an entrance from the platform there was a space for three urinals and a single WC cubicle. An awning which stretched the entire length of the building provided shelter for waiting passengers. The construction materials were referred to in the *Railway Modeller* article mentioned earlier (*see page 58*).

Even before taking over the Eyemouth line fully the North British draughtsmen were busy drawing-up plans for improvements at Eyemouth station. These plans indicated that the loading bank was to be extended with the siding adjacent to the headshunt on the platform line being shortened by the

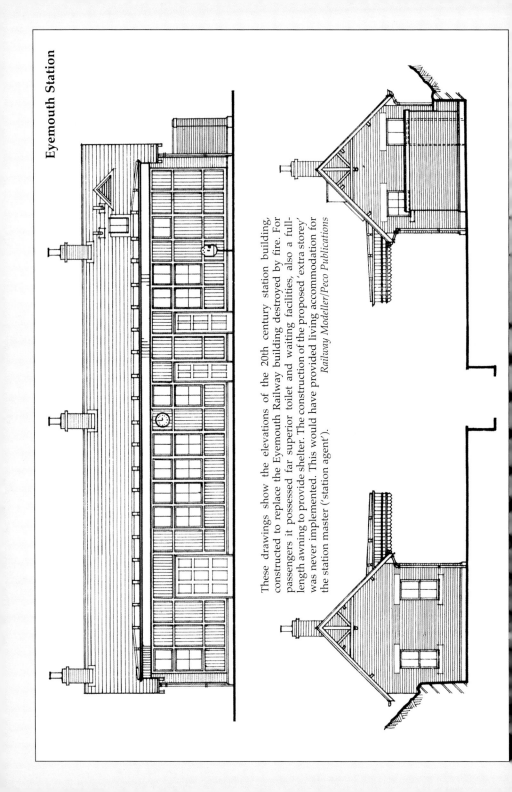

Eyemouth Station

These drawings show the elevations of the 20th century station building, constructed to replace the Eyemouth Railway building destroyed by fire. For passengers it possessed far superior toilet and waiting facilities, also a full-length awning to provide shelter. The construction of the proposed 'extra storey' was never implemented. This would have provided living accommodation for the station master ('station agent').

Railway Modeller/Peco Publications

same distance. The goods shed and store on the loading bank were to be removed, the goods shed being relocated beyond the buffers of the fish siding second from the river. A new siding was proposed to run alongside the extended loading bank with a frame for the point switches (levers) The work involved was costed at £341 including a contingency figure of £56 15s.

The 1901 census identified several NBR employees living (or lodging) at Eyemouth. Ninian Black and William Gillespie were porters whilst James Borthwick and George Miller were railway clerks. David Fairbairn and John Stewart were apprentice clerks. William Gordon was a railway surfacemen whilst David Spence and Archibald Spence were railway carters. Andrew Logan, listed as a 'visitor' was described as a railway labourer. On the 18th June, soon after the census, the *Berwick Advertiser* reported that Eyemouth passenger guard George Scott was married to Helen Fortune at Ayton Manse. Further good news was that Burnmouth station, under station master Mr Liddell, had been awarded a first class prize in the NBR's Best Kept Station competition. This was reported in the *Dundee Courier*.

The *Southern Reporter* of 10th May described the sad news that James Gordon, formerly station agent at Eyemouth, was killed on a level crossing at Leith. He had been run over by a train and suffered severe injuries to his arms and legs.

It was on the 26th November that the *Berwick Advertiser* reported the sad death of Colonel David Milne Home. Col Home had been a Director and Vice-Chairman of the Eyemouth Railway and had been a leading light in its inception. He had appeared to have been in the best of health and spirits but he died suddenly. The report of his death said that the interests of Eyemouth had always been very close to his heart, and nothing amid all the heavy public work and ceaseless activity of his life gave him greater pleasure than to help in promoting the welfare of the town. He was survived by three sons and one daughter.

The outlook from Eyemouth station looked to be improved in February 1902 when the *Berwickshire News* reported the sale of Eyecliffe Mill on the other side of the River Eye. This mill, at one time a distillery, had been out of use for some time and was looking derelict. The purchasers were the Globe Manufacturing Co. of London and Antwerp who were planning to introduce new machinery and electric lighting!

Two women were accused at the local court on charges of contravening the Tweed Acts. As reported in the *Berwickshire News* Helen Aitchison (also known as Wilson) of Partanhall, Burnmouth was accused of having illegal possession of one salmon and one sea trout at Eyemouth station on 29th October. Mary Anderson of Cowdrait, also part of Burnmouth, was found in possession of two salmon at the same station. Both were fined 10s. for each fish and 10s. of expenses, to be paid within seven days, or the alternative of seven days in custody. Each paid her fines!

It was on 18th August, 1903 that the *Berwickshire News* reported that on Wednesday 12th of that month, the East United Free Church from Duns had held a highly successful and enjoyable picnic at Eyemouth. The members had left Duns on a special train a few minutes after 9 am. The weather was kind and the children played in a park near Gunsgreen; there were sports, including races, and refreshments. Their special train arrived back at Duns soon after 7

EYEMOUTH STATION

This picture dates from the post-1900 North British era on the Eyemouth branch. Ready to depart from the terminus is, what appears to be, a mixed train, headed by 'Standard Goods' 0-6-0 No. 249. This was built at Cowlairs Works in 1887. It became part of the LNER class' J33' and was the last of the class to be withdrawn from service in December 1938, just prior to World War II.

Stenlake Publishing Collection

pm. The same newspaper reported that on Thursday 13th August the Provost Court tried an onion seller by the name of Joseph Gweguen who had been caught lodging in a third class railway carriage at Eyemouth in contravention of the Trespass Act. He pleaded guilty and was given the option of a 5s. fine or seven days custody. He paid the fine!

One of the long-standing station staff, George Miller, was treated to a fish supper, in November 1903, by both the Eyemouth railway staff and some of the local fishermen. George, who had been a clerk at Eyemouth station since 1893, had been promoted to a post at the NBR's headquarters in Edinburgh. He was presented with a travelling rug and gold studs by his station colleagues and a 'handsome gold curb chain' by the fishermen.

On 16th February, 1904 the *Berwickshire News* reported on an action in the small debt court, Ayton, which had been brought against the NBR by Eyemouth fish curers, Messrs Robertson & Son. They claimed a sum of £9 14s. 6d. in payment for damage sustained by the mis-delivery of a cargo of fish which had been delivered to the wrong auctioneer in Manchester. The railway company asserted that the fish would have attained a lower price had they gone to the correct auctioneers! The claim was lost and the railway recovered its expenses.

A much more light-hearted happening took place in the following October when a parrot took up its abode in the strip of woodland adjacent to Burnmouth station, obtaining its food from a nearby stubble field. The railway staff unsuccessfully tried to entice it within reach but eventually they offered a reward of half-a-crown for its capture. Two local schoolboys eventually made the parrot captive and took it to Eyemouth. It was believed to be a Patagonian parrot commonly found in Paraguay, Chile and Buenos Aires!

On the 3rd March, 1905 the *Berwick Advertiser* contained an article which described the paucity of harbour accommodation on the east coast of Scotland. It referred to Eyemouth harbour as being inconveniently small with the boats being aground at low-water. Steam fishing boats were practically unable to take advantage of the harbour. Whilst some other harbours had been improved those on the Berwickshire coast had not. The view was expressed that Eyemouth harbour should be improved to provide both a harbour of refuge and a low-water fishery harbour close to the fishing grounds. The railway station being in the vicinity of the harbour was stated to be an advantage: 'being on the level with the existing quays a line of rails could at little expense, be extended to any point of new works. Fish could be landed directly into trucks if so wanted'.

The *Berwick Advertiser* of the 24th March reported on an assault which had taken place in a railway carriage between Burnmouth and Eyemouth. The accused, William Paterson, a farm servant of Eyemouth Mill, pleaded guilty to assaulting George Cockburn, another farm servant of Hallydown, Eyemouth, whilst they were returning from the Berwick hirings on the day in question. They had changed trains at Burnmouth and both entered the same compartment on the Eyemouth train with 10 other men. Paterson called Cockburn 'a liar with an adjective' and struck him a blow on the head. Another passenger tried to intervene and a struggle developed which resulted in the train being stopped. Paterson was offered a fine of £1 or seven days in prison; he chose to pay the fine.

A passenger train composed of an NER 'C1' class 0-6-0 (later LNER 'J21') and NBR coaches crosses the Linthill (or Eyemouth) viaduct en route from Eyemouth to Burnmouth. The picture is a reproduction of a postcard sold commercially in the 1920s.   *David Anderson Collection*

This is a reproduction of another commercial postcard showing the buildings on Victoria Road, Eyemouth. The parish church is just out-of-view to the right. The steeply-graded approach to the station was initially used by both carts and passengers though later passengers could access the platform via a flight of steps.   *Author's Collection*

Later the same year, on 21st November, it was reported that two men, William Young and George Wynd, pleaded guilty to being drunk and disorderly at Eyemouth railway station. They were offered a fine of 7s. 6d. or seven days in prison and chose the former option.

Further court cases were reported in the first few months of 1906. The *Edinburgh Evening News* (of 12th January) and *Southern Reporter* (of 18th January) reported that at the Sheriff Court in Duns, an Eyemouth fisherman, William Young, perhaps the same man mentioned in the previous paragraph, had pleaded guilty to a charge of travelling on the on the NBR from Burnmouth to Eyemouth without a ticket and with intent to avoid payment. The amount of the unpaid fare was 3d. The Sheriff impose a fine of 2s. 6d. with expenses of £1 19s. 3d. No wonder the headline read 'A Bad Bargain In Railway Travelling'!

Two months later, on the 20th March the same paper reported a similar misdemeanour. David Robertson, a pedlar of Berwick, was charged with travelling on the line from Burnmouth with an improper ticket. He tendered a ticket, with the date erased, having used the same ticket on the previous day, but this was noticed by a vigilant ticket collector. Robertson was fined 17s. or 14 days imprisonment.

In January 1907 a plan (now held in the Scottish Archive) was drawn up by the NBR for 'Proposed Alterations at Eyemouth'. These, incidentally, indicated that the '1901 plans' had not been put into effect.

The new plan involved the purchase of about 0.2 acre of land from Mrs Topping to allow the railway sidings to be extended in an easterly direction in the direction of the harbour. The existing loading bank was to be demolished allowing the extension of the short siding next to the locomotive headshunt to be extended to accommodate an extra 10 wagons. A new, much longer loading bank would be constructed on the north side of the line taking up some of the space which had formed the station access road. The retaining wall of the former approach road would need to be moved. The second fish siding would be re-aligned away from the first siding (adjacent to the river) and extended to accommodate an extra seven wagons. This work required that the existing weigh-house and store be moved to a position in the new yard between the two extended sidings and for two new stores to be erected close to the site of the former loading bank. A new access road would be created to the newly formed facilities on an upward gradient of 1 in 16. The river wall adjacent to the Eye would require strengthening, also. The total cost of this work was estimated at £835 (to include land purchase) including an allowance of just over £75 for contingencies.

It is interesting to note that this plan, dated January 1907, still shows the locomotive run-round facility. The 25 in. Ordnance Survey map, surveyed in 1906 and published in 1908, indicates that it had been removed.

Shortly after the drawing up of these plans, Captain David Milne Home spoke at a local council meeting and moved the resolution,

That this Council strongly approve the Action of the Eyemouth Harbour Trustees in approaching HM Treasury with a view to obtaining a sufficient Grant of Money to enable them to construct a deep water harbour in connection with the existing tidal one and thus provide for the requirements and safety of the modern fishing boats ....

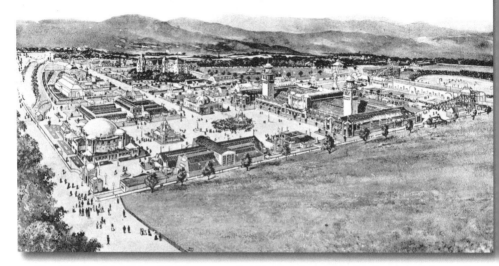

The 1908 Scottish National Exhibition was held in Saughton Park, Edinburgh and the North British Railway advertised a through train from Eyemouth to Edinburgh for the event with cheap tickets also being available on normal service trains. The reproductions of postcards show (*upper*) the extent of the exhibition in the park and (*lower*) the water chute ride (with its own railway lines!), one of many attractions which supplemented the industrial and commercial displays and exhibitions. *(Both) Author's Collection*

The Water Chute, Scottish National Exhibition, Edinburgh, 1908

The cost was estimated as about £75,000 and it was proposed that the Government should be asked for a grant of £50,000, that £10,000 should be obtained from the Jubilee Works Loan Board, and that £10,000 would come from the NBR provided the scheme went on in the current year. The size of the boats was increasing and the six steam drifters operating out of Eyemouth would move elsewhere to find better accommodation if the work was not done. Milne Home was reported in the *Berwickshire News* article as fearing that the fishing industry in Eyemouth would 'go down' if the effort was unsuccessful. (Capt. David Milne Home was one of the sons of Col Milne Home associated with the earlier history of the Eyemouth Railway.)

Meanwhile there was a change of station master at Burnmouth. David Watt, who had been 'agent' at Burnmouth for some five years was appointed as station master at Millerhill, Midlothian, having been through the grades including porter, signalman, passenger guard, and agent at Hallbeath before coming to Burnmouth.

The year 1908 began with the publication of a plan by the NBR for an agent's house to be built above Eyemouth station on the north side of Victoria Road in a gap between existing houses. The house was to have two floors and a substantial garden. The front door, at the end of a steep path from Victoria Road, led to a small lobby. To the right was planned the main living room measuring 16 ft x 12 ft. To the left was the kitchen leading to a scullery and wash house. In the scullery there was a recess for a bed. Straight ahead of the lobby was a bathroom with a WC. An integral coal house separated the bathroom and scullery. The first floor, approached via a staircase, had two bedrooms.

A second plan for an agent's house followed in July of the same year. Both of these plans form part of the Scottish Archive at Edinburgh Park. This later plan contained the designs for a house to be located on the west side of Coldingham Road, Eyemouth, a little further from the station. This house was also designed to be on two floors. The porched front door led to a small hall with a sitting room to the left and the kitchen to the right. There was a scullery, a store for coals and a pantry. Under the staircase there was a closet. Upstairs there were two generous bedrooms and a bathroom with WC at a slightly lower level than the bedrooms. The total size of the plot was nearly a tenth of an acre. Neither plan was proceeded with.

The same month the local press described an excursion from Eyemouth for the midsummer holiday. There was an early special train which set off with over 190 passengers. The ordinary service train leaving at 7.08 am carried at least another 50 who would have changed to an Edinburgh train at Burnmouth. At that time the Scottish National Exhibition was being held in Edinburgh in Saughton Park, between one and two miles from Princes Street station. The exhibition included an industrial hall, a concert hall, a fine arts gallery, a figure-of-eight railway and a water chute. In addition there were Canadian, Russian and Irish pavilions.

Burnmouth station once again celebrated receiving a first class award in the Best Kept Station competition in 1908. The station master (or agent) was a Mr Barnfather. This was reported in the *Berwick Advertiser* of 18th September. However, the following year, 1909, appears to have been very much a 'routine

This is a reproduction of another postcard entitled 'Victoria Road' but on this occasion the photograph was taken from Brown's Bank on the opposite bank of the Eyewater. Note the typical North British Railway train in the platform and the spare carriage in the siding next to the river. Platform lamps extend right along the platform. The old grounded carriage bodies act as stores in the yard. The gradient post indicates the start of the steep gradient at the platform end.

Author's Collection

year' in the history of the branch. The newspapers found nothing of note to report!

The *Berwickshire News* contained the first news-worthy report emanating from the Eyemouth line in the second decade of the 20th century. An item in the edition of the 28th February, 1911 commented on the provision, by the NBR, of facilities for Glasgow residents to visit some of the East Coast 'watering places', including the Fife coast towns, North Berwick and Dunbar. The article regretted that once again the North British had ignored Eyemouth's growing importance as a summer resort. 'The town receives many Glasgow visitors each year and they complain bitterly about the inadequate train service. The last train from Glasgow with a connection for Eyemouth leaves Glasgow at 2 o'clock in the afternoon'. The article argued the case for there to be a connection off the 4.15 pm Queen Street departure with an arrival time at Eyemouth of 7.40 pm.

The second reported event was the presentation, made on Wednesday 19th April, 1911, to James Black who had worked for the NBR at Eyemouth station for five years. He was given a travelling rug and a box of cigarettes by his colleagues. The station agent, Mr Mundell, wished Black every success in his move to Canada. The account appeared in the *Berwickshire News* of 25th April.

Surprisingly it was the *Yorkshire Post* of 9th January, 1912 which first referred to the proposed scheme to develop a new harbour at Eyemouth. The headline read: 'North East Coast Fishing: A Big Harbour Improvement Scheme'. It reported that an expenditure of £60,000 was contemplated; part of the sum was to be raised by Eyemouth, part by the NBR and part by Government grant. North British Railway engineers had already inspected Eyemouth, Berwick and Blyth and there was in view a scheme to provide adequate facilities for all of the four or five hundred boats using that stretch of coast.

However it was not long before this scheme foundered! A correspondent to the *Berwickshire News*, in its 13th February edition, indicated that the NBR had declined to give a grant towards the new harbour scheme. It would be necessary for Eyemouth, so dependent on the fishing trade, to investigate other sources of revenue such as attracting other summer visitors: 'Many towns, with but half of the natural beauties and the health-giving properties of Eyemouth have great numbers of visitors every year, because they are advertised as holiday resorts throughout the country. Why cannot Eyemouth do likewise?' The correspondent encouraged the town council both to develop a proper bathing pool amongst the rocks and to petition the NBR for better railway connections in the summer months.

Almost a month later the train service between Eyemouth and Burnmouth was reduced to just three trains per day in each direction as a result of a possible coal shortage arising from the national coal miners' strike. The *News* of 5th March indicated that this state of affairs would continue until the coal strike was settled. Under this arrangement the last train from Eyemouth to Berwick would be that leaving at 3.35 pm. There were reductions in the service on the main line. For example the 6.04 pm train from Reston to Berwick, which could have been used by Eyemouth inhabitants prepared to walk to Burnmouth, was also suspended.

The *Berwickshire News* of 25th June reported two matters of railway interest. Firstly it was announced that the popular Mr Mundell, who had been station master at Eyemouth since 1901, was shortly to leave the service of the NBR prior to his emigrating to Australia. Secondly it was reported that the NBR had offered cheap fares on the occasion of Eyemouth's midsummer holiday. A number of townspeople had taken advantage of the opportunity.

The NBR returns for 1913, the year before the outbreak of World War I, showed the increasing popularity of the Eyemouth line, some 25,593 passengers having used the line during the past year, though even this figure was eclipsed in the post-war years when, in 1920 for example, nearly 35,000 passengers travelled on the line!

The 1914 NBR Working Timetable contained an 'Important Notice', the consequences of which could have led to a widespread effect on train travel and revenue:

> In consequence of the European War Crisis, the Train, Coach and Steamer Services shown in this Time Table may be altered or curtailed at any time without notice and the Companies will not be responsible for any loss, injury, damage or delay through any failure to afford their ordinary services or any modified services.

For the duration of World War I the accounts in the press of happenings on the Eyemouth line were considerably reduced, perhaps because of reporting restrictions being in force. Accounts of matters and events relating to the stations and the train services did not appear. No mention was made, for example, of the 'takeover' of the station, late in the war, by the army following an aircraft crash nearby. The recovered parts were transferred to the station and taken away in goods wagons, or by horse-drawn transport, under the strictest of security! The army would not provide any further details at the time. The departure of the '7th Battalion of Welsh Cyclists' from Berwick did, however, receive a mention, together with the arrival of their replacements, the Royal Scots, at the vacated billets.

Plans dated 26th January, 1915 indicate that the NBR had not given up the idea of creating a house for its station agent at Eyemouth. This was the third scheme proposed within 10 years. From the company's financial point of view this plan had increased merit in that it would not involve costly land purchase. It was proposed that the agent's apartment be provided in a newly constructed upper floor above the existing station buildings. The approach would be via a 'staired' path from Victoria Road. The accommodation was to have a porch, with outer and inner doors, leading to a transverse lobby area (hallway). A door from the lobby on the right-hand side led into a parlour positioned over the booking hall on the lower, ground floor. Directly ahead of the porch was the pantry. To the left of the porch, on entry, the lobby formed a corridor, at the end of which was the bathroom with a bath and WC. On the right-hand side of the corridor was a door leading into the bedroom (above the booking office) with space for two beds. Further along the corridor was a door on the right leading into a large 15 ft x 12 ft kitchen (above the ladies' room) which had a cupboard and provision for another bed. There was a small scullery with sink off the kitchen, with a sink and tub. The parlour, bedroom and kitchen were all to have fireplaces. The windows of the parlour and kitchen formed bays projecting over the awnings built to shelter waiting passengers.

Somewhat surprisingly the plan for the agent's house still shows a locomotive run-round loop in the station several years after it was removed. The plan also shows the short loading bank, a crane and two 'bothies' (storage sheds) plus the weigh-house and weighbridge. Once again construction of the agent's house was not proceeded with!

One happy piece of news, reported in the *Berwickshire News* of 9th November, 1915, was the marriage of Thomas Collin, the younger son of the harbourmaster, to Miss Anne Leith. At the time Thomas was booking clerk at Eyemouth and had formerly worked at Berwick station.

In September 1916 the station at Burnmouth appeared in the NBR's list of awards for 'Best Kept Station', on this occasion receiving a fourth class prize worth the princely sum of £1. The station master was still Mr Barnfather. The list of local prizewinners appeared in the *Southern Reporter* on the 7th of the month. The station achieved the same result in September 1917, this time the report appearing in the *Berwickshire News*.

Not all of the published news was good news. Mr and Mrs Black of Paxton Terrace, Eyemouth, received the news that their son, James, mentioned earlier as having moved to Canada in 1911, had died after a long and painful illness. James had, of course, served his booking clerk apprenticeship at Eyemouth station. In the district he had been held in high esteem on account of his genial disposition and exemplary character. He had held a position with the Canadian Railway Company before working for a grain exporter. His obituary appeared in the *Berwickshire News* of 21st November, 1916. A year later the same newspaper mentioned that Robert Thompson, an engine driver on the Eyemouth line, received information from the War Office that his son, serving with the Scottish Rifles in France, had been wounded.

The *Advertiser* of 22nd December, 1916 announced some very welcome news. Until that month the cart road leading to Eyemouth station had been very rough. This edition of the paper recorded that the road had at last been metalled. 'We may now hope to reach the station without having to endure a compulsory mud bath.' Further to this the *Berwickshire News* of 16th January, 1917 published some partly contradictory information:

> The goods yard at the Railway Station is looking very clean now, having been well and truly laid with metal. The station road, however, is as muddy as ever on wet days. Of course, passengers are expected to emerge from and enter the station by the footbridge, and they would be acting sensibly if they did so, and their boots would tell a different tale.

The same article referred to the acute effect that the reduced train service was having on the local populace. However, the author of the article considered that the time of war was an ideal time for self-sacrifice, with most 'sensible' people thinking that they might be worse off if, for example, the train service were to stop completely. He reminded visitors to the town that the last train from Eyemouth to Burnmouth was the one that left shortly before 4 pm.

The *Advertiser* reported, in March 1917, that Eyemouth was having a 'Busy Curing Time', with large quantities of kippers being dispatched to various destinations. It was said that the station at Eyemouth presented a very busy and animated appearance. However, this was only partly good news for the town as

Station & Victoria Rd Eyemouth. 878.

This photograph, taken by Mr A. Edwards of Selkirk, provides a close-up of the steps linking the station platforms with Victoria Road. A mixed train appears to be ready to leave the station whilst the yard appears to be busy with crated and boxed goods traffic. The station staff appear to be lined up for the photograph. Note the large advertisement for Lifebuoy soap pasted on the wall of the gentlemen's toilet.

Stenlake Publishing Collection

the fish were only cured at Eyemouth, having been brought to the town from the safer fisheries of the Firth of Clyde district.

On 18th August, 1921 the *Southern Reporter* informed the public that the Government control of the railways, adopted as a wartime measure at midnight on 4th August, 1914, had terminated on Monday 15th August, three days previously. It explained that the main object had been to facilitate the movement of troops and munitions but at the same time maintaining services for the ordinary trade of the country as far as necessities would allow.

It was against this background that the *Berwick Advertiser*, quoting extensively from the *Windsor Magazine*, explained the background to the intended railway Grouping arising from the Railways Act 1921 which had received its third reading in the Commons on 9th August, 1921. It had then quickly passed through the Lords and received the Royal Assent. The advantages quoted were the breakdown of 'railway frontiers' where traffic was exchanged, reduced need for record keeping in connection with wagons and their contents, the elimination of the need for Railway Clearing House charges, the availability of locomotives and trains on both sides of the former frontiers and reduction in the number of locomotives, rolling stock and staff required to keep the railway running.

A year later, on 17th August, 1922 the same newspaper was very realistic about the state of the railways after the war:

> While other organisations are getting back to normal conditions, the railways are still a long way behind what they used to be, and are not fulfilling the high traditions of the past. Labour disputes, high wages, the eight hours day and the high cost of materials have all told against the reconstruction which we were led to believe would follow the ending of the war. ... Meanwhile great benefits are promised by the operation of the Railway Act 1921.

In the meantime the movement of workers from the Berwick district to the fishing ports of East Anglia had featured in several newspaper reports of 1922. A meeting of the Scottish Fishermen's Association executive council at Aberdeen, reported in the *Berwickshire News* on 7th February, discussed the question of high rates charged by the railways for the conveyance of the fishworkers to Lowestoft and Yarmouth. The association, with one of its liveliest branches, Eyemouth, sought to secure substantial concessions in ticket prices. Later in the year, on 19th October, the *Southern Reporter* indicated that for the previous couple of weeks the workers had been leaving Eyemouth in small parties but in the previous week a packed train had taken a large 'animated' party. The *Berwick Advertiser* expanded upon this three days later, referring to the fact that on Monday 9th October every square foot of Eyemouth station was occupied by those who were on the platform to wave farewell to the huge exodus of fishworkers. They departed on the local train changing to a special train to Yarmouth at Berwick.

The Railways Act of 1921 took effect on 1st January, 1923 when the 120 or so railway companies were merged into four large groups. The Eyemouth line, as part of the North British Railway, now became incorporated into the London and North Eastern Railway, the LNER.

An enlargement of part of an aerial photograph of the area around Eyemouth station taken in 1929. It shows the proximity of two of the sidings to the Eyewater and a variety of goods vans and open wagons, some of which appear to be carrying coal. The water tower is in the foreground. The yard is illuminated by a single large lamp. The weighbridge and weighhouse are visible near to the top of the picture. *Armstrong Railway Photographic Trust*

Chapter Seven

LNER days: 1923-1947

On 23rd August, 1923 the *Berwickshire News* recognized that Mr T. Barnfather, the station master at Burnmouth, was about to complete 40 years of railway service. He had started with the NBR at Langholm, working in the parcel office. In 1887 he was transferred to the parcel office in Edinburgh before being sent to Helensburgh as a shunter. Later he became a signalman in Fife. His first appointment in charge of a station was at Cardroma, near Peebles, before he took over at Burnmouth. During his time at Burnmouth the station won several Best Kept Station Awards, indeed on 23rd September the Southern Scottish Area of the LNER made another award, namely a third class prize, valued at £3!

The general index of the LNER Passenger Timetable for the period of '22.9.1924 until further notice' (in practice until 21st September, 1925) contained notes referring to the fact that 'both horses and carriages could be loaded and unloaded at Eyemouth and Burnmouth stations'.

At the criminal court held in Duns on Friday 20th February, 1925 Andrew Spratt, a game dealer, pleaded guilty to a charge of day poaching on the embankment of the LNER's railway bridge at Ferneyside [*sic*] where the Eyemouth branch left the main line. The prosecution was at the instigation of Captain Liddell Grainger of nearby Ayton Castle. One of Liddell Grainger's employees noted a man working traps on the railway embankment. He reported the incident to the head keeper and a watch was set for the next morning. The accused came along but did not approach the traps at first as there was a platelayer working nearby. Later he checked the traps and took two rabbits. He was apprehended by the men watching. He claimed that he had set traps there before and wasn't doing any harm. Presiding Sheriff, Macaulay Smith, handed him a £1 fine with £1 5s. 6d. court expenses. According to the report in the *Berwickshire News* of 24th February his traps were also confiscated.

Another record of long service to the railway was detailed in the *Berwickshire News* of 7th July, 1925. Thomas Dowens of Berwick had entered railway service as a boy in 1875, with the NBR. His first job was as a greaser, later moving on to become a cleaner, a fireman and finally an engine driver. In the late 1890s he was employed firing and driving engines on the Eyemouth branch. Later he was employed on the Berwickshire goods service before moving to Portobello in Edinburgh. He then switched to becoming the driver of pilot engines on the main line until the North Eastern Railway took over the running of the main line trains between Berwick and Edinburgh. He then transferred to Berwick where he continued as a driver. Sadly he lost a son in the Great War.

A brief note in the same newspaper reported in February 1926 that the LNER had been paid the sum of £3 6s. when the local council purchased a small piece of ground in connection with a minor road improvement scheme.

The year 1926 was the year of the General Strike. It was called by the general council of the Trades Union Congress in an attempt to force the Government of the day to resist reductions in miners' wages and worsening of their working conditions. Workers, especially those in transport and heavy industry, came out on strike in support of the miners. After no progress in the negotiations begun on 1st May, the strike commenced on at a minute to midnight on Monday 3rd May. It lasted for nine days and caused major disruption.

The *Berwickshire News* of 11th May reported that up to that date the strike had had little apparent effect on Eyemouth apart from the cessation of the train service and the curtailment of postal services. Buses, whose crews were not striking, were still running to Berwick. Arrangements were being made for two outgoing mails and two postal deliveries in the town. A few pupils had been unable to travel to school. Fish was still being landed but as the catches were scarce in nature there was no surplus beyond local needs. Fish hawkers with their motor-vans were covering a wide radius daily when fish were procurable. The staff of Eyemouth station, being non-union men, reported each day for duty. Motor-cycles and pushbikes were much used and the local woods were raided to provide sticks and branches to feed the domestic fires in view of the coal rationing.

On 12th May most employees returned to work though the miners maintained their resistance for several more months. It was not until the end of November that the strike was fully over. Because of the continuing threat to the supply of coal for locomotives and the dwindling stocks, the LNER issued a 'Timetable of Modified Train Services' on Saturday 29th May. On the Eyemouth branch this meant a reduction from six trains a day each way to just four, with only one train through to and from Berwick instead of two formerly.

On 13th August, 1926 the *Hawick News and Border Chronicle* reported on 'a large contingent' of Hawick residents having holidayed at Eyemouth. The two illustrative photographs showed a view of Eyemouth harbour and the party changing trains at Burnmouth on their return journey to return to Hawick, presumably having to travel onwards via the Reston to St Boswell's line. The train from Eyemouth appears, from the photograph, to have been strengthened by the addition of several extra carriages to cope with the many extra passengers. As a consequence it used the main line platform rather than the Eyemouth bay.

On the 15th November the *Berwickshire News* reported on a letter which was sent to the LNER by the Eyemouth School management committee. It referred to the inconvenience suffered by Berwickshire High School pupils as a result of the long wait that they had to suffer at Burnmouth station whilst on their way to and from Eyemouth. Some waited for one hour at Burnmouth in the mornings and ¾ of an hour on their way home in the evening. The timings of the pupils' trains were having an effect on the length of the school day at the high school. The timetable alterations had cut 35 minutes from the teaching day, ten minutes in the morning and 25 minutes at the end of the school day. The committee threatened that unless changes were made to the rail timetable to improve the service then the children would have to be conveyed by bus, there being enough of these at convenient times. It was considered that bus transport would not cost any more than the cost of season ticket purchase for the trains.

It is very noticeable that the arrival of the LNER succeeding the NBR resulted in greater use being made of the local newspapers for advertising excursion traffic and special train tickets, at reduced prices. The *Berwickshire News* of 21st December, 1926, for example, contained a large display advertisement. It referred firstly to 'Cheap Day Excursions' which were available over the Christmas and New Year holidays from Berwickshire stations (plus Berwick itself) to Edinburgh Waverley. The tickets were valid on any train on 25th December and the 1st, 3rd and 4th of January. The cost of an adult ticket from both Eyemouth and Burnmouth was 5s. 6d. For the return journey there was a puzzling note attached to the reference to Eyemouth: 'On Saturday 1st January connexion [sic] to Eyemouth will be given off the 6.25 pm train from Edinburgh Waverley to Glasgow (Queen Street)'. The second part of the advertisement referred to the availability of cheap fares from a variety of local stations to Berwick. The tickets were to be valid on any ordinary train on the day of issue only but would apply to all trains on 25th December and from 31st December to 8th January inclusive. The third class return fare from Eyemouth was 1s. 1d. whilst the first class fare was 1s. 10d. From Burnmouth the fare was 9d. third class and 1s. 2d. first class. Handbills advertising these excursion tickets were posted at all local stations.

The local council had been asked to support a request for there to be cheap return fares from Eyemouth to Edinburgh on Thursdays and Saturdays, with a connection to Eyemouth being provided from the train which left Waverley station at 6.25 pm on both days. This appeared in the *Berwickshire News* of 18th February, 1927. The next issue of the passenger timetable showed no additional evening train! Cheap fares had certainly been available every day between Eyemouth and Berwick throughout the summer months and this had been a popular arrangement, the facility being extended to Edinburgh later in the summer. Many Eyemouth residents were reported as having used the cheap tickets to visit Edinburgh on the day of the September monthly holiday.

An advertisement was placed in the *News* of 18th October, 1927 under the headline 'Transport by Road and Rail', in which the LNER stated that it would be prepared to arrange the collection and delivery of agricultural and other bulk traffic within a radius of 10 miles of Ayton, Burnmouth, Chirnside, Eyemouth, Grantshouse and Reston stations. They promised 'exceptionally low cartage rates' for farm traffic.

The *Berwickshire News* of 1st May, 1928 advised Eyemouth and Burnmouth passengers to be aware of the timetable changes that came into force on that day. The departure of the 9.00 am train from Burnmouth to Eyemouth was changed to an 8.30 am departure, whilst the 8.20 am from Eyemouth to Burnmouth was to leave at 8.10 am. (This would give the train crew just 13 minutes to perform their necessary manoeuvres at Burnmouth instead of the 40 minutes previously allowed.) The changes were a necessary consequence of changes in the timetable on the main line.

Special one-day excursion tickets were advertised in the local press for 20th July, 1928 on the occasion of the Berwickshire Agricultural Show held at Duns. Intending passengers could use the 8.10 am or 12.19 pm departures (changing trains at Burnmouth) and each third class ticket was priced at 2s. 3d. Passengers travelling from Burnmouth could choose either the 8.26 am or 12.57 pm trains and the cost of the return ticket was 1s. 10d.

The success of George Miller in becoming station master at Haymarket station, Edinburgh, was noted in the *News* of 18th August, 1928. Miller had started his career with the NBR at Ayton station in 1891. He then held a similar post at

Views of Eyemouth station are almost always dominated by the parish church. The steps linking the station and Victoria Road are clearly visible despite the picture's quality, and the steepness of the station approach road can be appreciated from this view as it climbs up towards the main road. The houses on the right were proposed for demolition when the extension of the railway towards the harbour was contemplated in the early 1900s. *Author's Collection*

Before the opening of the branch, Ayton was Eyemouth's 'local station'. Several railwaymen had careers involving both stations. Station master Bennett recalled in his book (*see Bibliography*) that in World War II some fish was received at Ayton by rail from Scotland's more northerly ports for processing (e.g. smoking) at Eyemouth. This fish was taken by road from Ayton to Eyemouth. *Author's Collection*

Eyemouth for 10 years. Later, after a period working as a relief clerk in the offices of the superintendent of the line, he returned to Eyemouth becoming station master for eight years. For six months he was the station master at the Exhibition station in Edinburgh during the period of the 1908 Scottish Exhibition. From 1920 he had been station master at Mallaig on the West Highland Extension line.

The practice of the LNER in advertising in the local press continued later in 1928. The *Berwickshire News* of 16th October targeted the dates of the Earlston, Burnmouth and Eyemouth holidays. Cheap excursions were advertised from these stations to all stations in Scotland including the Clyde coast and Loch Lomond Piers. Period excursion tickets were issued from Earlston on 19th and 20th October, and from Burnmouth and Eyemouth on 17th and 18th October. In addition there were 'One-Day Excursions' to numerous resorts from Earlston (on 29th October) and Burnmouth and Eyemouth (on 18th October).

In May 1929 the Berwick Boy Scouts held their Whitsuntide holiday camp at Netherbyres House in Eyemouth. The camp was held there both for the enjoyment of the participants and to promote scouting in the Eyemouth district. A party of between 60 and 70 scouts travelled on the train from Berwick to Eyemouth, a special train being provided for their return journey. The event was publicized in the *News* of 14th May.

The need for Eyemouth to advertise its tourist potential was recognized by both the LNER and the local council. Accordingly these two bodies maintained close contact and, as mentioned in the *Berwickshire News* for 8th March, 1930, the council took advantage of the LNER for the placement of advertisements in the various newspapers published in Glasgow, Edinburgh and Newcastle. The success of the advertising in attracting holidaymakers to Eyemouth was often reported in the *Berwickshire News*, such as that of 16th August, 1932.

History seemed to be repeating itself when a man was prosecuted for stealing rabbits from snares on a local railway embankment, as described in the *News* of 9th January, 1930. On this occasion, though, the crime took place between Eyemouth and Burnmouth. Benjamin Parker, a farm labourer from Eyemouth, pleaded guilty to stealing five rabbits from snares set by a local gamekeeper. He had taken them to Eyemouth where he had sold them. Parker was fined 30s.

A correspondent to the same newspaper, writing in March 1930, had visited Eyemouth and found it 'from the herring point of view and prosperity, very fair…' though he added that 'Something will have to be done for the bay if ever it has to attract visitors for holidays'.

On 9th September of the same year the imminent retirement, on 30th September, of the Burnmouth station master was reported. The *News* described the career of Thomas Barnfather from his first appointment at Langholm in 1883. He would have completed 47 years' service if he had worked until the month of November. He had spent eight years as station master at Burnmouth.

An edition of the *Berwickshire News* of January 1931 referred to the imminent retirement of railway guard, George Scott, of Eyemouth. He had completed 41 years' railway service. When the branch from Burnmouth to Eyemouth was opened Mr Scott was one of the first officials on the line, indeed he had the honour of acting as guard (before the arrival of the guard actually appointed for the duty) on the first train that ran from Burnmouth to Eyemouth. Some 39 years of his service (misprinted in the newspaper as 49 years) were spent on the Eyemouth branch, for the last 30 of which he had been a guard. He had served under four station masters at Eyemouth. He was described as courteous and well-liked and it was said that he would be missed by the regular travellers on the line. The same paper, on 7th June, said that Scott had finally retired and it named his successor as a Mr Gilchrist who had been residing lately at Tweedmouth. Meanwhile there was a report (10th April) of a Mr Uprichard from Edinburgh having been appointed station master at Eyemouth.

A 'different' type of holiday was advertised by the LNER in the *Berwick Advertiser* of 2nd April, 1931. The company had arranged a series of walking tours in its North East area. Amongst the tours in the Berwick locality was one in which participants travelled outwards from their home station to Eyemouth station by rail, then visiting local places of interest including Coldingham Priory and St Abbs Head. The return rail journey was to be made from Reston station, making the length of the walk 6½ miles.

Later that year the *Berwick Advertiser*, on 12th November, reported the conviction of a local apprentice engineer who was charged with the offence of committing an act of malicious mischief. John Gray Nisbet, on 7th October, was travelling in a group of seven boys in a carriage on a train from Eyemouth. They had begun to sky-lark and all were jumping about. However, the accused had 'tackets' in his boots and one of these had torn a cushion. On arrival at Burnmouth the guard at the train had to caution Nisbet, who was in a boisterous mood, for shouting. The Sheriff accepted that the damage had been caused as a result of high-spirits and thoughtlessness, not deliberate intent, but found Nisbet guilty and fined him 20s.

An unusual incident which could have resulted in a fatal accident occurred on 17th May, 1932 and was reported in the *Berwickshire News* of 24th May. As a southbound express train was approaching Burnmouth station on the main line a dining car attendant noticed a hand appearing through a joint in the canvas 'concertina' joining the corridors of two coaches. He immediately pulled the communication cord and the train was stopped. A bedraggled and distressed man was found on the buffer of one of the coaches! He could not explain how he had got himself into this predicament but declared that he had been asleep for the journey. He had travelled 54 miles from Edinburgh on the buffer before he was discovered. As he had no wish to travel to Newcastle he was returned to Edinburgh by the next train from Burnmouth, this time inside a carriage!

The passenger timetable for 1932 showed a change from that of earlier years as it contained a statement that motor cars, in addition to carriages, could be loaded at both Eyemouth and Burnmouth. The same document included information about the omnibus service operated by the Southern Scottish Area of the Scottish Motor Traction Co. Ltd. which was advertising services between Berwick, Burnmouth, Eyemouth and Edinburgh which would compete with the train service.

The *Berwick Advertiser* of 21st February, 1933 announced the retirement of John Lochhead as station master of Burnmouth. Their article stated that Lochhead had transferred to Burnmouth where he had succeeded Mr Barnfather (described as popular and painstaking) in October 1931. He had entered NBR service on 'The Old Monkland'* and after passing through various

---

* The Monkland and Kirkintilloch line.

grades he was appointed station master at Oxton, Berwickshire, when the Lauder branch opened in 1901. Later he was in charge at Steele Road on the 'Waverley Route' for seven years before taking up the Burnmouth post. Of his 48 years of service he had been a station master for 32.

Despite his having retired in February 1933 the *News* of 7th March, 1933 reported that John Lochhead had been appointed as Burnmouth's station master. The new appointment was actually Alexander Russell of Melrose. His career had started at Chollerton station on the North Tyne from whence he had moved to the booking office at St Boswells, remaining there for two years until he joined the Royal Navy at the start of the war. He returned to his job at St Boswells after the war ended but then moved successively to Millerhill station and then Melrose. He later interacted as relief station master to several stations including Burnmouth Junction [*sic*]. The surroundings of Burnmouth were therefore described as being 'not strange to him'. The edition of the *Berwick Advertiser* published two days later contained the same article.

In the editions of the *News* of June 1933 the LNER placed an advertisement for cheap rail facilities for travel to Dundee for the purpose of attending the Highland and Agricultural Society's Show. On 22nd June the price of a day return ticket from Burnmouth to Dundee was 10s. 6d. whilst Eyemouth passengers were expected to pay an extra 6d.

The year 1934 produced the appearance in the *Southern Reporter* (dated 1st March and 27th December respectively) of announcements, by the LNER, of new local station masters. Mr Dickson, the station master at Eyemouth, had been appointed to the position of station master at Jedburgh station, also in the Borders. Into his position as Eyemouth station master came Andrew Irving. He was station master at Belses and Hassendean stations, before he was appointed to Eyemouth.

A local celebration was reported in the *Berwickshire News* of 3rd December, 1935. John Hill Brown of Ayton Mill celebrated his silver wedding in his cottage next to the River Eye. Mr Brown had been a labourer on the construction of the Eyemouth branch railway and had worked on the section near Redhall. He later worked, for 35 years, on the Ayton Castle estate as a forester. Some sad news of another local railway employee was reported in the *Berwick Advertiser* of 6th June of the same year. This was the death of Ninian Jeffrey Black who had been employed as a porter-guard at Eyemouth station for over 30 years. He had retired on ill-health grounds 18 months previously. He had been popular in the community and endeared himself to the people he met. He had sung with the Eyemouth Old Kirk choir.

The *Berwick Advertiser* interviewed Burnmouth-born Adam Shearlaw on a bench on the platform at Burnmouth station just a few minutes before he was about to start his last shift, on 30th September, 1935, as signalman at the nearby signal box. Mr Shearlaw had followed in the footsteps of his father by working on the railway. He had joined the NBR in 1890 as a surfaceman (platelayer in today's parlance) but then became a porter and finally, in 1915, a signalman. His entire career with the railway was spent at Burnmouth station. The article appeared in the newspaper's next edition, six days after the interview. Another retirement was reported in the *Berwickshire News* on 19th November. George J. Miller, who had been station master at Eyemouth from 1912 to 1920, retired from the post of station master at Haymarket station in Edinburgh. He received a bureau from his colleagues and friends together with a handbag for his wife.

In 1936 the Berwickshire County Council drew up plans for the replacement of some of the bridges carrying roads across the Eyemouth branch railway. These plans were studied and approved by the LNER and copies exist in the Scottish Archives. The three bridges were those known as bridge No. 3 (Hillburn bridge, close to Burnmouth) and bridge No. 7 (at Biglawburn) plus the bridge over the line near the Toll Bridge known as bridge No. 9. Bridge No. 3 had new supporting girders which were 35 ft 9 in. long, with transverse girders, a top fabric mesh and concrete decking topped with tarmac. New wing walls were constructed. New parapets were made in pre-cast concrete and provided with a topping. The end-result was a bridge with a 20 ft roadway with a pedestrian footpath to one side and a grass verge on the other, the total distance between the parapets being 34 ft 6 in. The *Berwickshire News* announced that work had commenced in its edition of 22nd November. The other two bridges were rebuilt along similar lines but the *Berwickshire News* article stated that the work to complete all three bridges would take about six months to complete. In fact the work at Hillburn was not completed until well into 1939, with Biglawburn the next bridge to be worked upon. The new Biglawburn bridge was built in the same way and produced not only a stronger bridge, more suited to the increasing weight of road vehicles, but also a safer 20 ft-wide road with its curves adjusted and a footpath provided for pedestrians. Completion of the final bridge allowed the elimination of a slight 'dogleg' on the road thus improving visibility for drivers, made the road wider and created a pedestrian footpath as well as allowing heavier vehicle to use the Ayton Road. It was necessary for a complete road closure of the Eyemouth – Ayton Road between the Toll Bridge and Eyemouth Mill from Thursday 25th May to Friday 9th June, 1939. Later, as the works were being completed, traffic lights controlled single-line traffic over this part of the B6355 route. These notes appeared in various 1939 editions of the *Berwickshire News*.

Returning to 1936, the LNER drew up plans of its own for improvements at Burnmouth station. A Plan dated 20th October, 1936 provided for a new pedestrian pavement on each side of the Eyemouth Road. There were further plans dated 19th July, 1937. The subsequent work involved the reduction in length of the bay platform for Eyemouth trains by 10 ft 0 in. with new buffer stops being provided. New access steps were constructed from the adjacent road on the west side of the station building with the 'old' steps on the east side being demolished. The old access gate was closed. A new screen was placed at the end of the station building.

In 1937 two railwaymen, employed at Eyemouth station were separately accused of stealing coal, the property of their LNER employers. The accounts of the two incidents and the subsequent trials and court decisions appeared in various editions of the *Berwickshire News*. The first took place on 11th February, 1937 when James Ross Young, a railway guard, apparently removed a piece of coal, weighing 23 lb. The station master, Mr Irvine [sic], had apparently suspected that there had been some thieving going on at the station. The station master and a relief guard, Cessford Fairley, had seen the piece of coal secreted behind a barrel in the porters' bothy. Later the same day it had disappeared. Fairley was able to say who had wrapped it in brown paper and taken it away. Young was convicted of the crime and fined £1 (to be paid within 30 days) with the option of 10 days' confinement if he could not pay. The second event took place in September of the same year. John Patterson, a railway porter of Eyemouth, was also charged with stealing coal, on several occasions between December 1936 and 8th February, 1937, from the same bothy. Patterson had removed the coal, on the last occasion, in a small attaché case. Despite claiming that the coal was 'scrap coal' which had been lying on the ground, Patterson was also found guilty and fined 15s. with the alternative of 10 days in prison.

The frequency of LNER publicity items in the local press increased in 1938. On 18th January, 1938 a ticket was advertised for an evening excursion from Edinburgh to Burnmouth and Eyemouth. Another ticket was available from Eyemouth and Burnmouth to Chirnside where the local football team, Chirnside United, were taking on the team from Ross County. The same day the *Berwickshire News* advertised an evening excursion to Edinburgh. There were regularly advertised half-day excursions to Glasgow from stations to the north and north-west of Berwick. The Eyemouth departure was scheduled on the 10.18 am train, with a Burnmouth departure of 10.40 am. The departure on the return from Glasgow (Queen Street) was at 8.48 pm allowing a generous time in the city. Another Evening Excursion to Edinburgh was advertised for 23rd April and others to the same city took place later in the year.

The 10th June, 1938 was chosen for 800 scholars, from Berwickshire Schools, to visit the Empire Exhibition held at Bellahouston Park in Glasgow. This Exhibition marked 50 years since the first International Exhibition held in Glasgow in 1888. It was also designed to boost the economy of Scotland which was still shaky after the depression of the 1930s. Countries from the British Empire erected their own Pavilions on the site in addition to the British exhibits which included the Palace of Art and the Engineering Pavilion. Fortunately the weather on the chosen day was fine and the excursion passed off successfully according to the report in the *Berwickshire News* of the following Tuesday. Two special trains had been arranged by the Berwickshire Education Committee and Berwickshire Education Trust, with scholars being charged very moderate fares. The first excursion train started at Eyemouth and conveyed children from Eyemouth, Burnmouth, Coldingham, St. Abbs, Cockburnspath and Reston. Other children were conveyed on a train which came from the Duns line, picking them up from, for example, Chirnside, Paxton, Longformacus, Earlston and Greenlaw. All of the children were identified by rosettes or cards and carefully marshalled by their teachers.

A December 1938 edition of the *News* reported that 71 passengers had booked on an advertised Edinburgh excursion from Eyemouth and Burnmouth. Apparently 'quite a number' had visited the pantomime.

As the end of 1938, approached the *News* of 20th December announced that a former Eyemouth station employee, Andrew Spence, had been appointed as station master at Redding station (LNER). Whilst at Eyemouth he had been a station clerk, his later career involving Prestonpans, Reston, Innerwick, Peebles and Cockburnspath stations.

The plans for the summer 1939 joint newspaper advertising scheme were submitted by the LNER to the Eyemouth Council the following week. As well

A through working from Eyemouth to Berwick-upon-Tweed accelerates southwards from Burnmouth behind 'J21' locomotive No. 1562 of Tweedmouth depot. At this point the line is elevated and passengers have a good view over the North Sea. At this time the branch trains often consisted of two carriages, especially at weekends.   *Real Photographs*

This is the return working of the train shown in the upper photograph. The 'J21' class 0-6-0 was a regular locomotive at that time on the branch. It slows the two-coach train for its stop at Burnmouth. Some of the roofs of Lower Burnmouth houses can be seen on the left of the picture. The picture was taken in 1937.   *Real Photographs*

as Scottish newspapers, those from Newcastle were included in the list. It was commented that an increasing number of Newcastle holidaymakers were making Eyemouth the destination for their summer holiday. The pattern of excursions planned and advertised by the LNER in 1939 included the same origins and destinations as in 1938. One of the advertisements in the *Edinburgh Evening News* (of 1st May, 1939) described Eyemouth as a 'Beautifully situated Fishing Town on the East Coast. Safe Bathing. Golf. Tennis. Bowls. Fishing etc.' and referred to the availability of cheap monthly return tickets from Edinburgh (Waverley) to Eyemouth for 9s. 9d.

Local newspapers reported that Mr Burns, who had worked for the NBR, mainly at Burnmouth station, retired in January 1939. He was the local branch collector for the National Union of Railwaymen for 27 years.

The *Berwick Advertiser* reported the death of a former railwayman in its edition of 1st June, 1939. Adam Shearlaw of Burnmouth collapsed and died whilst wheeling a hand-cart on Tuesday 30th May. He had retired from the position of signalman at Burnmouth station just a few years previously and had received an engraved silver watch after 45 years of service. After his retirement he had become accustomed to wheeling the handcart of milk from Catch-a-Penny Farm to the station where it was placed on a train. He stumbled and fell when near to the station and did not recover after his collapse.

The *Berwickshire News* of 31st October, 1939 made reference in its '50 Years Ago' column to the blasting accident at Burnmouth, during the construction of the Eyemouth line, which had damaged the 'Flying Scotsman' express. It referred to the fact that the signals were not able to be placed against her and that the locomotive was severely damaged, but fortunately not derailed, by debris from the blast.

By November 1939, two months after the start of hostilities the Education Committee, as reported in the *Berwickshire News*, was becoming concerned about the transport of pupils as a result of the reduction in the local railway service. A further '*News*' article reported the Transport Minister as saying that under the present conditions of working of trains it would not be possible to operate a system of seat and carriage reservations. Wartime conditions were beginning to have an effect on train travel.

By the start of 1940 World War II had been in progress for several months and, as in World War I, reporting restrictions were imposed upon the press. As a result during the period of hostilities there were few reports emanating from the Eyemouth branch, and, indeed, the nearby East Coast main line. Most items that did appear were related to railway employees rather than matters to do with train operations.

However, John Bennett, the then Ayton stationmaster, in his book, *Random Reflections of a Roving Railwayman,* referred to a happening in October 1939 which was not able to be recorded by the local press. The staff at his station reported to him that they had seen a crippled Heinkel bomber hedge-hopping across the local countryside and heading out to sea over Eyemouth. Apparently there had been a bomber attack on the Forth Bridge earlier that day. Bennett also referred to incidents of bombs being dropped near Ayton, one of which had landed upon the railway embankment. It did not explode and was removed by the local bomb disposal team to Coldingham Moor where it was detonated, creating a 'terrific bang'. He also remembered at least one trainload of evacuated children, all with identification labels around their necks, from Edinburgh and Portobello being allocated to homes in the coastal area between Ayton and Eyemouth.

John Crow, a former employee at Eyemouth station, was appointed station master at Stow and Bowland stations on the Waverley route, an article appearing in the *Southern Reporter* of 2nd May, 1940, whilst the *Berwickshire News* of 11th June recorded that Andrew Irving, the station master at Eyemouth, had been appointed acting station master at Penicuik, Auchendinny, Eskbridge and Pomathorn south of Edinburgh.

The winter of 1940-41 included a storm, described by the *Lanarkshire Daily Record* as 'the worst in 56 years'. It lasted for three days (18th-21st February) and snow fell to a depth of 17 inches. Many roads became almost impassable. One bus, between Eyemouth and Berwick, was said to have taken three hours to cover the eight miles between the two locations! However, the railways managed to cope, even running additional trains, including one to Berwick from Newcastle.

On 9th October, 1941 the promotion of a former Burnmouth station employee, Robert Crombie, was announced in the *Southern Reporter*. He had recently become station master at Milnathort station in Kinross. The final reported item for 1941 for the Eyemouth line appeared in the *Berwickshire News* of 30th December. The LNER advised that from 5th January, 1942, the 1.30 pm from Edinburgh to Berwick, the 1.30 pm from Berwick to Edinburgh and the connecting train into the latter, the 1.45 pm from Eyemouth, would run on Saturdays only, thus 'clearing the line for the passage of essential freight trains and to relieve engines and train crews to assist in the working of such traffic'.

Just three items featured in the pages of the local 1942 newspapers, all in the *Berwickshire News*. In April the LNER announced that Mr A. Spence, a clerk at Eyemouth station, had been appointed station master at Ayton, whilst in December Mr D. Dougan was reported as being appointed station master at Burnmouth (a position he was to hold until June 1943). However, the most dramatic report concerned an incident which occurred on the 9.30 pm train from Berwick to Eyemouth in the month of February. The incident involved two men by the names of Aitchison and Collin. Aitchison had already got a criminal record, having been convicted, in January 1939 at Eyemouth Burgh Court, of a breach of the peace. The Procurator Fiscal, G.S. Morrison, said that the two men, under the influence of drink, had boarded the train, entering a compartment that was already full, being occupied by eight persons, namely five soldiers, a married couple and another woman. One of the two women remarked that there was no room in the compartment. On hearing this remark Aitchison commenced to use the filthiest language to the woman and her husband. The two accused then began to fight with one another. The soldiers tried to intervene, at which point Aitchison threw off his coat and challenged the soldiers to a fight. The aggression continued all the way to Burnmouth with the soldiers doing their utmost to restrain the two men. Aitchison and Collin continued to use filthy language throughout the journey. At Burnmouth station Aitchison, standing in his shirt and trousers, challenged a civilian to a fight and aimed two blows at him. The man avoided these and struck Aitchison in self-defence. The whole event was reported by the Burnmouth station master to the station master at Eyemouth, who proceeded to inform the police. The police constable who attended clearly knew

Aitchison for he stated that whenever he was drunk the accused would go 'fighting mad', becoming a terror to everyone within reach.

The Sheriff thought that this was a very bad case. In earlier situations, where various accused were drunk, but simply making a noise and not harming people, he would dismiss the case and issue a warning. However, this was the worst case he had dealt with in a long time. Both Aitchison and Collin pleaded guilty and were fined £3 and £2 respectively.

An incident which took place over the night of 11th-12th December, 1943 was reported in the *Berwickshire News* following a court case held at Duns Sheriff Court in February 1944 before Sheriff J. Macgregor. The accused before the court was James Alexander Dalgetty, a railway shunter of Carlisle who had acted in concert with an unnamed soldier causing five separate acts of criminal damage. These acts included removing a gate from its hinges at the entrance to Biglawburn railway siding and damaging the military bridge classification signs at the Biglawburn and Mill Bank bridges. The other acts included damage to farm gates at Eyemouth Mill Farm, removing a farm gate at Linthill Farm and multiple acts at Millbrae House: damaging a fence, bursting open locked gates and removing double gates. The trial of the soldier involved, presumably a court martial, was not reported but Dalgetty was found guilty and fined for his actions.

In November 1944 an interesting advertisement appeared in the *Berwickshire News*. A 'clerkess' was required by the LNER to work between Eyemouth and Ayton stations. The wage offered would be in the range of 51s. 6d. per week for someone aged 18 up to a maximum of 84s. for an older person. Applicants were to get in touch with the goods and passenger manager at Waverley station in Edinburgh.

The newspapers of 1945 found nothing of local railway interest to report. However, a 1946 newspaper mentioned that on the anniversary of 'Victory Day' many passengers availed themselves of a stroll 'down the brae' when their northbound train broke down at Burnmouth and was held up for three hours. The 'brae' is the steep road leading to Lower Burnmouth.

A month later, in June 1946, the *Berwickshire News* reported a court case in which the LNER prosecuted 20 persons for trespass on the Eyemouth to Burnmouth branch. The incident had taken place on Sunday 21st April when, of course, there were no trains on the branch. David Collin (a private in the Kings Own Scottish Borderers) David Rattery (RAF, of Eyemouth Mill) and Donald Monro (of Commerce Street, Eyemouth) were charged along with 17 young persons. When the accused were seen and apprehended they said that they had been on the adjacent main road when they were caught in a heavy thunder shower and had taken to the bridge for shelter. Eleven of the group had pleaded guilty to the charge of trespass. Each of the accused was fined the sum of 5s. by Sheriff Reid.

Under the Transport Act of 1947 the railways were nationalized and British Railways was formed, divided into six regions for operations purposes. The Eyemouth line passed from the LNER into its Scottish Region. The Act came into effect on 1st January, 1948.

In the late 1950s the branch train from Eyemouth, hauled by a 'J39' class 0-6-0, has arrived at the bay platform at Burnmouth station. After unloading the locomotive will propel the single carriage into the loops to the west of the station before running round and moving it back into the platform for the next train down the branch.   *R.M. Casserley*

This photograph, previously attributed to Henry Casserley, is claimed by his son Richard. Often-photographed 'J39' class No. 64843 is in the Burnmouth platform with the branch BCK carriage, though its headlamp will need repositioning before the train departs. In the 1950s this locomotive was a regular on the branch trains.   *R.M. Casserley*

Chapter Eight

British Railways days: 1948-1962

A correspondent to the *Berwickshire News*, identified as 'Borderer', wrote an article published on Tuesday 30th March, 1948. In his text he described the inequalities between the services on several of the British Railways' branch lines in the area of the Borders. He pointed out that the inhabitants formerly served by stations on the Cornhill-Wooler-Alnwick line had no train service and an inadequate bus service whilst the line joining Eyemouth and Burnmouth, just three miles away, had a service of nine or 10 trains a day in each direction. In addition Eyemouth had a frequent bus service of nine or 10 each way on the Berwick-St Abbs route. He considered that either the inhabitants of the Coldstream-Wooler-Alnwick area were getting a poor deal or that there was a considerable wastage of costly rolling stock, manpower and petrol near to Eyemouth!

Mr Thomson had been station master at Eyemouth station throughout most of World War II, having been appointed to the post in August 1940. The *Berwickshire News* of Tuesday 13th April, 1948 announced that Scottish Region of the Railway Executive had appointed him to a similar post at North Berwick station. His railway career had commenced locally at Reston station where his first post had been as a clerk, though later he gained experience at other locations including Leith Walk Goods, Gordon, Glenfarg and Largo before his Eyemouth appointment. The information was repeated in the *News* of 18th May, perhaps this being the date when he moved to his new post.

The temporary closure of the Eyemouth branch from 13th August, 1948 as a result of what is now sometimes called 'The Great Borders Flood', the damage to the viaduct and its subsequent repair are described in Chapter Fourteen. However, here we can resume the local newspaper reports by referring to the ceremonies associated with the line's reopening which appeared in the *Berwickshire News* of Tuesday 5th July, 1949.

The line was officially reopened by Provost J.S. Collin on the afternoon of Wednesday 29th June. Also present was Mr T.F. Cameron, the Chief Regional Officer of the Scottish Region of British Railways, Mr R.W. Rose, the district commercial superintendent, Mr G. Crabtree, the district operating superintendent, Mr J.B. Innes, the assistant district engineer and Mr A. Beaton, the Eyemouth station master and his clerk Mr J. McIntosh. Local dignitaries present included Mr J.C. Muir, the Eyemouth Town Clerk, Mr J. Burgon, representing the local fish curers, J. Burgon Ltd, and Sir Christopher Furness from a distinguished North-East family. The Provost was introduced to the train crew, namely William Finney (driver), J.A. Purvis (fireman) and James Purvis (guard) before the first train departed.

The same report went on to describe the damage to the viaduct, the embankments and bridges. It had been estimated that a year would be necessary for the repairs but the newspaper commented that the finish time of just 10 months reflected greatly on the engineers and workers for getting the work done so speedily.

After the opening a film was shown of the damage caused by the floods in the Home Arts Hotel and the repairs carried out by the engineers. Immediately following the film a lunch was held at the same hotel. Mr Cameron made a short address to those present commenting on the hard and efficient work carried out both on the Eyemouth branch and on the main line between Berwick and Dunbar. He thanked the Railway Executive for providing an excellent meal and proposed a toast to 'The future of Eyemouth'. Provost Collin replied explaining the hardship that the branch closure had caused to the fishing industry, to the daily workers and to visitors to the town. Sir Christopher Furness expressed a personal inconvenience that he had suffered; the 7 am and 8 am trains had been good 'timers and wakeners' for his family and whilst the line had been closed he had been forced to rely on alternative methods! What the assembly thought of that comment was unrecorded! Mr Burgon expressed his pleasure on the line's reopening and Provost Collin wound up the proceedings with a comprehensive vote of thanks.

British Railways took no time in advertising the new train service for the branch, an advertisement having been placed in the local press on 30th June. A further advertisement of the introduced service appeared on the 5th July and special day excursion fares to Berwick were announced. On the 8th August special excursion tickets to Edinburgh were also announced in the press, valid on Thursdays and Saturdays, giving up to several hours in the Scottish capital for just 8s. 6d. These tickets were available until the end of 1949.

The reporting of the Eyemouth line in the 1950s started with an article on the new station master appointed at the branch terminus to replace Mr A. Beaton. Archibald Spence, as reported in the *Berwickshire News* of 1st August, 1950, was a native of Eyemouth. He started his career with the LNER as a clerk at nearby Ayton station before his first appointment at Eyemouth in 1920. After 22 years' service there he was appointed back to Ayton, this time as station master. In 1945 he was transferred to a similar post at Newcastleton on the Waverley route before being posted to the LNER head office staff at Edinburgh. During the late 1940s he acted as relief station master at various stations in the Borders. In his early years at Eyemouth he was goalkeeper for Eyemouth Rangers Football Club.

British Railways continued to try to promote passenger traffic on the Eyemouth branch. Various newspaper editions in 1950 contained advertisements for cheap tickets to Edinburgh Waverley in particular.

Somewhat surprisingly in view of the time of year the railway embankment caught fire at Burnmouth (*Berwickshire News* 18th December, 1951). Both the Eyemouth and Berwick fire brigades sent appliances and the fire was soon extinguished. The Berwick unit quickly returned to base leaving the Eyemouth team to supervise.

The 8th April, 1952 edition of the *News* reported on the retirement of Robert Gilchrist of Spittal, Berwick, who had, between 1931 and 1937, been a guard based at Eyemouth. He had joined the North Eastern Railway in 1912 starting as a porter. After war service in France he returned to being a porter. He worked for a time on passenger trains before being made redundant from his post. He transferred to Tweedmouth marshalling yard before his Eyemouth appointment. After leaving Eyemouth he returned to Berwick sometimes acting as a 'link guard' which involved trips to Alnwick, Coldstream and St Boswells.

Local newspapers from 1951 into 1953 continued to advertise cheap tickets to Waverley on Thursdays and Saturdays, the cost for adults being 8s. 6d. from Eyemouth leaving on the 7.05 am train, with a change of trains at Burnmouth. Return could be made from Waverley at either 2.30 or 3.45 pm. Reduced price tickets were also available from Burnmouth, Ayton, Reston and Grantshouse, though in the case of the first three of these stations a return journey could be made as late as 6.30 pm from Waverley. It was the summer 1952 timetable which included the dramatic reduction in services on the Eyemouth line (see Chapter Ten). This eliminated the possibility of an evening return to Eyemouth from Waverley, the last departure from Burnmouth for Eyemouth being at 5.15 pm.

The illustrated article on the arrival of a new carriage and the role of Mrs Mavin, the carriage cleaner, in the 22nd July, 1952 edition of the Berwickshire News, will be recorded in Chapter Nine. The condition of the previous passenger carriages must have been deplorable as once the new carriage had arrived then 'word spread throughout the town so more and more of the residents arrived to the station to view it'.

Football supporters were encouraged to use the train when Berwick Rangers played an away cup game (at Rangers or Third Lanark depending on the result in the previous round) on 9th March. Reduced price return tickets, advertised in the News of 9th March, were available at 11s. from Burnmouth, but, of course no ticket was available from Eyemouth. Passengers would have been unable to return home directly to Eyemouth as they would have missed the last branch train!

In 1953 the local press and the British Railways in-house newspapers reported the success of the Burnmouth (Lamberton) track gang in winning the award for the best maintained length of track in the whole of Scotland. The gang's responsibility stretched from the Border to East Linton and included the Eyemouth branch. The team leader was ganger Aitchison with the rest made up of lengthmen Gillie and Anderson (of Burnmouth), Clark (of Berwick) and sub-ganger Wallace of Eyemouth. On 6th May, 1954 the Berwick Advertiser reported that this team had, once more, been successful, this time gaining second place in the whole of Scotland.

Under the headline 'Nest Under Rail Van' in its 8th June, 1954 edition, the Berwickshire News reported an unusual happening. A number of fish vans had arrived at Eyemouth station from Hull. A female blackbird was seen hovering near to them and a nest was discovered under one of the vans. It contained five eggs. The van was shunted onto one of the sidings and labelled 'Not to be moved'. The five eggs successfully hatched and the blackbird was reported as having a busy time feeding her brood. Her mate was not to be seen, presumably having been left behind in Hull!

A few weeks later, on 3rd August, the News reported that the circus of Messrs Robert Brothers was to make two performances, one in the afternoon and one in the evening, at Acredale Farm at Eyemouth on Friday 6th August. The circus elephants presumably arrived by train at Eyemouth for the public were invited to see the elephants walk from the station to the circus ground at 12.30 pm. The circus moved to Duns for two performances on the following day and at Coldstream on the following Monday. In each case the elephants were to walk from the local stations.

No. 64843 with its 52D (Tweedmouth) plate carried on its smokebox door prepares to leave Eyemouth station with a mixed train including a van or two behind the single carriage. The branch 'spare' carriage is parked at the end of the siding. The gradient board indicates that in the station it is 1 in 300 but this changes to 1 in 50 at the platform end.

Armstrong Railway Photographic Trust

It has not been possible to trace the identity of the photographer who took this impressive view of No. 64843 and its one-coach train emerging from the road overbridge on the Ayton road, or the date when it was taken, though it is likely to have been in the late 1950s as the locomotive has the early British Railways logo on its tender. Note the legend 'J-39 Tweedmouth' on the locomotive's buffer beam.

Nigel Blagburn (Alnwick Auctions) Collection

The press reported that the national rail strike of May 1955 had caused newspapers to be distributed by road. By this time the number of passengers using the Eyemouth trains had declined dramatically and the local bus services no doubt profited from the strike!

A late train returned to the Eyemouth branch on Saturday 27th August of the same year when a special excursion train connected Eyemouth and Edinburgh Waverley stations. It was run in connection with the Edinburgh Tattoo. The train left Eyemouth at 5.15 pm and returned at 1 am the following day, a rare Sunday train on the line. As this departure time was the normal scheduled departure of the last Eyemouth to Burnmouth train it is likely that the excursion also carried any intending passengers between these two points. The excursion party included 15 members of the Eyemouth High School Pipe Band. The event was recorded in the *News* of 30th August.

The same newspaper reported that James R. Young, of Eyemouth, had commenced duties as a porter at Burnmouth station. He had previously served at Dirleton, Eyemouth and East Fortune before his Burnmouth appointment. In the war he had served with the Kings Own Scottish Borderers.

Cheap return tickets from local stations to Edinburgh were advertised in the autumn of 1955. However, the availability was extended from just Thursdays and Saturdays to 'Any train, any day', though this was qualified by the statement 'where services permit'. The branch timetable required an early return from the capital! By 1955 the price of the return ticket from Eyemouth had increased to 9s. third class and 13s. 6d. first class.

In November 1955 both the *Southern Reporter* and the *Berwickshire News* recorded the retirement of a local railwayman who had amassed 49 years railway service. John Dougal, of Duns, started as a cleaner at Berwick station in the days of the North British Railway. He became a fireman and then an engine driver, a post he held for 35 years. He worked mostly on the Berwick to St Boswells line until that line was closed after the 1948 floods. On the night of the floods he had great difficulty in driving the train to St Boswells taking some risks during a dreadful run. The weather conditions meant that he could not return home that night and he spent the night at St Boswells station! He then transferred to driving between Berwick and Eyemouth, driving the locomotive that, in July 1952, first hauled the new coach on the branch. He also drove between Berwick and Kelso. He planned to take things easy in his retirement.

A few weeks later, in December 1955, Burnmouth station, under the supervision of station master Mr C. Guthrie, was once again awarded a third class prize in the best kept station competition.

Football supporters were, once again, encouraged to travel by train when British Railways advertised, in the *Berwickshire News*, special return tickets from Eyemouth and Burnmouth for a trip to see the Scotland versus England match to be played at Hampden Park, Glasgow, on 14th April, 1956. The return fare was 14s. 6d. from Eyemouth (depart 10.10 am) and 14s. from Burnmouth (depart 10.26 am), with the special train, complete with cafeteria car, arriving at Glasgow (Queen Street) at 1.21 pm. Intending

This is the first of two photographs of Tweedmouth's 'J39' class 0-6-0 No. 64844 at the head of the branch train in Eyemouth's platform. In this view the train has at least one fish van behind its solitary carriage. The 'old' running-in station name-board is visible beyond the lamp-post on the left-hand side. It is believed that this was replaced by an enamel board in the years before the line closed. The year of the photograph is probably 1954.

T.G.Hepburn/Rail Archive Stephenson

The train crew of No. 64844 need to position a headlamp on the upper bracket before the train departs in this July 1954 view. Like most of its sister locomotives based at the local depot it has the legend 'J-39 Tweedmouth' on its buffer beam.

R.S. Carpenter

participants then had to make their way to Glasgow Central to catch a connecting service (at a cost of 8*d*. return) to Mount Florida station for the stadium. It is not known how the football fans returned from Burnmouth to Eyemouth. The score in the match was 1-1.

Two months later, on 19th June, the *Berwickshire News* published the timetable for Her Majesty the Queen's forthcoming visit to Eyemouth and Duns on 7th July. Accompanied by the Duke of Edinburgh the Royal Train was to arrive at Berwick, from Dunbar at 11.15 am. Clearly it was not considered advisable for the train to traverse the Eyemouth branch as the Queen transferred to a car for her short journey to Eyemouth where she was to arrive at 12 noon. Her schedule required her to leave Eyemouth after a stay of just 10 minutes, so as to arrive at Duns at 12.40 pm, also by car. Her route then took her on to Mellerstain and Lauder via Earlston. Quite a whistle-stop tour!

The *News* of 4th September, 1956 had much, of railway interest, to report. A Burnmouth railway porter, William Patterson, who had held the post for some 3½ years transferred to Berwick where he became an assistant linesman. The vacancy at Burnmouth was filled by Robert W. Miller of Eyemouth who transferred from agricultural work.

The same edition reported on the dreadful storms that had hit the Borders region on Tuesday 28th August, resulting in a 'miniature Niagara' at Eyemouth. The swollen Cast Burn near to the East Coast main line had burst its banks and flooded half a mile of track, and the station, at Grantshouse. A section of cutting wall had collapsed and main line trains were subject to diversion via Carstairs and Carlisle or via Hawick. Some trains were cancelled. The 'Flying Scotsman' was nine hours late leaving Newcastle after its diversion. Passengers from Berwick and Burnmouth were taken by train to Reston where they transferred to a bus for Dunbar. Here they were able to board a train for Edinburgh.

On the Eyemouth branch there was a landslide of 50 tons of rock and earth which buried the track near Hillburn bridge. Fortunately much of the water was able to escape to sea via the Eyewater though it was necessary to evacuate some homes and one small boat was sunk by the onrush of water. The level of the flood was some three feet below the Great Flood of 1948. Once the water level subsided the job of clearing the quayside of the accumulated silt could commence and the evacuated persons could return home.

Special return excursions from Burnmouth, Eyemouth and other local stations were on offer to Edinburgh from December 1956 onwards (again marked 'where services permit'). Once again there was evidence of inflation in the ticket prices, the Burnmouth return fare having increased to 14*s*. and the Eyemouth fare to 14*s*. 8*d*. (first class) and 9*s*. 4*d*. and 9*s*. 9*d*. respectively for what had become second class! The tickets were valid on any train though an early morning departure would have been necessary from Eyemouth to produce a worthwhile amount of time in the Scottish capital. The advertisements for the excursion tickets appeared in the *News* editions of 2nd and 24th December, 1956.

In February 1957 Sir Christopher Furness submitted a letter which was discussed at a Meeting of the Eyemouth Town Council on the third of the month. Sir Christopher's letter was reported in the *News* of 4th February. In it he wrote that the train service to Eyemouth had become so bad that he could only conclude

It is interesting to compare this photograph, taken by C.J.B. Sanderson in October 1954 with the earlier photograph (*upper, page 48*) taken in 1903 in NBR days. The track layout and station show very few changes though there are additions to the buildings on the skyline. The original lattice bracket signal post with its finials now bears upper quadrant signals, the lower arm being for trains accessing the Eyemouth branch.   *Armstrong Railway Photographic Trust*

Burnmouth signal box controlled the station, its sidings and access to the Eyemouth branch. On 16th May, 1954 No. 64844 passed the signal box and entered the bay platform with a train from Eyemouth: the regular BCK and a fish van. The upper quadrant signal in front of the box was the 'starter' for the Eyemouth branch whilst the shunt signal controlled the propelling movement when the locomotive propelled its train out of the platform prior to running-round in the loops (just out-of-sight).   *T.G. Hepburn/Rail Archive Stephenson*

that it was the avowed aim of British Railways to close the line. He quoted two examples to support his assertion. Firstly the former 3.45 pm train from Edinburgh now waited at Dunbar for half an hour and the former 2.30 pm waited a full quarter of an hour at Burnmouth. He added that the netting in the luggage racks of the branch trains was so rotten that it wouldn't bear even a light weight. Councillors in their discussions were informed that the 3.45 pm train had to wait at Dunbar to allow the express, 'The Talisman' to pass and that this could not be avoided. The 2.30 pm train, arriving at 4.15 pm, had been altered to arrive a quarter of an hour earlier at 4pm, thus allowing passengers from this train to catch the 4.07 pm to Eyemouth. The main line train then continued on to Berwick at 4.15 pm after its 15 minute wait art Burnmouth. The council agreed to send a letter to Sir Christopher.

Later that month the *News* contained the same small British Railways advertisement that had appeared in December 1956. It reappeared again in the *News* edition dated 1st October, 1957. It would be interesting to know how many passengers availed themselves of this offer bearing in mind the nature of the branch train service, the only possible arrival in Edinburgh being at 9.05 am, with the latest departure on weekdays being at 3.20 pm (half an hour later on Saturdays).

A road accident was reported in the 25th February, 1957 edition of the *Berwickshire News* which was indirectly attributable to the poor train service on the branch. As a result of the inconvenient train times the transport of Eyemouth High School pupils living in Burnmouth and Ayton had been switched from train to bus. Fortunately there was no-one hurt when the school bus skidded over 150 yards down a steep icy hill on the Eyemouth-Ayton road on 18th February. The vehicle had come to rest against a concrete pillar bordering a 30 ft drop into the River Ale. Otherwise the consequences would have been much more serious.

There were several press reports of encouraging numbers of holidaymakers visiting Eyemouth that summer although almost every one referred to the visitors arriving by bus. Otherwise the amount of reporting of railway matters declined, with the next item of note not appearing until the following year, 1958. On 17th June the *Berwickshire News* described the presentation by British Railways to a long standing railwayman, James McIntosh JP, who received a gold watch to mark the completion of his 50 years of service to the railway. The presentation took place at the Regional Headquarters in Edinburgh. Although a native of the village of Uddingston in Lanarkshire, Mr McIntosh had resided in the fishing burgh for many years. He had always taken a keen interest in the affairs of the town. He had served on the Eyemouth town council for 24 years. He was Provost for five years and honorary treasurer for nine years. He was one of the oldest members of the Eyemouth Bowling Club and still bowled regularly!

On 26th May, 1959 a party of pupils and staff from Eyemouth High School travelled on a chartered special train for a day out on the River Clyde. The party numbered 200 pupils and 13 teaching staff. The special left Eyemouth at 8am for Glasgow and the party travelled down the River Clyde to Tighnabruach. The weather, according to the *News* report of 2nd June, was favourable and a good time was had by all! The party reboarded the special train at Gourock for the

'J39' class 0-6-0 No. 64843 has arrived in Berwick's up platform with the early morning through train from Eyemouth on 27th June, 1957. The fireman appears to be caught in the act of preparing to pass some coal through the signal box window for the fireman's stove. The train will transfer the single coach into the down platform before running round and almost immediately hauling the train back to Burnmouth and Eyemouth. *Les Turnbull*

No. 64843 runs parallel to the Eyewater as it emerges from beneath the Toll Bridge just over 200 yards from the platform end at Eyemouth on 19th August, 1957. As always the departure was 'spirited' though in this case the dramatic smoke effect may have been requested by the photographer! The train was the 5.07 pm departure which was allowed just eight minutes for its journey to Burnmouth. *W.J. Verden Anderson/Rail Archive Stephenson*

return journey. It arrived back at Eyemouth station at 10 pm, well after the day's last timetabled train on the branch.

On 25th August of the same year the Eyemouth town council invited the Burnmouth Representative Committee to its meeting. On the Agenda was the matter of the Eyemouth to Burnmouth rail service. A committee member believed that there was a threat of closure of the Eyemouth line and that a diesel train could have been used on the line, making the case for the continuation of the service. The member wondered if the Council could take up the matter with the Transport Commission. The Provost said that there was a plan for the electrification of the Berwick to Edinburgh line between 1963 and 1970. Another member of the committee said that every opportunity should be taken to popularize the line. He added that passengers using the morning train to Berwick could not get back by train in the evening. He thought that through excursion trains to Eyemouth could be run in the summer months. The Provost, Mrs Jackson, wondered if a more frequent service would get much support. He added that it might be worth trying to see what the result would be. Councillor Mrs Fairbairn asked how many people were currently using the train. Bailie Dougal said there were about 20 passengers a day. Others were using cars to get to Berwick. The Provost said that they should ask the Transport Commission for a better service. Bailie Mrs Blackie said 'We should ask for something for the workers'. Councillor Dunnet asked if there was an immediate threat to the service. The Provost replied that it was felt that the service would be 'taken off'. It was, however, pointed out that it was cheaper to travel from Eyemouth to Burnmouth by train rather than bus. In conclusion the Council agreed that they should press for a better rail service, especially during the summer and on Saturdays.

At the monthly meeting of the Eyemouth council held in the first week of December 1959, the *News*, which had reported the August meeting described above, also briefly reported on this meeting. The council were told that the General Manager of British Railways, Scottish Region, had replied saying that, in addition to the Council's letter, he had received one from the local MP, Sir William Anstruther-Gray. He said that the matter was currently under consideration.

A month later, in the *News* edition of 15th December, 1959, the regular columnist under the pen-name of 'Onlooker', produced an item under the heading 'Mixed Feelings'. He said that diesel engines were being used on the express trains from Newcastle to Edinburgh and that 'these sleek looking monsters' were attracting crowds of trainspotters to the local bridges over the railway. He conceded that they were faster and cleaner than the more familiar steam engines but doubted that the diesels were as quiet as they were claimed to be. The strident notes of their horns could jolt people from their slumbers.

On 8th March, 1960 a further meeting of the Eyemouth town council met with a deputation from the Burnmouth Representative Committee and the Eyemouth district council. The subject was the future of passenger traffic on the Eyemouth branch line. The meeting was reported in the *News* a week later. The various suggestions that had been put forward previously were once again aired: making the line more poular, summer excursions and a better passenger service in summer and on Saturdays, and a better service for workers including

'B16' class 4-6-0 No. 61410 based in the York area heads a southbound goods train on a bright November day in 1958 just south of Burnmouth. The train contains an interesting mixture of four-wheeled and bogie vans and open wagons. The train is running with Class 'E' headlamps which indicate that there are a few vehicles immediately behind the locomotive which have operating vacuum brakes.   *C.J.B. Sanderson*

Two Tweedmouth locomotives are present in this picture taken at Burnmouth on 9th June, 1960. 'K3' class 2-6-0 No. 61952 is on a southbound stopping train on the main line whilst 'J39/2' class 0-6-0 No. 64925 rests in the bay with its connecting single-coach train for Eyemouth. The photograph was taken from the Burnmouth Road bridge over the railway.   *H.B. Priestley*

a later train back to Eyemouth. However, no further suggestions were put forward and no decisions made.

In September 1960 the *Berwickshire News* reported on the summer visitors to Eyemouth with many having come from the North of England and Glasgow. There was also a growing need to cater for South of England visitors on their way to the Edinburgh Festival or to tour the Highlands. A frequent complaint was the inadequate *bus* service to Berwick from Eyemouth, the buses running at inconvenient times. No mention was made of the train service which could have been described in the same way!

Further reporting of railways in the local newspapers was scanty in 1960 but the *News* reported on a meeting of the parish church guild in early December. It was attended by Mr J. Pringle representing the British Railways district manager in Edinburgh and he was assisted by Mr J. Duncan. They presented a series of colour films made by British Railways featuring the county of Northumberland, Blackpool and the continent. They were thanked by the Guild's vice-president.

The *Berwickshire News* of 10th January, 1961 reported on a meeting of the local roads committee at Duns, at which it was stated that there was a need for a new Toll Bridge at Eyemouth, to cross both the railway line and the River Eye. As things finally turned out the new bridge was required to cross the river only!

The same newspaper dated 28th February, 1961 contained the obituary for Archibald Spence who had died aged 58. He had been station master at both Ayton and Eyemouth as mentioned earlier. At the time of his death he was living with his wife at Paxton Terrace in Eyemouth.

On Thursday 25th July, 1961 an 'A3' Pacific locomotive left Eyemouth for Berwick. No, it was not a standard gauge machine but was a model, 3 ft in length and built to a scale of ½ inch to the foot, which had been engineered by Mr S.J. Wishart, a retired Eyemouth grocer. The locomotive, in NER green livery, numbered 717 and named *Border Lass*, worked on 'live steam' and was the latest in a series of model engineering projects of Mr Wishart who had a workshop in Eyemouth. A ceremony was held at Berwick station, as reported in the *Berwick Advertiser*, when the locomotive was presented to Berwick station. At the ceremony were Berwick Alderman, Mr T. Evans. Mr G. Davison, the shedmaster at Tweedmouth locomotive depot, Mr G. Smith, the Berwick station master, and Mr W. Dendy, the assistant superintendent at Newcastle. Mr Smith accepted the engine on behalf of British Railways and, in particular, Berwick

Table 21		BURNMOUTH and EYEMOUTH					

Miles		Week Days only					
		am	am K	pm	pm E	pm S	
20	Edinburgh (Wav.) dep	..	6 50	..	2 25	3 30 3 48	..
20	Berwick-upon-Tweed ,,	7 20	8 52	..	..	.. ..	..
—	Burnmouth .. dep	7 35	9 12	..	4 05	25 5 40	..
3	Eyemouth arr	7 43	9 20	..	4 85	33 5 48	..

Miles		Week Days only					
		am	am N	pm	pm E	pm S	
—	Eyemouth .. dep	7 58	03 30	..	5 05 10		..
3	Burnmouth arr	7 13 8	93 39	..	5 95 19		..
8½ 23	Berwick-upon-Tweed arr	8 18 4	0	..	5 23 5 37		..
55 20	Edinburgh (Wav.) ,,	9 5	..	..	..		..

E Except Saturdays

K Through Train between Berwick-upon-Tweed and Eyemouth
N Through Train between Eyemouth and Berwick-upon-Tweed

S Saturdays only

Extract from the passenger timetable for 1951.   *Author's Collection*

The Eyemouth bay platform is empty as 'A4' Pacific No. 60025 *Falcon* speeds through Burnmouth with a non-stopping southbound express. Whilst the platforms appear to be devoid of passengers an interesting group of individuals watch the passage of the train from the end of the up platform and part of the boarded crossing. *G.M. Stadden*

An Edinburgh to Berwick three-coach stopping train of LNER stock is in the hands of 'V2' class 2-6-2 No. 60833 of Gateshead depot as it approaches its stop at Burnmouth on 26th August, 1960.. The pictures on pages 106-8 illustrate the variety of trains and locomotives that could be seen by waiting passengers on Burnmouth station. *Armstrong Railway Photographic Trust*

station. A previous model, constructed by Mr Wishart, was of HMS *Hood* and this had been presented to Eyemouth Harbour.

Though not directly connected with the Eyemouth branch the *News* of 17th August, 1961 produced an illustrated article on an accident at Grantshouse, between Burnmouth and Dunbar, involving an English Electric diesel locomotive (later called a class '40') with a train of some 45 wagons in tow. This caused a complete blockage of the Berwick to Edinburgh main line and would have necessitated any passengers from Eyemouth or Burnmouth taking a train to Berwick to catch an Edinburgh service diverted via St Boswells and the Waverley route.

British Railways published the closure notice for the Eyemouth branch in *The Scotsman* newspaper in September 1961. It did not appear in the newspapers published in Berwick. Large closure notices were pasted up at the stations involved. On Tuesday 19th September the *Berwickshire News* published an article under the headline 'Eyemouth protest at closing of railway, County Council support objection by Burgh'. The article both informed the readers of the British Railways' proposals and detailed the courses of action that the objectors were planning to take.

Firstly the article stated that the Eyemouth town council, supported by the Berwickshire County Council, were to lodge an objection to the closure of the Eyemouth branch. The Eyemouth council had been forced to call an extra meeting to discuss this matter as it would have been too late to lodge an objection had they left the matter to their next scheduled meeting. The council had agreed at their special meeting to forward their objection to both British Railways and to the Transport Users' Consultative Committee (TUCC). Their objections had to have been received by Tuesday 19th September.

The decisions of the council were unanimous. They felt that the decision to close the line at that time was inopportune in view of the imminent harbour developments which were expected to start in early 1962. They deplored the decision suggesting that the closure plans should have been postponed until the effect of the harbour developments could be ascertained. They felt that the closure would adversely affect the prospect of any firms starting up a business in the harbour area if rail facilities were withdrawn and would hinder any major expansion of the town's industry and economy. The Provost, Mrs J.R. Jackson, expressed the council's views to the press. On the passenger side she felt that the line's closure would cause hardship to the 30 or so Eyemouth residents who used the early morning train to get to work in Berwick, there being no suitable alternative bus service. The first train of the day from Eyemouth, the 7.25 am, also provided a good connection for Edinburgh at Burnmouth. She added that holidaymakers often investigate whether a potential holiday destination has a train service before making bookings. She confirmed the council's views regarding the harbour and potential goods traffic.

The proposals were for a complete closure of both Eyemouth and Burnmouth stations for passengers. Goods, including large items such as coal, would be delivered from Ayton station to Eyemouth, though passenger trains would cease to call at Ayton. The very limited amount of fish traffic emanating from Eyemouth would be dealt with at Berwick.

BRITISH RAILWAYS

CLOSING OF

BURNMOUTH AND EYEMOUTH

PASSENGER AND GOODS STATIONS

AND

WITHDRAWAL OF PASSENGER TRAIN SERVICE FROM

AYTON STATION

On and from MONDAY, 5th FEBRUARY 1962, with the approval of the Transport Users' Consultative Committee for Scotland, Burnmouth and Eyemouth Stations will be closed; and the Passenger Train service will be withdrawn from Ayton Station. Biglawburn Public Siding, Eyemouth (full truck loads only) will also be closed.

Thereafter the following arrangements will apply:

PASSENGERS

Alternative rail facilities are available at Berwick-upon-Tweed at which point bus services operate to and from the areas served by Burnmouth, Eyemouth and Ayton Stations.

PARCELS AND OTHER MERCHANDISE TRAFFIC BY PASSENGER TRAIN (Except Fish Traffic), AND FREIGHT TRAIN TRAFFIC

Alternative facilities for traffic in less than truck loads, and in truck loads requiring a collection or delivery service by railway motor, are available at Reston Station from which point a collection and delivery service will be provided, as required, to and from the area now served by Burnmouth and Eyemouth Stations.

Alternative facilities for fish traffic by passenger train or other similar service are available at Berwick-upon-Tweed from which point a collection and delivery service will be provided, as required, to and from the area now served by Burnmouth and Eyemouth Stations.

Traffic not requiring a collection or delivery service by railway motor will be dealt with at Ayton Station where arrangements for dealing with all parcels and other merchandise by passenger train and freight train traffic will remain unaltered.

The notice of closure issued by BR for the stations at Burnmouth, Eyemouth and Ayton stations.

The council case was hardly a strong one as, apart from the first train of the day, patronage was very low. Even the 30 'souls' reported as using the first train to Berwick had to return, after work, by bus! They even suggested that in the event of closure of the train service would require a change to the bus service. The 'evidence' as regards the harbour development was largely speculative and existing rail-borne fish traffic from Eyemouth was already almost negligible in comparison with the fish travelling by road. The continuing dwindling population of the Borders area also did not bode well for an increase in passenger traffic. None of the local newspapers contained 'Letters to the Editor' deploring the proposed closure and the newspapers themselves refrained from any editorial comment. The *News* of 3rd October did contain a very brief report of a meeting of the Eyemouth and Berwick Labour branch at which the prospective Labour Party candidate for the Berwick constituency, Mr James Stewart, said that he was firmly opposed to the closure of the Eyemouth to Burnmouth line. There was no other political comment.

The *Berwickshire News* of Tuesday 31st October, 1961 contained an article headed: 'Transport Committee agrees to closing of Eyemouth-Burnmouth line, county to fight decision'. It reported that, on receipt of this information by letter on 26th October, the county clerk, Mr J.B. Smith, noted that it was intended that an early morning bus would be provided to take workers to Berwick but asked the TUCC to delay the lifting of the line for 12 months. This last item was ignored. Less than a month later, the Minister of Transport, Ernest Marples, speaking in the House of Commons on 28th November, emphasised the need for a severe rationalization of train services in the Borders region, describing the 8.00 am train from Berwick to Edinburgh (which called at Burnmouth) as a 'ghost train' and the evening Edinburgh to Berwick stopping train as a 'white elephant'. The Government position was clear!

Though not affecting the Eyemouth line directly there was a fire at the Tweedmouth locomotive depot where the branch locomotives were stabled overnight. This fire took place on 13th November, 1961 and was reported in the *Berwick Advertiser*. It affected a building adjacent to the main shed. The fire caused some damage to the roof and its supporting beams. The prompt arrival of the Berwick fire brigade allowed the fire to be extinguished in just 30 minutes.

The *Advertiser* of 21st January, 1962 contained a brief article which confirmed that the fish traffic from Burnmouth, which was described as 'still substantial', would be handled at Berwick station when Burnmouth station closed on 5th February.

Although 5th February, 1962 was the scheduled closure date for Ayton, Burnmouth and Eyemouth stations, along with the whole of the Eyemouth branch line, British Railways had clearly purchased an advertising slot to appear in several successive editions of the *Berwick Advertiser*, starting in late 1961 and extending into late March of 1962. It advertised special day return tickets from Berwick station to many stations in Northumberland and the Borders. Although Eyemouth did not appear in the advertised list of stations, Ayton and Burnmouth did, even in newspaper editions dated after their February closure! This may, on occasions, have caused some embarrassment to the booking clerks at Berwick station!

The *Berwickshire News* of Tuesday 6th February reported on the final trains on

'J39/2' class 0-6-0 No. 64917 waits in the Eyemouth bay at Burnmouth station with the 8.52 am service. The train conveys a parcel van and a fish van ahead of the passenger coach. The signal in the foreground indicates the imminent passing of an Edinburgh bound train. The date is 3rd February, 1962, the last day of services on the line. *Edwin Wilmshurst*

Also taken during the last week of service is this second photograph of No. 64917, this time awaiting departure from Eyemouth station with the one-coach passenger train on what looks like a wet day. Clearly the local coal merchant had been 'stocking up' with the imminent cessation of all traffic on the line. *Jim Sedgwick*

the Eyemouth branch under the heading: 'Sentimental journey to the end of the line'. Two photographs illustrated the article. The first was captioned: 'All aboard – and the one carriage is crowded as the Eyemouth-Burnmouth train prepares to pull out for the last time'. Fifty passengers travelled on it.' The second bore the caption: 'Mr. George Robertson prepares to board the Eyemouth-Burnmouth train on its last run on Saturday. He was a child of six months when he travelled on the train on its first run in 1891'.

The text of the article started with the last run down the branch to Eyemouth which had left Burnmouth to the sound of cheers and the crack of detonators. It consisted of locomotive 64917 and the branch's single 'dedicated' coach bearing 'Eyemouth-Burnmouth' boards on the side. It was undoubtedly a sad occasion and no-one felt it more keenly than local farmer William Bell, who lived by the side of the line. As the train steamed past he stood, bare-headed, cap in hand, paying his last respects. Mr Bell had watched the trains steam past for all of the 71 years that the line had been open. There were also memories for local fish-curer, George Robertson, who recalled that he had also travelled on the first train in 1891. 'It was a great day when the line opened and for all of us it is sad to see it going,' he said. Also on board for the Saturday night finale was James McIntosh JP, a former Provost of Eyemouth, and a clerk at Eyemouth station for 41 years. 'I just could not miss this trip!' Both gentlemen recalled how the herring season had meant an annual boom for the line. There were many people involved in the industry who travelled to and fro on the train and on top of that there was formerly a very substantial freight business. Plus there were special trains which ran down to Eyemouth.

There were 50 people aboard the train for the last historic runs though almost half of these were a party of schoolchildren. In the words of the newspaper reporter:

At 5.10 precisely Guard James Purvis of 4 Wellbraes, Eyemouth – guard on the line for 15 years – waved away the engine and its passengers. One blast from the whistle, an answering cheer from the passengers leaning out of the windows and it was shunting out of Eyemouth station on its last return trip.

ROUSING SEND OFF

As it went, detonators on the line gave it a rousing send-off. People stood on the bridge which carries the road over the line to wave it away and others stood looking over a high wall to see it leave.

Eight minutes later, dead on time, it was steaming into the siding beside the main line platform at Burnmouth.

Thousands and thousands of passengers had made the same short trip to catch connections all over the country from 1891 until the present day. They will be able to do it no more.

The men, women and children who had travelled on this final run stood on the platform at Burnmouth and tried to keep out the biting cold wind as the train was shunted into position and at 5.32 amid more cheers and detonators it began its return trip to Eyemouth.

Soon afterwards engine 64917 was on its way back to the sheds at Tweedmouth. The coach will later go on to Edinburgh. Driving the engine on this final run (back to Tweedmouth) was Mr. Arthur Dixon, 3 Osborne Crescent, Tweedmouth; his fireman was Mr. Joe Pringle of St. Bartholomew Crescent, Spittal Hall. Many of the passengers stopped for long enough to say that the decision to close the line – taken on economy grounds – was too hasty.

But the authorities ordered the closure after considering and rejecting the protests from Eyemouth Town Council. Many believed that the death throes of the Eyemouth-Burnmouth line – operated at first by the North British Railway following agitation by fishermen and merchants who felt that it was necessary to develop the trade of the port – began when the August floods swept down in 1948. They damaged the red-brick viaduct which carried the line over the River Eye. For 10 months the line was closed while repairs were carried out. And in that time many people found alternative means of transport for their fish and for other freight. When the line re-opened in June 1949 neither passenger nor goods traffic ever attained pre-flood volumes.

On Saturday night in a cloud of smoke and steam, the death knell sounded.

In an earlier era the railway had advertised excursion tickets from Eyemouth and Burnmouth to many events and destinations in, for example, Edinburgh. It was a sign of the times that a June 1962 edition of the *Berwickshire News* advertised day excursions using the buses of the Scottish Omnibus Co. to take visitors to the Highland Show. Departing at 7.40 am from Eyemouth, the cost was 10s. That month Eyemouth recorded a large influx of visitors from both Tyneside and from Glasgow, all, of course, arriving by road!

Finally on Tuesday 18th September a large advertisement with a cartoon-style picture of a small station and train appeared in the *News* with the heading 'The End of the Line'; it was placed by the makers of Drybrough Scottish beer.

On 19th June the same newspaper reported that a start had been made to the uplifting of the rails at Eyemouth station. A similar item appeared in *The Railway Observer*, a railway society journal.

Plans survive in the Edinburgh Archives which show the extent of the work at Burnmouth after closure and lifting of the rails between Burnmouth sidings and Eyemouth. Most of the Burnmouth signalling associated with the branch was to be removed except the branch-arm on the bracket at the end of the Burnmouth main line platform, as the facing crossover towards the branch was to be left in position (for a time at least). The branch was to have a pile of sleepers erected as a buffer stop, before the exit from the north end of the branch line sidings. The tracks of the branch line thus became a short siding. The arm on the bracket signal, formerly allowing trains from Eyemouth to access the main line platform, now controlled movement from the newly created siding. The points connected to the other former branch sidings were disconnected from the signal box and the facing points were spiked and clamped in the 'normal' position. A small seven-lever ground frame in the sidings, used during shunting operations, was also taken out of use. The three sidings on the opposite side of the main line and their shunt signals were not affected by the closure of the branch.

Eventually the main line was realigned and all of the former sidings, on both sides of the main line, were lifted. The platforms, including the Eyemouth bay, were largely demolished and Burnmouth signal box disappeared, its signals replaced by centrally controlled colour-lights.

A casual visitor looking from the bridge on the Burnmouth road, or a passenger in a passing modern high speed express, would not suspect that there had once been a busy railway junction at this location.

Chapter Nine

Depots, locomotives, carriages and personnel

Although nominally a separate railway company until it was absorbed into the North British Railway the Eyemouth branch was, from its opening, worked by locomotives of the NBR. No locomotive shed was provided at either Eyemouth or Burnmouth, the line's locomotives being based, until its closure, at the North British Railway's Berwick depot. However, it was necessary for there to be a supply of locomotive water available at Eyemouth as, for some years, a locomotive was stabled there overnight. Initially, in August 1891, the Directors decided that they would accept the offer of James Gibson of Gunsgreen who undertook to supply water at a cost of £10 per year, for the first five years of operation. However, by September 1892 the Directors decided that the water should come instead from Eyemouth Mill Farm (a farm belonging to Colonel Milne Home) for a payment of just £5 per annum.

The NBR arrived in Berwick in 1846. Its locomotive depot was built to the west of the line a short distance to the north of Berwick-upon-Tweed station. It is recorded as being built by 18th June, 1845. It was a stone-built semi-roundhouse with a continuous pitched roof. There were 13 roads leading from the turntable. This turntable was open to the elements. A coal stage (known as the coke platform) and a water tank were provided for locomotive servicing. On a map of 1852 it appears that there was a ramp leading from this platform above the tracks to facilitate fuelling of the locomotives on one of the two roads adjacent to the platform. On the same road as the ramp was an ash pit with a nearby crane, presumably to aid emptying of loco ash from the pit. The water tank was mounted centrally above the shed roof. A chimney next to this water tank seems to indicate the presence of a stove below to prevent the water freezing in winter. Behind and to the west of the shed, in a separate building, were a store, a smith's shop, a pump house and a boiler house. To the north of the shed was located a small gas works with a gas house, coal shed, purifiers, a gasometer and a tar pit [sic]. A coal siding provided the necessary fuel. Access to the main lines could be made either from a head shunt beyond the fuelling facilities or from a road leading from the turntable. The turntable area was illuminated by several lamps on columns, presumably gas lit. Until about 1900 a curling pond was located a few yards outside the railway boundary.

The LNER came into existence at the start of 1923. The existence of two locomotive sheds near to Berwick was obviously considered a luxury and rationalization resulted in the closure of the former NBR's depot and the concentration of all locomotive stabling and servicing at the former NER's Tweedmouth shed. Most of the former NBR shed was demolished in late 1924 in association with the works to rebuild Berwick passenger station, though the roof-mounted water tank survived until later.

Tweedmouth locomotive shed was located on the south side of the River Tweed. It was built at the east end of Tweedmouth station on the south side of the main line. It was completed on 1st July, 1847 for the Newcastle and Berwick

This is the only known photograph of the North British locomotive depot at Berwick-upon-Tweed. It was located to the west of the main lines just to the north of Berwick station. It was a 'half roundhouse' with tracks radiating from the turntable. The photograph shows the centrally placed water tower with the shed clock beneath. Note the impressive lamp column next to the turntable.   *R.W. Lynn Collection*

The appropriately named 'A1' class Pacific No. 60161 *North British* enters Berwick station from the Edinburgh direction with a London-bound express. The date is 16th July, 1954 and some 30 years after the closure of Berwick's NBR shed, its water tower survives by the sidings on the left of this picture. Note the fish vans and containers on the right.   *R.S.Carpenter*

Railway which reached the south bank of the river in March 1847. This railway became the York, Newcastle & Berwick Railway until 1854 when it merged with two other large companies to form the North Eastern Railway.

The 1847 shed at Tweedmouth was straight and single-ended, with just four tracks. Other facilities included a turntable, coaling stage and a water tank. These facilities were proving inadequate by the 1870s and in 1877 a second shed was erected to the east of, and close behind, the first shed and turntable. At this time the depot had an allocation of 20 locomotives. This shed was a stone- and brick-built single roundhouse with a triple-gabled, pitched style roof. The cost of the works was £8,465 1s. 6d., plus a further £305 for a, presumably new, turntable from Messrs Ianson & Sons of Darlington. In 1881 rebuilding of the old shed took place which cost £1,570 1s. 6d. During this rebuilding the old shed received a single-gable pitched style roof. In 1907 the nearby goods shed was re-assigned for locomotive purposes and was converted into a repair shed. It also housed the Tweedmouth breakdown equipment. The cost of conversion was £1,833.

Its allocation at the start of 1923 was some 44 locomotives though by the start of 1939 this had swelled to 53, this number including a dozen locomotives of classes 'J35' and 'J37' which had been transferred from the NBR shed at the time of its closure.

The Tweedmouth depot (coded 52D) continued to serve the locomotive needs of the area until it was finally closed on 19th June, 1966 as the end of steam traction on British Railways approached. During its life it provided motive power for local trains to Alnwick via Coldstream, Alnmouth and the Alnwick branch via Belford (on the main line), trains to Kelso and St Boswells, and, of course, the Berwick-Burnmouth-Eyemouth trains. It also housed some large engines which could substitute for, or assist, failed or ailing locomotives on main line express trains. Trains on the Berwick-Reston-Duns-St Boswells line were largely in the hands of Duns-based engines.

In 1968 the original straight shed at Tweedmouth was demolished and the roundhouse was sold for private industrial use. It is still extant (2018) although it was badly damaged by fire on 21st June, 2008. Fortunately a private video film was made of the shed remains in 2012 in which it is possible to see most of the original cast-iron support girders and transverse beams and braces still in place. Some of the original windows, arches and doorways survive; others have been bricked up. Some of the slate roof survives, albeit in a precarious condition. On the walls are the remains of electrical equipment and a pulley wheel which may date from railway days. Various bits of debris litter the floor, including some very short lengths of rail. The building and yard are in the hands of a builder's merchant. All notices on the outside of the building date from its industrial use.

On 1st January, 1923 the North British depot at Berwick had an allocation of 27 locomotives. Whilst most of these, some sources say 21, were transferred to Tweedmouth depot, some were transferred elsewhere (for example Duns) or met an appointment with the scrapman. This was the fate of the two Wheatley-designed 'J31' 0-6-0s which had worked on the Eyemouth branch. No. 1134 (originally 336 and built by Dübs & Co.) and No. 1195 (originally 246 and built

'J39' class No. 64813 stands amidst piles of ash at the side of the straight shed at Tweedmouth depot. The picture is unfortunately not dated.   *C.J.B. Sanderson*

From left to right the locomotives inside Tweedmouth's roundhouse are' J25' class 0-6-0 No. 65706, 'J39' class 0-6-0 No. 64941 and 'J39/3' class 0-6-0 No. 64843. The class 'J39s' were the replacements for the 'J25s' which had formerly worked trains on the Eyemouth branch.
                                                    Armstrong Railway Photographic Trust

at Cowlairs Works) were both scrapped in 1924. Two class 'J82' 0-6-0Ts had also been employed on the Eyemouth branch, namely Nos. 1333 (formerly 162, named *Milngavie/Loch Leven*) and 1351 (formerly 49 *Sunnyside/Gretna*) which dated from 1887-88 and were of a Drummond design built at Cowlairs. No. 1333 was reported as being seen on the branch when carrying 10333 later in LNER days. A 'J83', No. 828, had been photographed on the Eyemouth branch back in North British days but was transferred away from the area before the start of 1923. This was a relative 'youngster' compared with the 'J31s', being built to a Holmes design in 1900-01. It became LNER No. 9828, and then BR No. 69828, ending its career at Neasden and then Hornsey depots. Another photograph, dating from NBR days, perhaps the year 1914, shows No. 249 at Eyemouth heading a passenger train. This locomotive was built for the NBR at Cowlairs in 1887. Later classified by the LNER as belonging to class 'J33', it received the number 9249 in 1926. It was withdrawn in December 1938. It has also been recorded that a rather similar 'J34' 0-6-0 (designed by Drummond for the NBR) worked on the line around this time.

It was not long before former North Eastern Railway locomotives, based at Tweedmouth, took over the Eyemouth branch trains. Ken Hoole, the noted NER historian and author, records the date as 1st August, 1924. In 1923 Tweedmouth had an allocation of three 'J21' 0-6-0s (formerly NER class 'C1'). These had the same sized driving wheels as the 'J31s' but were more powerful, but also nearly 10 tons heavier. These took over the branch trains and by the 1930s, 'J21' No. 1562 had become the established branch engine though sister engines Nos. 5039 and 5083 were also seen on the line. Records show that four 'J21s' were shedded at Tweedmouth in 1933.

It must be remembered that the LNER originated a 'route availability' system which identified the classes of locomotive which were allowed to operate on each line of its system. Thus a line described as Route Availability 1 could only employ the smallest and lightest of locomotives as a result of the nature of its embankments and bridges: the higher the route availability number, the greater number of locomotive classes that could work on a line. The appendices to working timetables list the Eyemouth to Burnmouth line as being 'RA3' in LNER days which thus allowed locomotives of RA1-3 to work on the line. However, this was clearly not followed rigidly, as, for example, the 'J83' class tank engines were placed in Group 4. The 'J21s' were rated as RA3. It is suggested that a 'D20', No. 2354, was working on the line in the 1930s, a photograph of it on a train having been taken on the main line between Burnmouth and Berwick. As this was a locomotive of RA6 a special exception must have been made if it indeed had worked to Eyemouth. It is, perhaps, more likely that this locomotive, when photographed, was working a train originating on the Duns and St Boswells branch. For some years, on this branch, locomotives of RA6 were permitted subject to a speed limit of 25 mph.

In 1935 there were locomotive problems on the Darlington to Penrith line over the Pennines and a former Great Eastern Railway 2-4-0 of class 'E4', No. 7496, was tried on the line with great success. A total of six of this class were then transferred from East Anglia to the North-East area. On the 8th January two of these locomotives were transferred to Tweedmouth shed, No. 7463 from

No. 64917, a 'J39/2', is seen adjacent to the coal stage at Tweedmouth. Its tender carries the later design of British Railways crest which it may have received during its last works visit. A young trainspotter is seen by the tender. Perhaps he was responsible for the class 'A' headlamps on the buffer beam brackets! The photograph was taken on 5th June, 1959.

Armstrong Railway Photographic Trust

'C16' 4-4-2T No. 67497 of St Margarets shed in Edinburgh, was used to haul an engineers' inspection special as far as the loop sidings at Burnmouth station where it was photographed. This class of locomotive was introduced by the NBR during World War I. As was usual for locomotives on such trains it was in pristine condition.   *R.W. Lynn Collection*

Darlington and No. 7496 from Kirkby Stephen. Darlington received 'J21' No. 570 in exchange for 7463. They were tried out on the Eyemouth branch. Their stay lasted only until 9th April, 1942 when they were transferred away to the Southern Area of the LNER. Their larger driving wheels and inferior tractive effort compared with the 'J21s' may have precipitated this transfer. As replacements for the 'E4s' transferred away, Tweedmouth received 'J21' Nos. 807 and 1559 (from Sunderland) for the Eyemouth services.

At the time of nationalization of the railways the number of 'J21s' at Tweedmouth was four. These 'J21s' continued as the mainstay of motive power on the line though 'J25' No. 3039 is reported as visiting in June 1947. An unusual visitor on 30th May, 1948 was 'J37' 0-6-0 No. 4606 on a ballast train; this locomotive and its crew were from St Margaret's shed in Edinburgh.

The rebuilding and strengthening of the Eyemouth viaduct in 1948/9 contributed to locomotives of RA6 being allowed onto the branch for the first time. This, in theory, allowed locomotives of classes 'J39', 'B1' and 'C16', amongst others, to operate on the branch.

Although it was 'J21' No. 65039 which hauled the first train over the rebuilt viaduct it was the 'J39' 0-6-0s which played an increased role on the line. Although two 'J39s' had been allocated to Tweedmouth for a period in 1939 it was not until BR days that Tweedmouth received a substantial allocation of the class. In 1953 there were seven of the class at the shed, now coded 52D. Others were sub-shedded at Alnmouth depot. Apart from their use on Eyemouth services the 'J39s' could be seen working passenger or goods trains on the branch lines to St Boswells (either via Kelso or via Duns) and on the main line. The Alnmouth examples worked not only on the Alnwick branch (on both passenger and goods services) but also to Amble and destinations further south such as Heaton.

Apart from the 'J39s' which were well-photographed on the branch and on the other local lines, a visit was paid by 'C16' No. 67497 on an officers' special train from Edinburgh in 1952. A local platelayer, Ian Moffatt, can recall that when trains of this type passed it was necessary for the track gang members to stand back from the rails and wave to the dignitaries on board the inspection carriage. Woe betide any member caught not doing this. Ian can also recall the varnished wood of the special inspection carriage. Ian's team worked on the main line on weekdays and looked after the branch on Saturdays. He also recalled that the engines would run round the train at Burnmouth loop before heading back to Edinburgh.

The largest locomotives seen on the branch were the various 'B1' 4-6-0s which appeared on special excursion trains in the late 1950s and early 1960s. For example, 'B1s' arrived at Eyemouth station with ramblers excursions from Newcastle in 1957 and 1958, pilot locomotives being attached for the return journeys from Eyemouth as far as Burnmouth. On 14th August, 1960, 'B1s' Nos. 61199 and 61238 double-headed a long train down the branch to Eyemouth, the pilot engine having been attached at Burnmouth to provide extra brake power. After the passengers had left the train to enjoy the delights of Eyemouth and St Abbs, the empty stock was propelled back up the gradient to Burnmouth. The carriages were stabled in the sidings there until it was time for them to be

The tender of 'J39/3' class No. 64843 is lettered in the immediate post-nationalization style as the locomotive waits in Eyemouth station with an afternoon train for Burnmouth. The carriage received its Sc32400E number in the LNER renumbering of 1943. The new BCK, often seen in the mid- to late-1950s was yet to arrive on the line. *David Anderson Collection*

It was the usual practice for locomotives to haul trains from Burnmouth to Eyemouth running tender first. Here, on a part of the line which is difficult to identify, No. 64844 heads a train down the gradient? The photograph is dated 26th August, 1960, that is, just 18 months before the line's closure. Note the position of the locomotive headlamp which should be on the bracket towards the top of the tender! *Armstrong Railway Photographic Trust*

worked down to Eyemouth for the evening return journey of the 'special'. An equivalent train in the previous year was photographed leaving Eyemouth hauled by 'B1' No. 61007 *Klipspringer* piloted by a 'J21' class 0-6-0. Finally a '2MT' 2-6-0, possibly Tweedmouth shed's No. 46476, is known to have positioned wagons on the branch to assist in the demolition of the line and track reclamation in the summer of 1962. The *Railway Observer* of August 1962 made its final reference to the Eyemouth line: 'The Burnmouth Eyemouth line is in course of being lifted, wagons being placed on the branch for the contractor by the "Berwickshire Goods" or Tweedmouth-Duns branch goods usually a "2MT" 2-6-0.' The last of Tweedmouth's 'J21s', No. 65070, had long since left the depot for South Blyth back in October 1959.

There are numerous records of the classes and individual numbers of locomotives which appeared on the Eyemouth line but detailed observations of the carriage stock are more difficult to come by.

A document held in the Eyemouth Museum lists three carriages which formed the 'NBR branch train'. These are four-wheeled third class brake No. 342, a six-wheeled full first No. 341 and 6-wheeled composite No. 351. It is, perhaps, surprising that three carriages of different types should carry numbers close together in a sequence, though these numbers may be the ones carried by this set after the formation of the LNER when carriages allocated to the Southern Scottish area were given numbers commencing with '3', including 300-399. These are most likely the carriages appearing in some of the early postcards photographs of Eyemouth. It is possible that some refurbished or replacement carriages arrived for the line in about 1916, as a contemporary newspaper article refers to a 'brand new engine and newly painted carriages' albeit as part of a humorous aside. The identity of the 'brand new engine' is not known.

The former NBR carriages survived into LNER ownership but were replaced at Eyemouth in the mid-1920s by two bogie coaches built at the York carriage works. Their arrival was recorded in a somewhat unusual way by an anonymous poet writing in the 'Local Poet's Corner' of the *Berwickshire News* on 11th February, 1930:

PUFF PUFF

When I went up on Eyemouth train
The seats were hard, their covers plain.
The word had lost its pristine stain,
On Eyemouth train.

The carriages were old and bare,
They seemed fatigued and full of care,
They were indeed beyond compare,
On Eyemouth train.

When I came down on Eyemouth train,
From wonder I could not refrain,
I stared, and stared, and stared again,
On Eyemouth train.

This image shows part of the station yard with the 'spare' carriage in the siding next to the Eyewater. Various LNE and LMS vans are present. The buildings on the right are those formerly owned by Mrs Topping. The proponents of the extension of the railway to the harbour planned to demolish her house and develop the property for the railway including the extension of the sidings. *Author's Collection*

An extract from an LNER 'carriage working' roster. Carriages based at Tweedmouth for use on the line were branded 'Sc (number) E'.

SCOTTISH AREA SETS. WEEKDAYS

325 EYEMOUTH—BURNMOUTH

ATTACH	STATION	Arr	Dep	DETACH	ATTACH	STATION	Arr	Dep	DETACH
	325								
		am	am				pm	pm	
	Eyemouth.........		7 7			Burnmouth	4 2	4 20	
	Burnmouth.......	7 15	7 48			Eyemouth	4 27	5 12	
	Eyemouth.........	7 56	8 5			Burnmouth......	5 21	5 46	
	Burnmouth.......	8 13	8 50			Eyemouth.........	5 53		
	Eyemouth.........	8 59	10 13			Eyemouth	.	6 10	
	Burnmouth.......	10 21	10 35			Burnmouth	6 17	6 36	
	Eyemouth.........	10 42	pm			Eyemouth	6 44		
	Eyemouth.........	pm	12 45			Eyemouth.........			8 15
	Burnmouth ...... { SX	12 53	1 25	SX		Berwick............	8 35	9 30	SO
	Burnmouth ...... { SO		1 45	SO		Eyemouth.........	9 51		
	Eyemouth ...... { SX	1 33	3 10			Eyemouth		8†15	
	Eyemouth ...... { SO	1 53	3 10			Burnmouth	8†22	8 45	SX
	Burnmouth	3 18	3 40			Eyemouth	8 52		
	Eyemouth	3 47	3 55						

Works daily
Additional Brake Vehicle to be available at Eyemouth for working mixed trains

Sweet pictures met my startled gaze,
Soft cushions tempted me to laze,
Their velvet ease showed a new phase,
On Eyemouth train.

On Eyemouth train, on Eyemouth train,
I fear it quite has turned my brain,
The sudden change be dazzling, vain,
When I came down, on Eyemouth train.

The first of the two York-built coaches, originally numbered 3480, was a brake third built under Diagram 62 in 1924/5 (Order No. 62). This vehicle was 51 ft 1½ in. long and 9 ft wide. It had five compartments in addition to the guards and luggage area and had seats for 50 passengers. In 1943 it was renumbered 86020. The second vehicle was a lavatory composite numbered 32344 built under Diagram 50 in 1926/7 (Order No. 150). It was the same length as the brake carriage but of slightly greater width, 9 ft 3 in. It had three first class compartments seating 19 and four for third class passengers, seating 33 persons. At least one other carriage must have found employment on the line as a surviving postcard from the 1930s shows a 9-compartment vehicle against the buffer stop in the siding adjacent to the River Eye. At this time many of the trains were formed of just a single carriage and it may be that this was the place where this coach was kept pending for strengthening trains when necessary. Carriage No. SC32400E (*see page 122*) was photographed at Eyemouth in the 1950s, behind a 'J39', the vehicle showing its 1943 LNER number.

By the early 1950s these carriages were showing their age, and, according to the lady carriage cleaner based at Eyemouth, were becoming increasingly difficult to keep clean. A new single steel-bodied replacement coach was ordered for the branch built to Diagram 360. The carriages of this type were of LNER design and were brake composites (BC) with two first class compartments (capable of seating 16 passengers) and four third class, later second class, seating 40. The carriages were built by the Birmingham Carriage & Wagon Co. and measured 52 ft 4 in x 9 ft 3 in. They were numbered in the 80332-80391 series with carriages Nos. 80332-80342 being allocated to the Scottish Region. A second batch was built in 1951 with the number sequence 80392-80421. It was SC80334E which was seen on the Eyemouth branch train hauled by 'J39' class 0-6-0 No. 64925 on 3rd July, 1959, though whether this was the 'new' carriage from the early 1950s, or a later replacement, is not known.

The *Berwickshire News* of 22nd July, 1952 contained an article, with two illustrative photographs, entitled 'The Eyemouth Express' describing the role of the Eyemouth carriage cleaner, Mrs M. Mavin, of the Highfields Estate, Berwick. Mrs Mavin had been employed by the railway for 12 years. She commenced her career as an oiler and greaser of carriages and wagons, only relinquishing that job when former employees returned at the end of the war. She transferred to cleaning duties in the offices and waiting rooms at Berwick station before becoming carriage cleaner. Her 'gleaming new carriage' entered service on the branch on Monday 21st July, 1952. Mrs Mavin commented that 'this was not before time'! This view was shared by the branch footplate crew

No. 64844 makes a spirited start on the adverse gradient out of Eyemouth station with its train for Burnmouth. This photograph was taken from the opposite side of the River Eye near to the Toll Bridge in 1957. Unlike some of its sisters, this engine still carried the early British Railways crest on its tender: the often-called 'cycling lion'.   *Armstrong Railway Photographic Trust*

This July 1954 photograph of Eyemouth station platform shows several items of interest, including the 'old' station nameboard, the spare composite carriage in the siding, and fish boxes stacked in the yard between the sidings. The repaired platform face in the centre of the view is at the location where the edge collapsed may years before, though this looks like a recent repair.
Armstrong Railway Photographic Trust

for the day, namely guard Robert Hay of Eyemouth, driver Robert Dougall of Duns and fireman T. Fullerton of Burnmouth. When the news of the new carriage spread around Eyemouth more and more residents came to the station to view it. However the newspaper reported that there were defects in the carriage's electrical system and that it would have to be taken out of service in the near future for repairs to be carried out. One of the photographs depicted Mrs Mavin with her bucket of hot water which was obtained from the engine. The other showed the carriage, having arrived at Berwick, behind the train engine, a 'J39' 0-6-0. Each weekday morning she awaited the arrival of the 'Eyemouth Express' at about 8.15 am and cleaned the carriage before it departed back to Burnmouth and Berwick-upon-Tweed. This early train normally carried about a dozen people to their place of work in Berwick.

Various British Railways Mark I carriages appeared on the branch on excursion trains towards the end of the 1950s and in the early 1960s. These were the most modern passenger vehicles to appear on the line.

For much of the Eyemouth branch history the line was worked by tender locomotives rather than tank engines, though in early years photographs show tank engines in use. As there was no turntable at either end of the branch 50 per cent of the journeys made by the enginemen were thus run in tender-first mode. So as to keep the water level above the firebox crown the branch tender locomotives almost invariably faced up towards Burnmouth, though some special trains, late in the branch history had one of the locomotives facing towards Eyemouth when double-headed.

In the early days until World War I, the locomotives for the Eyemouth branch were always allocated to Berwick NBR shed. However, as the first branch trains each day started from the Eyemouth end of the line, the locomotives were stabled at the branch terminus overnight. Despite this the NBR, whose locomotives and engine crews worked the trains from the date of opening, never saw fit to provide Eyemouth with any locomotive facilities such as an engine shed, coaling facility or ash pits. The only provision for the locomotives was the water tank which was located at the Burnmouth end of the Eyemouth platform.

After the early years there were no run-round facilities at Eyemouth and the crews therefore had to be adept at the gravity shunting of both carriages and wagons. The branch locomotive crews in these early days were resident in, or lodged in, Eyemouth. Relief crews were sent from Berwick when necessary though as the crews, until after World War I, were required to work a day of 10 hours, one crew sufficed for the train service. Relief enginemen could take the train from Berwick to Burnmouth but then could have faced a three mile walk to the branch terminus.

Prior to 1919 an engine cleaner was employed at Eyemouth, working continuous night duties which involved not just cleaning but coaling the engine, not an easy task in the absence of proper facilities. Following the coaling the fire would be lighted with kindling, followed by wood and coal. The only shelter and warmth during rest periods could be gained in the room below the water tank where there was a stove. The locomotive fireman was required to be with the locomotive at least two hours before the departure of the first train. As

No. 64844 awaits departure from the Eyemouth bay platform at Burnmouth station whilst the train crew relax and put their feet up! This photograph shows the detail of the LNER-designed BCK carriage with its four doors leading into the third class (later second class) seating area, and the two doors for first class passengers, plus the space for the guard and luggage.
Author's Collection

This photograph, taken at Tweedmouth shed in 1953, shows driver Jimmy Mackintosh with his 'J77' class 0-6-0T , also his fireman, Mr T. Piercy. Jimmy retired from service just three years later after a long railway career.   *John Burgon Collection*

the first Eyemouth departure was at, or before, 7.00 am, this meant an early start to the working day. Amongst the fireman's responsibilities was the examination of the firebars to ensure that they were straight and in good order. He had to tend the fire so that it was in good condition, and make sure that the boiler pressure was raised, ready for the first train. The fireman had a special dispensation in that if the first train was scheduled to run before six o'clock in the morning then he need be at the locomotive just one hour before the service started, but in these circumstances he must check and straighten the firebars the previous evening before signing off. The driver's special role was to be responsible for boiler washouts and to oversee routine maintenance such as oiling round. The regular driver during World War I was Robert ('Bob') Thompson and his fireman was Charlie Morrison. The cleaner at this time was Alex Gilchrist.

From 1919 onwards the length of a shift was reduced from 10 to 8 hours. This necessitated two crews sharing the day's work on the branch. Lawson Wood's book records that at that time the Eyemouth station master was George Miller assisted by porters Nean Black, Peter Nisbet and William Tait, plus booking clerk Jimmy Mackintosh. Archie Spence joined as a booking clerk in the early 1920s and he eventually became station master at Eyemouth. Alex Gilchrist became a fireman in 1918 and eventually became a driver during World War II.

The initiation of the eight hour shift produced changes in the way that the Eyemouth branch was operated. Instead of overnighting at Eyemouth as had been the usual procedure, the branch engine travelled light engine from its Berwick shed each morning and returned there each evening. Of course, until August 1924 the home shed was the NBR depot to the north of Berwick station but after this depot closed the branch locomotive started its day at Tweedmouth, crossing the Royal Border bridge on its way north to join the Eyemouth branch. Eyemouth thus ceased to be a signing-on point for crews. This pattern of operation continued until after World War II. Jimmy Mackintosh later became a footplateman at Tweedmouth depot before retiring in 1956. Because of the two shift pattern and the need for light engine movements it was hardly an economic way to operate the branch.

In the 1950s there was a drastic reduction in the branch timetable but two shifts were still worked. The morning shift worked the first couple of return trips then returned the locomotive to Tweedmouth. A second locomotive and crew would cover the afternoon passenger train workings plus the evening fish train to Burnmouth or Berwick. One role for the crews during the light engine workings was to convey cans of water to the rather isolated Marshall Meadows signal box in the morning and collect the empties on the way back to Berwick in the evening.

Chapter Ten

The passenger train services

The years up to 1900: Eyemouth Railway

Burnmouth station at the start of the Eyemouth branch had been served by train services for almost 43 years before the branch opened. Firstly there were stopping trains linking Berwick and Edinburgh and secondly there were the trains on the branch to Duns which diverged from the main line at Reston to the north of Burnmouth.

Until the opening of the Eyemouth branch, Ayton was considered to be the station of first choice for the inhabitants of Eyemouth wishing to take a train. A certain Mr Brack of Eyemouth operated a carriage (or 'car') service between Eyemouth and Ayton on the direct road between the two places. On weekdays there were five departures from Eyemouth starting at 5.30 am with the last leaving at 7.50 pm. There were five services in the reverse direction, the first at 6.20 am and the last at 8.31 pm. On Sundays Brack ran an 'as required' service of two journeys each way, leaving Eyemouth at 7.00 and 9.30 am and returning at 8.45 or 10.20 am.

All of Brack's services took 35 minutes between Eyemouth and Ayton (generally uphill) whilst in the reverse direction they took slightly less time, some occupying just 30 minutes. The carriages made good connections with trains on the main line: four of the journeys from Eyemouth connected with trains for Berwick and four with Edinburgh trains. In the reverse direction four connected with Berwick trains and three with Edinburgh trains. On Sundays there was one connection with a Berwick train and one with an Edinburgh train. A through journey by carriage and connecting train allowed Edinburgh to be reached in about three hours. An Eyemouth to Berwick journey could take as little as 1 hour depending on the length of wait at Ayton station. Brack's service last appeared in the NBR's timetable for March 1891. The Eyemouth branch, opening on 13th April of that year, put an end to this.

When the branch railway opened an initial service of seven trains in each direction was provided by the North British Railway which operated all of the trains on behalf of the Eyemouth Railway Company:

Up direction		BE	D	B	B	BDE	BD	BDE
		am	*am*	*am*	*am*	*pm*	*pm*	*pm*
Eyemouth	*dep.*	7.35	8.35	9.10	10.30	1.00	3.30	5.25
Burnmouth	*arr.*	7.42	8.42	9.17	10.37	1.07	3.37	5.32

Down direction		B	BD	E	D	BD	BE	BDE
		am	*am*	*am*	*am*	*pm*	*pm*	*pm*
Burnmouth	*dep.*	8.00	9.03	9.30	10.50	1.45	4.05	6.30
Eyemouth	*arr.*	8.07	9.03	9.37	10.57	1.52	4.12	6.37

Key: B - Connection to Berwick; D - Connection to Duns; E - Connection to Edinburgh.

This service is shown in the NBR's passenger timetable for June 1891. Duns was the administrative centre of the former Berwickshire county, later the county town, and was thus a place of some importance holding a market and being the site of the Berwickshire Sheriff Court.

To promote passenger traffic on the railway the introductory ticket prices were set at 3*d*. for a third class single between Eyemouth and Berwick and 6*d*. for a return. First class passenger singles cost 6*d*. with the return being just 9*d*. By November of the same year the prices had risen to 8½*d*. for the Eyemouth to Berwick third class single (1*s*. 5*d*. return) whilst the corresponding first class prices were 1*s*. 7*d*. and 2*s*. 5*d*.

In June 1892 the service became eight trains in each direction with the addition of an early morning train from Eyemouth at 6.00 am with a return from Burnmouth at 6.25 am. Other trains showed slight retimings compared with 1891.

The working timetable which came into force on 1st July, 1896 provides some more insight into the train services. By this date the number of trains in each direction had reverted to seven. Trains left Eyemouth at 6.00, 7.35, 8.35, 10.25 am, 12.30, 3.30 and 5.35 pm. In the reverse direction there were departures from Burnmouth at 6.25, 8.00, 9.25, 10.45 am, 1.30, 4.10 and 6.35 pm. One locomotive could therefore cover all of the workings. All of the trains were shown as carrying first and third class passengers but the 8.00 am and 1.30 pm down trains were identified as being mixed trains, conveying goods as well as passenger vehicles. In the up direction the trains leaving Eyemouth at 12.30 and 6.43 pm were designated as 'Mixed'. Once again there were good connections advertised in each direction: six to/from Berwick, and four each to/from Duns and Edinburgh.

Towards the end of the 19th century there was still a service of seven trains in each direction on the branch with light engine movements being required at the end of the day and two trains in each direction being identified as 'Mixed'. Minor timetable changes had been necessary as a result of changes in the timings of connections on the main line.

On 6th August, 1900 the Eyemouth Railway ceased to exist as a separate entity, being wholly taken over by the NBR though the trains were made up of the same carriages and locomotives.

1900 to 1922: North British Railway

This summary, based on information gleaned from both the surviving passenger and working timetables, provides an outline of the scheduled train services on the branch during the days when the NBR was in sole charge. Unfortunately for some of the early years of the 20th century years copies of the timetables appear not to have survived and so the record is incomplete.

The train service in 1900 carried on from that of the previous year, with seven passenger trains being provided in each direction. The timetable dated 1st January, 1901 continues to show seven trains each way but the first train of the day started at Eyemouth even earlier than in previous years, at 5.40 am, with its return working from Burnmouth starting at 6.05 am.

At the start of 1902 there were still seven trains in each direction but in July the two earliest trains were dropped from the timetable, thus reducing the service to six trains in each direction.

Information for the years 1903-07 appears not to be available but the working timetable for 1908 shows that the service was of six trains in each direction, the earliest departure from Eyemouth being the 7.08 am passenger, with the 8.00 am mixed train being the first to leave Burnmouth. The last trains of the day were the 5.22 pm mixed from Eyemouth and the 6.28 passenger train from Burnmouth. These services ran on weekdays only; no Sunday service was provided on the branch.

The year 1909 produced no dramatic changes to the train service, simply a few slight alterations to timings. By 1910 ticket prices remained largely unchanged though there was a ½d. reduction in the price of a third class Eyemouth to Berwick single. The January 1910 timetable shows five trains in each direction, with one of the down trains (departing at 1.10 pm) being a mixed train. Two of the up trains (the 12.33 and 5.12 pm) were designated 'Mixed'. It is interesting to note that at this time there was still a 'road coach' connection between Coldingham and the main line at Reston, rather than with Eyemouth, though the Sunday service ceased to operate after 1910.

In 1911 the train service was increased slightly with seven trains in the up direction and six trains down the branch. Because of the unbalanced working it was necessary for an empty carriage train to return the stock to Eyemouth once per day. The earliest train was still the 7.08 departure from Eyemouth with the first Burnmouth departure being at 8.05 am. The last train of the day became a Saturdays-only train leaving Burnmouth at 8.05 pm and Eyemouth at 8.47 pm. Later that year the service was reduced to six trains in each direction on all days of the week.

An event then took place which resulted in a dramatic change to the Eyemouth line service. This was not the start of the Great War, as might have been expected, but the 1912 national coal strike. This momentous event seriously affected both shipping and rail transport. At this time trade union members nationally were becoming angrier with their poor working conditions and the failure of wages to keep pace with rising food and commodity prices. In 1911 and leading into 1912 there was a succession of dock strikes, rail strikes, local coal strikes and strikes in the jute and cotton weaving industries. The national coal strike which started in Alfreton, Derbyshire, spread rapidly until nearly a million miners were involved. It lasted from the end of February until 6th April, 1912. It ended when the Government rushed a Bill, the Coal Mines (Minimum Wage) Act, through Parliament. The Bill provided for local arbitration to settle the level of minimum wages. Though its details were poorly received, the union executive called off the strike, the first national strike by miners in Great Britain.

The NBR responded to the strike by bringing into force a lowering of the number of timetabled trains on its lines published in the March 1912 timetable. This referred to a 'Modified Train Service'. For the Eyemouth branch this meant the reduction in the train service to just three trains in each direction. Departures from Eyemouth were made at 8.30 am, 3.25 and 5.25 pm, whilst in the reverse direction trains left Burnmouth at 9.00 am, 4.25 and 5.45 pm. By October the same timetable was still in force on the branch albeit with slight retimings of some trains. In April 1913 the service was cut even further to two trains each way (one morning and one afternoon train in each direction) but by October the three-trains-each-way service resumed.

The May and July 1914 working timetables for passenger trains showed that there was a return to the service level of February 1911 though the former empty carriage train became a passenger train, the last trains of the day departing at 7.50 pm from Eyemouth and 8.47 pm from Burnmouth (both Saturdays only).

By October 1914 the late trains, the 7.50 and 8.47 pm departures, were withdrawn. In July 1915 the service was of six trains in each direction but the March and July 1916 timetables showed just five, the earliest trains having being dropped making the 8.35 from Eyemouth and the 9.30 am from Burnmouth the first trains of the day. In 1917 there was, again, a service of just five trains each way. Some retimings took place to fit in with main line trains and the last trains were the 4.20 pm from Eyemouth and the 4.48 pm from Burnmouth. A train at 12.10 pm ran through to Berwick returning to Eyemouth at 1.32 pm. This train continued into the 1918 and 1919 timetables when it was scheduled to cover the 5½ miles from Burnmouth to Berwick in a start to stop time of just seven minutes! 1919 saw the introduction of earlier morning trains starting from Eyemouth at 7.23 am and Burnmouth at 8.08 am. The same timetable indicated that there were still coaches from Coldingham linking with the main line at Reston: seven a day in each direction.

After about 1919, and the introduction of the 8 hour day, it was necessary for light engine movements to take place at the start and end of each day to fetch and return the locomotive from and to Berwick depot where it would overnight. Presumably on Saturdays the locomotive would have been returned to Berwick after the last train from Eyemouth and then travelled back to Burnmouth early on Monday morning as there was no Sunday service.

The 1920 working timetable showed the same pattern of trains as 1919 with the 12.05 pm (a slight timing adjustment from 1919) again running through to Berwick. Biglawburn Siding (2 miles and 25 chains from Burnmouth) was now open and appeared in this timetable. There was a special note regarding the 8.07 mixed from Burnmouth to Eyemouth: 'This train must start punctually from Burnmouth'. In this year four trains from Burnmouth were indicated as mixed with just two in the reverse direction but including the 12.05 pm through to Berwick. The very brief stop at Burnmouth for this train suggests that any wagons, such as fish vans, on this train were taken through to Berwick. A working timetable special notice of Monday 25th October indicated the discontinuation of many trains, 18 between Berwick and Edinburgh, for example. On the Eyemouth branch just the 10.18 am from Eyemouth and the 10.40 am from Burnmouth disappeared from the timetable.

The 1st March, 1921 timetable again followed that of 1919 with minor timing adjustments. However, this timetable had been in force for just two months when industrial action in the mining industry caused a more drastic effect on the Eyemouth line timetable than even the 1912 strike! Miners had been

EYEMOUTH RAILWAY.

DOWN TRAINS. Stations and Sidings.	Distance from Burnmouth	WEEK-DAYS. 1 Pass. 1 3 Class.	2 Pass. (Mixed) 1 3 Class.	3 Pass. 1 3 Class.	4 Pass. 1 3 Class.	5 Pass. (Mixed) 1 3 Class.	6 Pass. 1 3 Class.	7 Pass. 1 3 Class.	8
	Mls. Chs.	a.m.	a.m.	a.m.	a.m.	a.m.	p.m.	p.m.	
Edinburgh ... ... depart	... ...	...	...	7 0	...	10 20	s 1 50	4 35	...
Duns ... .. ,,	... ...	...	7 15	...	10 0	12p30	...	5 20	....
Berwick ... ... ,,	... ...	6 0	7 35	8 40	...	1 10	3 30	5 40	...
Burnmouth ... ... depart		6 25	8 0	9 25	10 45	1 30	4 10	6 35	......
Eyemouth ... ... arrive	2 72	6 32	8 7	9 32	10 52	1 37	4 17	6 42	...

UP TRAINS. Stations and Sidings.	Distance from Eyemouth	WEEK-DAYS. 1 Pass. 1 3 Class.	2 Pass. 1 3 Class.	3 Pass. 1 3 Class.	4 Pass. 1 3 Class.	5 Pass. (Mixed) 1 3 Class.	6 Pass. 1 3 Class.	7 Pass. (Mixed) 1 3 Class.	8
	Mls. Chs.	a.m.	a.m.	a.m.	a.m.	p.m.	p.m.	p.m.	
Eyemouth ... ... depart	Mls. Chs.	6 0	7 35	8 35	10 25	12 30	3 30	5 35	...
Burnmouth ... ... arrive	2 72	6 7	7 42	8 42	10 32	12 37	3 37	5 42	......
Berwick ... ... arrive	... ...	...	...	8 3	9 28	10 53	1 20	4 15	6 48	...
Duns ... ... ,,	... ...	...	...	...	9 35	...	2 0	4 35	6 43	......
Edinburgh ... ... ,,	... ...	8 35	9 52	...	...	2 55	...	8 25	...

Branch timetable, 1896.

BURNMOUTH and EYEMOUTH.—North British.

Miles.	Down.	mrn	mrn	mrn	aft	aft	aft	aft				
	Burnmouth .....dep.	8 0	9 30	1040	1e10	1s15	4 8	6 28	...	...	...	...
3	Eyemouth.......arr.	8 7	9 37	1047	1e17	1s22	4 15	6 35	...	...	...	...

Miles.	Up.	mrn	mrn	mrn	aft	aft	aft					
	Eyemouth ....dep.	7 8	8 35	1020	1233	3 35	5 22	...	...	...	...	...
3	Burnmouth 794..arr.	7 15	8 42	1027	1240	3 42	5 30	...	...	...	...	...

e Except Saturdays.   s Saturdays only.

Branch timetable, 1910.

Table 21		BURNMOUTH and EYEMOUTH				
Miles		Week Days only		Miles		Week Days only
		am	am K	pm	pm E	pm S			am	am N	pm	pm E	pm S
---	---	---	---	---	---	---	---	---	---	---	---	---	---
20	Edinburgh (Wav.) dep	..	6 50	..	2 25	3 30	3 48	..	Eyemouth . ... dep	7 58	8 0	3 30	..	5 0	5 10	..
20	Berwick-upon-Tweed ,,	7 20	8 52	...	...	...	3	Burnmouth ... ... arr	7 13	8 9	3 39	....	5 9	5 19	..
—	Burnmouth . ... .. dep	7 35	9 12	..	4 0	5 25	5 40	..	8	2	Berwick-upon-Tweed arr	..	8 18	4 0	..	5 23	5 37	..
3	Eyemouth .... arr	7 43	9 20	..	4 8	5 33	5 48	....	55	20	Edinburgh (Wav.) . ,,	9 5	....	....	....	...

E Except Saturdays

K Through Train between Berwick-upon-Tweed and Eyemouth

N Through Train between Eyemouth and Berwick-upon-Tweed

S Saturdays only

Branch timetable, 1961.

pressing nation-wide for the nationalization of the coal industry. However, the Government, which had been considering the matter, suddenly abandoned the idea. This precipitated 'The Great Lock-Out' of the miners. Industrial strife began nationally and lasted for three months when the police, and later the military became involved. The miners went back to work on 1st July, 1921.

The strike caused the service to be cut to just two trains in each direction. The only morning trains were the 8.30 am from Eyemouth arriving at Burnmouth seven minutes later, and the 9.15 return arriving back at 9.22 am. The sole afternoon train was the 3.15 pm which called at Burnmouth (3.22 pm-3.34 pm) before continuing to Berwick arriving at 3.42 pm. It returned from Berwick at 3.55 pm arriving back at Burnmouth at 4.04pm. This state of affairs did not last for long and the 20th July timetable indicates that the train service on the line was essentially returned to that of July 1919. The August, October and November timetables of the same year, and continuing into 1922 show the same six trains each way, with four from Burnmouth able to operate as 'Mixed', but with just two mixed trains from Eyemouth. The middle-of-the-day train from Eyemouth continued to work through to Berwick together with its return working.

1923 to 1947: London & North Eastern Railway

The Railways Act 1921 which gained the Royal Assent on 19th August of that year provided for the 'grouping' of Britain's railways into four major bodies to replace the more than one hundred smaller companies that existed at that time. The North British Railway therefore became part of the London and North Eastern Railway on 1st January, 1923 though at first, there were no changes to stock used on the Eyemouth line.

Initially the Eyemouth branch continued to follow the NBR timetable of October 1922 with six trains running in each direction. The first LNER passenger timetable continued to show the six trains each way. The same number of mixed trains operated though there were now two through trains in each direction serving Berwick. The 12.05 pm train from Eyemouth to Berwick continued but there was an additional through train at 3.00 pm. Their return times of departure from Berwick were 1.32 and 3.55 pm respectively. The working timetable of 1st January, 1923 showed a repeat of the service for October 1922 with just one two-minute retiming. A notice in this timetable refers to a 'Stores Train' serving stations on the main line. It made a brief stop at Burnmouth but did not appear on the branch. Presumably any station stores for Eyemouth were handled by the branch train. The working timetable of 9th July, 1923 showed the same service as January 1923 but with some slight retimings and the service was broadly of the same pattern through to 1926, the year of the General Strike.

The working timetable issued in September 1926 showed the continuation of the pattern of six up trains of which four were 'Mixed', with two of the six down trains also being mixed. There was an interesting note relating to the 3.18 pm mixed train from Eyemouth. This was scheduled to stop at Burnmouth at 3.25

pm and leave for Berwick after a four minute wait, arriving at Berwick at 3.37 pm. However, on days when the van traffic was heavy the train would leave Burnmouth at 3.29 pm but not arrive at Berwick until 3.55 pm, an 18 minute addition to the schedule! There is another interesting footnote: 'The Eyemouth Branch Passenger Engine and Guard, when required, will make a Goods trip at about 2.00 pm to Burnmouth and back'. This trip would have been fitted into the space between the arrival of the passenger train at Eyemouth at 1.39 pm and its departure at 3.18 pm. The timetables issued on 16th May, 1927 and 26th September, 1927 were similar, and, with minor changes to timings the pattern continued until 1932.

The 1932 timetable indicated that at Eyemouth station horses, carriages and motor cars could be loaded and unloaded! The same timetable indicated that Scottish Motor Traction Co. Ltd. operated services between Berwick, Burnmouth, Eyemouth and Edinburgh: competition for the railway. Another reference was to a certain Mr French operating eight motor omnibus services each way between Coldingham and Reston station.

In the timetable from 11th September, 1933 an extra early evening train was added to the Eyemouth service in each direction. This provided Eyemouth departures at both 5.13 and 6.10 pm for Burnmouth, the return trains leaving at 5.35 and 6.40 pm. A similar service operated until 1937 when an extra late evening return service was introduced on Saturdays. This left Eyemouth at 9.29 pm and returned from Burnmouth at 9.44 pm, both being seven minute journeys. The service continued to include two through trains each day to Berwick running in each direction.

The summer timetable of 1938, starting in July, showed a reduction to just one train in each direction to or from Berwick, running Saturdays excepted. On Saturdays the train ran as far as Burnmouth only, then making a return trip to Eyemouth before running in the times of the weekdays through train back to Eyemouth. This extra return train was dropped from the timetable in September 1938. Thus, in 1939, as World War II approached the service between Eyemouth and Berwick consisted of eight trains in each direction plus the late evening Saturdays-only (SO) return trip.

The start of hostilities resulted in the introduction of an emergency timetable dated 2nd October, 1939 ('until further notice'). This reduced the branch service to just five trains each way with an extra late evening SO train which ran through, to and from, Berwick. One further train, the 1.15 pm from Eyemouth ran through to Berwick. Throughout the period from 1940 to 1941 the service settled down to six trains each way including the late through Berwick trains. The working timetable of October 1943 shows seven trains each way (eight on Saturdays) with four from Burnmouth to Eyemouth being labelled as 'Mixed' with one mixed train in the opposite direction. The 'mid-day' through trains linking Eyemouth and Berwick had been removed from the timetable. There was a note in the timetable which read: 'The Eyemouth Branch Passenger Engine and Guard, when required, will make a Goods trip at about 2.20 pm to Burnmouth and back'.

In May 1944 there was an unbalanced working on the line. Saturdays excepted the carriage, which had arrived at Eyemouth on an earlier train, was worked as empty stock to Burnmouth at 8.15 pm forming the 8.40 pm train from there to Eyemouth. On Saturdays the train was available to passengers running in the same path and then onwards to Berwick. Continuing into 1945 and 1946 four of the Burnmouth to Eyemouth trains were designated as mixed trains with just one mixed train from Eyemouth. The empty stock train still ran Saturdays excepted. The only return Berwick through service was that in the late evening.

In 1947, as nationalization of the railways approached, the pattern was similar: seven trains each day ran Mondays to Fridays. In addition the 8.15 pm worked to Burnmouth continuing to Berwick on Saturdays only. The Monday to Friday return was now timed to depart from Burnmouth at 8.45 pm. The Saturday train left Berwick at 9.50 pm with a three minute stop at Burnmouth before arriving at Eyemouth at 10.11 pm.

1948 to 1962: British Railways

The transfer to British Railways did not produce immediate changes to the Eyemouth branch timetable, that of the LNER continuing through until the cessation of services on the branch following the storm damage to the line's viaduct. The 1949 timetable for 23rd May to 25th September, 1949 contained the following: 'Burnmouth and Eyemouth: The train Service is meantime withdrawn but a substitute Road Motor Coach Service is provided between Berwick and Eyemouth'.

A similar road coach service was introduced between Berwick, Duns and St Boswells. The actual closure dates for the Eyemouth branch, for all services, were 13th August, 1948 to 29th June, 1949. During this time all freight traffic was transferred to road and Berwick became the point at which fish traffic was transferred into rail vans. This was inconvenient and added to both costs and the journey times.

There is no doubt that the 10 month closure of the line had a profound effect on the future of the line. During the period of closure passengers had to use the train-replacement coach services which were very acceptable as they allowed Berwick to be reached without a change of vehicle.

Now the 1948 passenger timetable had shown eight trains from Burnmouth to Eyemouth (including one Saturdays Excepted and one, the late train, Saturdays only). Four trains provided connections from Glasgow, six from Edinburgh and six from Berwick (seven on Saturdays). In the opposite direction there were seven trains from Eyemouth to Berwick (eight on Saturdays) with five connections onward to Glasgow and Edinburgh, and six to Berwick (seven on Saturdays).

In September 1949, after the branch trains were reinstated, the initial service appeared to be encouraging in that there were nine trains between Burnmouth to Eyemouth in each direction (one each way was Saturdays only). Connections were still good: four trains from both Glasgow and Berwick connected into Eyemouth trains at Burnmouth. In the reverse direction there were five connections for Berwick and three for Edinburgh and Glasgow.

In 1961 a special train, 'The Northern Venturer', arrived at Eyemouth station behind two 'B1' class 4-6-0s, the pilot engine being added for braking purposes at Burnmouth station. Passengers could either visit Eyemouth or take the motor coach, waiting on the platform, for a return trip to St Abbs, via Coldingham. The locomotives were recorded as Nos. 61014 *Oribi* and 61241 *Viscount Ridley*, both Tweedmouth engines.　　　　　　　　　　*North British Railway Study Group*

Class 'J39/2' no. 64917 waits in the platform ready to depart for Burnmouth. The picture dates from the late 1950s. Note the vans in the platform which will depart on a later afternoon train, perhaps one of the two timetabled class 'C' fish trains.　　　*Armstrong Railway Photographic Trust*

However, the service between Berwick, Reston, Duns and St Boswells had also been affected by the storm. The line had been severed between Greenlaw and Duns, a gap that was never reinstated. The surviving passenger service between Reston and Duns was ended on 10th September, 1951. It was, however, to or from these trains that many Eyemouth passengers had changed at Burnmouth. After the Duns line's closure the number of trains serving Burnmouth became reduced to a handful and the number of connections to and from Edinburgh, Glasgow (Queen Street) and Berwick was severely depleted.

Table 21 of the British Railways Scottish passenger timetable (for summer 1952) provides a dramatic contrast in the fortunes of the Eyemouth line. Burnmouth trains for Eyemouth were reduced to four in number and there were just three trains daily leaving Eyemouth for Burnmouth. Burnmouth trains departed at 7.30, 9.08 am, 4.07 and 5.40 pm, each train taking eight minutes. Returning up the branch departures from Eyemouth were at 7.05, 8.00 am and 5.15 pm. Only the first two morning trains provided connections from Berwick and there were fewer connections for trains from Edinburgh and Glasgow. At Burnmouth there were only two connections for Berwick and one each for both Edinburgh and Glasgow. A passenger leaving Eyemouth for Berwick at 8.00 am arrived in Berwick at 8.20 am on a through train but had to leave at 8.45 am to get back to Eyemouth by train on the same day!

The Edinburgh District working timetable for the summer of 1952 shows the same service. The 7.05 and 8.00 am were designated as class 'B' passenger trains whilst the 5.15 pm was mixed and carried fish vans on the rear. There were two additional up trains, both were class 'C' goods (fully fitted with continuous vacuum brakes) leaving Eyemouth at 3.40 and 6.53 pm with neither carrying passengers. All trains were allowed, at this time, eight or nine minutes for their journeys between Eyemouth and Burnmouth, rather than the traditional seven minutes.

This timetable pattern continued throughout the 1950s with just minor timing alterations. There was just the one through working from Eyemouth to Berwick at 8.00 am with an almost immediate return. In the evening it was possible to catch a train from Berwick to Burnmouth but the last train on the branch had departed around an hour and a half earlier! It was a sad end to passenger services on the line and therefore no surprise when closure notices were posted. The line closed to both passenger and goods services on 5th February, 1962. Although passenger services between Reston and Duns had closed some 11 years earlier a freight service on that line struggled on until the line finally closed on 7th November, 1966. With the final closure of the St Boswells to Kelso line in 1968, branch line train services completely disappeared from the far south-east of Scotland!

Today passengers between Eyemouth, Burnmouth and Berwick (also Edinburgh) can use the frequent service provided by Berwick-based Perryman's Buses Ltd., now merged with the Edinburgh-based firm of Border Buses and operating under their name. Their service 253 provides eight buses each way between Berwick, Burnmouth, Eyemouth and Edinburgh, with the service also serving Coldingham and Reston. A second route, Service 235, also provides a frequent service, seven days a week in each direction, between Berwick, Burnmouth, Eyemouth and Coldingham/St Abbs, though there are fewer buses on Sundays. The Eyemouth branch railway had never provided a Sunday service and there were no timetabled direct trains to Edinburgh.

A single-decker, operated by Perryman's Buses, scurries along Victoria Road above the site of the former Eyemouth station on route 235 which links St Abbs, Eyemouth Burnmouth and Berwick, taking just eight minutes for the Eyemouth to Burnmouth part of its journey: the same timing as the former passenger trains. With the Berwick to Edinburgh buses (route 253) also now serving Burnmouth and Eyemouth these places now have a very good transport service. *Author*

Perryman's (based in Berwick) recently merged with Border Buses of Edinburgh and the new company trades under the latter's name. Here a route 235 Borders bus pulls away from the bus stop adjacent to the former station site in Upper Burnmouth and heads towards the bridge over the main line railway. The road leading to Lower Burnmouth, 'The Brae' is signposted on the bend in the road. *Author*

Chapter Eleven

Eyemouth's fishing industry and the fish trains

Some information on the local fishing industry will provide a background to events and details which will be touched upon later in the Eyemouth branch line story.

Eyemouth is one of the few safe landing places on the Berwickshire coast. As a result it has had links with the sea and sea-fishing. Although there are records of fish being landed at Eyemouth dating from the 13th century it appears that until about 1800 the fishing industry was relatively unimportant, the export of grain being the most important activity. However, things changed in the 19th century when herring fishing, using drift nets, and line-fishing, for cod, haddock, whiting, halibut, ling and various flatfish increased dramatically.

Herring overwintered principally near the Norwegian coast, many making their way to Scotland, then to England in a migration associated with feeding and spawning. It was necessary for the Eyemouth boats to follow this migration. The herring season off the Scottish coast lasted for about two months, but by fishing as far south as East Anglia the season could be prolonged. The principal type of boat used for herring fishing off the Scottish coast, using very long drift nets, was the 'Fifie'. These two-masted vessels of around 70 ft in length initially lacked decks. As an illustration nearly 68,000 barrels of herring were loaded at Eyemouth in a single year in the 1880s. Steam drifters first made an appearance in Eyemouth by the middle of World War I; there were 13 local steam drifters by the late 1920s.

The 'Zulu' fishing boats were introduced from 1879 onwards and were around 80 ft in length. Their numbers increased as they were faster than the fifies and could carry a greater catch. From the 1880s they were fitted with steam-powered capstans and steering wheels replaced tillers. Zulus were used for both herring and line-fishing. Smaller vessels used two short lines of up to a mile in length to which were attached shorter pieces of line terminating in hooks (often numbering 1,200) each baited with shellfish, often mussels. These hooks were often baited before the ships left harbour by the womanfolk. Larger vessels could have 'great lines' with up to 5,000 hooks. Whilst smaller lines could often be baited with mussels collected locally the larger lines required the import of mussels from elsewhere. Eyemouth received wagonloads of mussels gathered on the north-east coast of Scotland or the east coast of England, principally Boston. In 1881-82, for example, Eyemouth received, by rail to a local station (probably Ayton), some 900 tons of mussels for use as bait.

The fish was craned from the boats in baskets then it passed successively to the gutters and the curers. The fish were packed into barrels and then these were sealed. Each barrel contained about 1,000 fish. Apart from the fish that left Eyemouth by rail, much left by sea. White herring was exported to Ireland, the Baltic (Poland and Russia) and even to the West Indies, whilst smoked fish often went to Newcastle, London or Hull.

Towards the end of the 19th century steam-powered drifters and trawlers made the earlier boats more inefficient; these vessels could power-haul the ropes of their nets and could make a quicker and more reliable return to port. However, they were much more expensive and some of the older boats lingered on well into the 20th century. The zenith of the herring fishery took place between 1900 and the start of World War I. After the war the development of the white fish industry and later still the landing of shellfish and crustaceans were to maintain the importance of Eyemouth as a fishing port.

Fish trains from Burnmouth – pre-branch days

A report on a railway accident at Burnmouth provides some insight into the transport of locally-caught fish from that station some 40 years before the Eyemouth branch railway opened, at a time when fish had to be taken up the hill to Burnmouth (or Ayton) for loading onto rail wagons.

The report was written by Col William Yolland of the Railway Inspectorate. The accident occurred when a special mail train heading northwards from Berwick was in collision with a line of wagons which were being shunted from the sidings adjacent to the up line on the west side of the station.

The report contains the following:

> During the herring season there is considerable traffic from Burnmouth, and there are sidings on the east and west sides of the down and up lines; but those lying east of the down line are principally used for empty waggons [sic], while the loading of herrings is carried on in the sidings lying west of the up line ... The porter, who had to attend to the signals, was, at the time when the train passed, engaged in loading fish into the waggons in the sidings lying west of the up line ... About 10 o'clock a fish train from Dunbar, consisting of 10 trucks, arrived at Burnmouth, where it had to leave one truck, and to take on 15 others from that station to Berwick ... Nine trucks were left standing on the down line, and the tenth was taken across the up line and placed in one of the sidings ... The engine was in the act of drawing the 15 waggons intended for Berwick out of the sidings lying to the west of the up line and had nearly the whole of them onto the up line, when the special carrying the mails from the south, which left Berwick at 9.55, came up and ran into the fifth truck from the tail of the train ...

Clearly the station layout at Burnmouth was not the most desirable for handling the fish traffic with the constant need to shunt empty wagons from the single siding to the east over to the west side of the station for loading. After loading the full wagons had to be shunted back across the main line tracks for the second time so that they could travel in a goods train on to Berwick. All of this manoeuvring had to occur at a time when the station was protected only by distant signals, no 'station signals' being provided on the line by the NBR, a situation unique to British double-tracked lines at the time! Inspecting officer, Colonel Yolland, commented as follows: 'This in my opinion is very objectionable and dangerous, and such a system of signalling could not be passed by an inspecting officer at the present time'. Subsequent maps show that the line became fully signalled!

(As a sideline it is worth commenting that between the date of this accident, the 25th July, 1861, and the opening of the Eyemouth branch in February 1891, there were at least 15 recorded accidents on the North British line from Berwick to Reston which were reported in the local press!)

Fish transport via the North British Railway – the early days

Although there will be passenger traffic, the fish trains will be the feature as Eyemouth now sends her fish all over the Midlands and to Liverpool, London and even Brighton. The port has almost recovered from the disaster of 1881, as there are now nearly 40 winter boats and 50 yawls registered there, and in the season thirteen fish curers are working in the quays. It is to be expected, however, that this year the railway will increase the number of curers and draw boats from other ports'
Edinburgh Evening News, 13th April, 1891

As a result of the additional fish traffic starting to be generated by the Eyemouth branch a new 'runs when required' fish train was laid on which ran on Tuesdays to Fridays, commencing on Friday 17th July, 1891. It started at Berwick at 2.45 pm and called at Burnmouth for the Eyemouth fish traffic, the last of which could have arrived on the 1.00 pm mixed train from Eyemouth arriving at Burnmouth at 1.07 pm. It then picked up Dunbar fish at Reston before taking the line to Duns and St Boswells. If there were sufficient vehicles to warrant it, then the train carried on to Carlisle; normally the minimum number of wagons for this was six. If there were fewer than six wagons then the fish train terminated at Hawick with the vehicles being taken forward to Carlisle on the next Edinburgh to Carlisle train. From Carlisle the fish progressed onwards, mainly to Birmingham for W.S. Scott, the large fish dealer based in Jamaica Row.

A study of the NBR working timetable which came into force on 1st July, 1896 provides a more detailed picture of the role that the recently-opened branch railway, and the main line, played in distributing fish from Eyemouth.

The Eyemouth branch timetable indicates two 'mixed' passenger trains which conveyed loaded fish wagon traffic. These left Eyemouth at 12.30 and 5.35 pm, each arriving at Burnmouth seven minutes later. In the return direction, trains, also 'mixed', returned the empty fish vehicles to Eyemouth, leaving Burnmouth at 8.00 am and 1.30 pm, both also taking seven minutes for the journey. (The *Edinburgh Evening News article*, quoted above, referred to trains heading down the branch as taking seven minutes, with trains heading up the grade taking 12 minutes to arrive at Burnmouth.) Clearly at this time there was normally insufficient fish traffic to warrant the running of regular, separate, fish trains, on the branch though in later years this was sometimes to happen. Various 'Notes' accompanied the Edinburgh to Berwick tables in connection with traffic for the Eyemouth line. It is beneficial to look at these in some detail as they illustrate the provision that the NBR (and NER) made for the fish traffic. (All grammar and capitalization are presented as they appeared in the original documents.)

Trains on the main line received an identification number. On weekdays Trains 20 and 27 in the down direction, that is, from Edinburgh towards Berwick, were both subject to the note which read: 'Burnmouth and Ayton must advise Reston by telegraph daily, not later than 5pm, how many wagons they have for this train to lift so that room may be left'. Train 20 was a Mondays-only goods train which left Sighthill (Edinburgh) at 7.15 am, calling at Burnmouth at 5.47 pm and arriving at Berwick at 6.00 pm and Tweedmouth at 6.20 pm. Train 27 ran Mondays-excepted and left Sighthill at 9.05 am, making its Burnmouth call at 7.07 pm and arriving at Berwick at 7.25 pm.

NORTH BRITISH RAILWAY COMPANY.
ADDITIONAL TRAIN ALTERATIONS
TO BE IN FORCE ON AND AFTER
WEDNESDAY, 1st JULY 1914.

Station		1 Fish Runs when required
		p.m.
Berwick	depart	3 15
Burnmouth	arrive	3 25
Do.	depart	3 55
Berwick	arrive	4 5
Berwick	depart	4 20
Burnmouth	arrive	4 30
Eyemouth	depart	4 30
Burnmouth	arrive	4 37
Burnmouth	depart	5 0
Reston	,,	5 10
Chirnside	,,	5 17
Duns	,,	5 25
Greenlaw	,,	5 38
Earlston	,,	5 56
St Boswells	arrive	6 5
Do.	depart	6 15
Hawick	arrive	6 40
Do.	depart	7 5
Riccarton	,,	7 30
Longtown	,,	8 3
Carlisle (Citadel Station)	arrive	8 25

Station		2 Runs when required Empty Coaching Stock and Fish Wagons (M)	3 Runs when required Empty Coaching Stock and Fish Wagons	4 Runs when required Empty Coaching Stock and Fish Wagons (8 0)
		p.m.	p.m.	p.m.
Carlisle	depart	9 20		
Riccarton	,,	10 30		
Hawick	arrive	11 0		
Do.	depart		12 30	7 25
St Boswells	,,	Stop	1 0	7 55
Earlston	,,		1 10	8 5
Greenlaw	,,		2 5	8 28
Duns	,,		2 25	8 45
Chirnside	,,		2 35	9 7
Reston	,,		3 0	9 15
Berwick	arrive		3 20	9 35

No. 1.—On first run from Berwick to Burnmouth works back Fish traffic to Berwick for the East Coast Route and Eyemouth must wire Berwick in good time number of wagons to go forward. Meets at Chirnside the Berwick and Duns Goods train and at Duns the 3·55 p.m. Passenger train ex St Boswells. Passes also at Duns the St Boswells and Duns Goods train, which must be kept back to allow this train to get a clear road.

No. 2.—The Carlisle and Bathgate Goods will shunt where required for this train.

No. 3.—Meets at Greenlaw 12·50 p.m. (1-0 p.m. 8 0) Passenger train from Berwick.

No. 4.—When the Fish train from Berwick is run on Saturday the Engine, Guard and Van will be exchanged at Hawick.

J. BLACK,
Superintendent of the Line.

OFFICE OF SUPERINTENDENT OF THE LINE,
EDINBURGH, 27th June 1914.

Train 31 was a fast passenger train operated by the NER under its running powers between Edinburgh and Berwick. This train left Edinburgh Waverley station at 5.15 pm and arrived at Berwick at 7.52 pm. It was timed to stop at Burnmouth at 7.38 pm. The accompanying note read: 'Takes on Fish Traffic from all stations where timed to call'.

Train 34 was a goods train from Portobello (Edinburgh), leaving at 5.30 pm and arriving at Berwick at 10.15 pm and Tweedmouth at 10.30 pm: 'It lifts but does not leave off Traffic at Burnmouth'.

Finally Train No. 40 was a goods departing from Leith Walk (Edinburgh) at 8.10 pm, arriving at Berwick at 2.20 am and Tweedmouth at 2.35 am. The accompanying note read 'Calls at Burnmouth except Sunday mornings to leave off Mussel and other perishable traffic. On Sunday mornings Mussel traffic for Eyemouth must be taken forward to Berwick'. Its call at Burnmouth was scheduled for 12.05 am. On Sundays there was just one train with traffic for the Eyemouth branch, but as the branch was closed on that day of the week the traffic had to be dealt with at Berwick and forwarded the following day. The 12.05 am goods train from Sighthill arrived at Berwick at 6.45 am and then Tweedmouth at 7.05 am taking 'Mussel traffic for Eyemouth forward to Berwick'. (Mussel traffic was, of course, wagons carrying fishing bait to Eyemouth.)

In the up direction there was a goods train, Train 13, leaving Reston at 5.20 am to Portobello, 'Traders Empties' being required to be sent on this train. 'Berwick, Burnmouth and Ayton to send such wagons to Reston, not later than the 12.55 am Train from Berwick'; this train, No. 2, called at Burnmouth at 1.05 am and presumably carried the empty mussel vans.

Train 21 was a passenger train from Berwick to Edinburgh (leaving at 7.35 am) which called at Burnmouth at 7.47 am, then proceeding on to Edinburgh Waverley where it arrived at 9.52 am, having been combined with a North Berwick train en route. The accompanying note read: 'Does not convey Fish Wagons except Wagons from Burnmouth for Dunbar and stations north thereof and from stations south of Berwick. Leaves off all Fish Traffic at Dunbar to be brought forward from Dunbar by No. 23'. Train 23 was an empty coaching stock train, starting from Dunbar and working through to Edinburgh Waverley.

Train 46 was a goods from Berwick to Kipps (Edinburgh), leaving Berwick at 5.50 am and calling at Burnmouth at 6.10 am. 'On Mondays takes Fish and other Perishable Traffic for Glasgow and the West'.

Train 50 was a 'through goods' which ran 'Mondays excepted'. It was timed to leave Berwick at 7.40 am, calling at Burnmouth at 8.00 am before proceeding northwards to Sighthill where it arrived at 3.05 pm. This train '… lifts Fish Traffic from Burnmouth for Edinburgh. Lifts also Fish Traffic at Burnmouth for Leith Walk and North Leith and leaves it at Dunbar to go on from there to Niddrie West by the 8.30 pm train from Berwick'. This last train was numbered 51 and was a 'through goods' from Berwick to Dundee which ran Saturdays excepted. The accompanying note read: 'Calls at Burnmouth and Reston on Mondays only for Glasgow Traffic which it will leave off at Niddrie West. Lifts also from Burnmouth on Mondays Fish Traffic for Edinburgh also to be left off at Niddrie West … Takes on from Dunbar to Niddrie West Fish Traffic from Burnmouth for Leith Walk and North Leith left at Dunbar by the 7.40 pm Train

The importance of the fishing trade for branch revenue can be seen from this picture, taken at Eyemouth, in North British Railway. The two sidings next to the Eyewater are full of vans awaiting loading, whilst the far end of the platform is holding loaded vans prior to their leaving for Burnmouth. This rather poor quality picture has been included for historic reasons.

Eyemouth Museum Collection

The first of two postcards from LNER days. With the station sidings being visible in the distance this picture illustrate how advantageous it would have been for the fishing industry if the railway had been extended for a few hundred yards towards the harbour. The photograph shows the Eyewater on the left and the extended harbour on the right. Weatherhead's boatyard is in the left distance beside the River Eye.

Author's Collection

from Berwick.' No Sunday trains in the up direction were involved in Burnmouth goods traffic.

At this time, early photographs of Eyemouth station and trains show that fish was transported in open rail wagons. These were mainly wagons with low sides of about five planks depth. The barrels or boxes were covered with tarpaulins. All of the wagons used on the branch would have been fitted with piped brakes so that they could be used on mixed trains coupled to the passenger carriages. At least one early photograph show the fish wagons placed between the locomotive and the passenger carriages. It has been reported that liquid, leaking from the fish wagons onto the rails, caused problems with adhesion of the locomotive wheels, especially in winter when the liquid froze. On the steeply-graded branch this could have been a major problem for locomotive crews.

Fish transport in LNER days

During early LNER times the majority of the fish wagons seen at Eyemouth would have been vans of the pre-Grouping companies, with the former open fish trucks, carrying fish in ice-covered crates or barrels, being phased out in the very early 1920s. There were some LNER 9 ft wheelbase fish vans with outside frames, built in 1924-25, but these could not travel in the fastest goods trains and were superseded by 10 ft and 12 ft wagons before the start of World War II. Several of these latter types appear in Eyemouth station photographs taken up to and after nationalization. Their doors bore small cast plates bearing the word 'FISH'. Some of the pictured vans were of the ventilated type. Whilst most of the vans were from the LNER and its constituents some vehicles of other companies such as the London Midland & Scottish Railway (LMS) have been pictured at Eyemouth.

During the early part of World War II, some fish, mainly filleted haddock, was actually brought *to* Eyemouth from ports on the east coast of Scotland, particularly Aberdeen. The then station master at Ayton, John Bennett, recalled the spectacle of a line-up of seven or eight fish merchants vans lined up outside his station, every Monday to Friday, awaiting the arrival of the 8 pm train bringing in their fish. When the train had arrived at the platform, several of the merchants entered the rail vans and handed out dozens of fish boxes to those waiting on the platform. The boxes were loaded onto barrows and taken to the waiting road vehicles. This particular fish train was always referred to as 'The Mail'!

Fish transport in British Railways' days

In the British Railways' era pre-nationalization vans continued to be seen at Eyemouth. In 1949 some LNER-designed vans, later adopted as a standard BR-design, were introduced for the newly-nationalized railway. These were of 15 ft wheelbase and could run in fast trains. Their plywood bodies, coated with aluminium sheet, were painted white to reflect heat and they received insulated roofs. The doors were draught proofed and boxes of dry ice were used to keep the fish chilled. However, at the same time advances in refrigeration technology

The postcard view shows the upper end of the harbour with the slipway. The parish church, above the station, as always, provides a point of reference. *Author's Collection*

This picture is dated towards the end of 1959, less than two years before the line closed. In the Eyemouth station platform is the afternoon train for Burnmouth, consisting of one coach and three vans laden with fish attached at the rear. It is to be hauled by a clean No. 64711. The fish traffic is clearly still important as there is a large number and variety of four- and six-wheeled vans in the two sidings next to the Eyewater. *Armstrong Railway Photographic Trust*

were being introduced and fish began to be processed, packed and frozen at the ports. New large, refrigerated road lorries were introduced and were allowed to travel at greater speeds on the improving road network thus providing a commercially attractive alternative to rail transport. The problems associated with the damage to the viaduct and the line's consequent closure certainly contributed to the decline in the movement of Eyemouth's marine harvest by rail. If the branch had survived for a few more years the already dwindling traffic would have disappeared completely.

At the time of nationalization some separate fish trains, of up to six or so vans, were still being worked up to Eyemouth but in the 1950s the vans were hauled as part of the passenger trains, the official number per train being two. Most fish vans were worked on to Berwick with occasional ones bring detached at Burnmouth for onwards movement to Edinburgh. Empties were returned to Eyemouth attached to passenger trains.

Former Burnmouth porter, Alan Craig, can remember a type of incident which happened on more than one occasion! In the mid-1950s, 'shellfish', which included prawns and crabs, arrived 'up the brae' from the Burnmouth harbour in barrels carried on the station's delivery lorry. The barrels were unloaded onto a platform barrow in Burnmouth station yard and then taken down the platform ramp and across to the down platform for loading onto a northbound passenger train sometime after 4 pm. Occasionally the porters would lose control of the heavy barrow on the ramp and it would run away and overturn. The lids of the barrels would sometimes come off and the still-live crustaceans would make a run for freedom! Apparently it took quite a time to catch them all and return them to their barrel. First priority was, of course, to make sure that the barrels or lids did not foul the main lines; the catching of the escaped creatures was the second priority!

Replacing the fish trains of old, an articulated lorry of D.R. Collin & Son waits by the harbour side for its turn to be loaded with seafood. These lorries are a common site on the A1 road taking their valuable cargo for consumption in the adjacent countries in Europe and in the south of England. Smaller vans make local deliveries in Northumberland and the Scottish Borders.   *Author*

The two pictures on this page are not of the highest quality but have been included because of the interesting wagons in the Eyemouth sidings. The first, taken in pre-nationalization days, shows some LMS cattle wagons next to the 'spare' carriage. Were they commandeered for carrying boxes of fish when vans were in short supply or had they been worked down from Biglawburn after unloading a load of cattle? The second view, dating from the 1960s, shows a variety of six- and four-wheeled vans, mostly of the ventilated variety, awaiting loading. Numerous fish boxes lie in the yard adjacent to the wagons.

Eyemouth Museum Collection (upper), Author's Collection (lower)

Chapter Twelve

Freight traffic and Biglawburn siding

Freight traffic on the Eyemouth branch

In addition to the wagonloads of fish, the branch generated substantial freight and goods traffic. Most of the loaded vehicles were 'inwards' towards Eyemouth though there was some farm produce and livestock traffic 'outwards'.

Inward coal traffic was considerable. The year 1914, when World War I started, showed an inward movement of 4,022 tons of coal. This figure fell slightly during the time of hostilities but increased to 6,099 tons in 1920. Much of this was the high-quality coal from Shilbottle Colliery, near Alnwick in Northumberland, but some emanated from the Scremerston Colliery to the south of Berwick. This coal was handled at Eyemouth station, some being for the Eyemouth Gas Works (on the far side of town and without a rail connection) and some for the local coal merchants to sell for domestic purposes in the town. No 'private owner' coal wagons were operated by these merchants. Some 800 tons of other mineral traffic arrived at Eyemouth in 1914 rising to 1,454 tons in 1918.

Other inward traffic included livestock. 1914 produced just 86 head of cattle (compared with 811 the previous year) but by the end of the War the figure had increased to 775 animals. As well as the movement of livestock there was an inward traffic for agricultural machinery and parts, for animal feedstuffs and fertiliser for the fields.

The fishing industry also contributed to the inward goods: mussels, imported from Boston in Lincolnshire or the east of Scotland were brought in as fish bait and salt for the curing and preserving of the locally landed fish catch by merchants such as Burgon & Sons.

A developing traffic was the inward transport of fuel oil, both for the fishing boats and for agricultural and road vehicles. The traffic not specifically listed under coal or mineral traffic was listed under the heading of 'General Merchandise' which included much of the above. This amounted, in total, to 8,742 tons in 1914 and 7,280 in 1918. After the construction of Biglawburn siding much of the general merchandise and fuel oil was handled there rather than at Eyemouth station.

There was an inevitable decline in the goods traffic on the branch as road vehicles became larger and more efficient. The death knell for freight traffic was sounded when the branch was closed for the repairs to the flood-damaged viaduct in 1948. Alternative arrangements were made for most of the goods traffic and much of this continued to be carried by road when traffic was reinstated on the branch, the major exceptions being the inward movement of coal (for local merchant Mr J. Lough) and fuel oil, plus the outward movement of fish for the Fishermans' Mutual Association and Polar Foods. Photographs, dating from the early 1960s, show part-emptied coal wagons in the siding to the side of the platform road at Eyemouth.

The final workings on the Eyemouth branch were the short trains used by the contractors for the removal of track items when the rails were lifted in the summer of 1962.

This is a view of Biglawburn siding, on the right, with the line towards Burnmouth curving up the gradient towards Linthill viaduct, visible on the left of the picture. At the end of the siding, beneath the tree, is the oil storage tank which stored fuel oil for Weatherhead's road tankers to distribute to the Eyemouth fleet and to local farmers. The photograph was taken during the last week of trains on the branch and the siding had probably seen its last traffic.   *Jim Sedgwick*

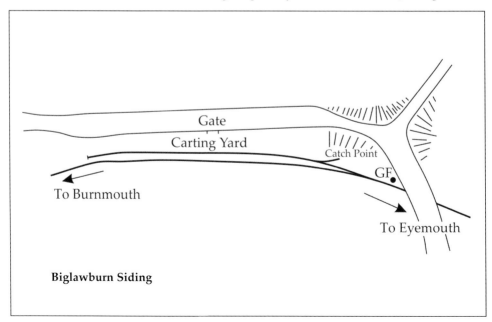

Biglawburn siding

The station layout at Eyemouth was always cramped. Apart from the provisions of the fish sidings and unloading of coal there was little room for loading and unloading of other goods and commodities. The perishable fish traffic required priority and other goods had to take second place.

Accordingly on 13th September, 1907 the NBR, perhaps following pressure from local merchants and farmers, produced plans for the construction of a siding and carting yard, to be located at Biglawburn, which would provide facilities for loading and unloading of items for local businesses. As well as merchants in Eyemouth receiving consignments, local farmers could then receive their fertiliser, agricultural parts and animal feedstuffs via this siding. The siding was designed to accommodate 18 wagons.

Biglawburn siding and gated carting yard were to be constructed on the north side of the line between the railway and the Eyemouth to Ayton road. The siding, according to the plan was located 2 miles and 26 chains from Burnmouth and 46 chains from Eyemouth. (In later Working Timetables it was referred to as 2 miles and 25 chains from Burnmouth.) An accompanying gradient diagram shows the siding points as being located on the short level section of track passing beneath the Biglawburn bridge, at the foot of the 1 in 50 incline leading down from the Eyewater viaduct. The gradient of the siding itself was indicated as being 1 in 200 up from the points, the rails at the buffers thus being several feet below the level of the adjacent branch line.

A surviving document describes the 'Estimated cost of proposed siding at Biglawburn near Eyemouth'. The siding involved forming a bed for the rails of 165 yards in length at a cost of £16 10s. 0d. The permanent way was to be formed of 'good, old materials' (presumably rails and fittings) plus new sleepers. The cost was forecast as £160 7s. 6d., with the additional cost of £18 15s. 3d. for an old 'switch' (point) and £8 11s. 0d. for a 'safety switch' (marked on the plan as a 'Catch Point'). A ground frame was to be provided located close to the bridge walls on the north side of the line. This was to be locked and unlocked through the use of the keys attached to the single line staff. At the end of the siding a buffer stop was to be constructed from old sleepers at a cost of £12 0s. 0d. The cost of forming and metalling of the carting yard (for 'light carting traffic') was set at £78 and the gate to this yard was costed at £6. Finally £42 was allocated for 'Ballast Engine Time'. With an amount allocated for contingencies, it was planned to spend £380 on the installation of the siding.

The work did not proceed for several years. Records indicate that the siding was not in operation until towards the end of World War I, when it started to appear in the NBR's working timetables. At this time some of the fishing vessels, using oil as a fuel, were using Eyemouth port. It was a local man, William Weatherhead, who realised there was an opportunity for supplying both these vessels and local farmers with fuel oil, and he established an oil depot, known as the oil store, at the end of Biglawburn siding.

The Weatherhead family's association with Eyemouth began when a Tweedmouth man, James Weatherhead, established a boat building company at Eyemouth in partnership with his uncle, James Lee. This firm built over 100

Included purely for historical reasons, this poor quality photograph shows the depot and offices of William Weatherhead at Port Seton. On the original print can just be made out the details on the enamel signs, including advertisements for Russian vaporising oil and Pratt's, the American oil company.   *Jim Hickie/Alex Weatherhead Collection*

boats at Eyemouth. In 1880 James' eldest son William left Eyemouth to set up his own business at Port Seton and later Cockenzie. In World War I his concern built motor launches, landing craft and cabin cruisers for the Admiralty and War Office. In addition the firm supplied equipment such as wire, ropes, cables and spares for fishing vessels.

The precise date of the establishment of the oil storage tanks at Biglawburn has not been identified. However, William Weatherhead bought two road tankers for the local delivery of oil to the harbour and the local farms. Fortunately a small photograph survives showing one of the tankers outside Weatherhead's depot at Port Seton. The oil storage facility survived at the siding until the closure of the branch but no photographs of a train discharging fuel from rail tankers has been traced. The administration of the firm's business and accounts was conducted, according to William's descendant Alex Weatherhead, by Jim Hickie. Initially the oil was supplied by Scottish Oils Ltd, based at Broxburn, but later by Shell Mex.

The working timetables relating to the Eyemouth branch included Biglawburn siding from its opening until the line closed. However, there were no goods trains scheduled to stop on a regular basis. Some of the timetables refer to a goods train running when required from Burnmouth to Eyemouth, usually around 2.00 pm when there was a gap in the passenger train timetable. The reverse working had to return to Burnmouth in time for the locomotive to bring the next passenger train to Eyemouth so any shunting time, at Biglawburn and Eyemouth, would have been brief! The siding could only be shunted by a train heading from Burnmouth towards Eyemouth. The siding did not appear in the timetable for trains heading in the reverse direction.

One pencil-annotated plan, in the Edinburgh archive, indicates that at some time there had been the idea of converting Biglawburn siding into a loop, though nothing came of this. In any case the height difference between the rail levels of the branch and the siding, at its Burnmouth end, would have made this difficult and costly. Another plan, dated October 1936 was drawn up by the county council in connection with proposed changes to the nearby road layout. These included improvements to the road junction adjacent to the bridge, and widening of both the road and the rail overbridge. The plans were approved by the LNER. The corner of the plan shows a small part of the Biglawburn yard and indicating that by this date a gate had been constructed in the fence producing a second, or alternative, entry. A small shed is shown within the yard fence, perhaps serving as a small store or office.

One photograph survives of a different use being made of Biglawburn siding. This photograph, dating from early BR days, shows an old twin-bogie railway carriage, possibly of NBR origin, parked in the siding attached to a train of several five-planked wagons plus at least one van. The carriage was formerly a seven-compartment vehicle, possibly with a toilet at one end. Whilst the small size of the original photograph makes it very difficult to read all of the information on the coach-side panel it is possible to make out that the wagon belonged to the Engineer's Department and was in use as a sleeping van. It appears to have been based at Riccarton Junction. The vehicle was fitted with a large tubular chimney emanating from the central area of the roof, no doubt leading from a stove inside the coach. The photograph is undated but may have been taken when the work was taking place on the restoration of the viaduct, and associated track work just a short time after nationalization.

The name of the siding had disappeared from the line's working timetables by 1955 but was still listed for the rest of the life of the branch in the Railway Clearing House *Handbook of Stations* when its sole use was for the inward fuel oil traffic. It is fortunate that at least one photographer visited the line on the Eyemouth branch's last operational day and paused to take a photograph of the siding and its oil tanks.

Biglawburn siding appears to have unusual visitors. A former NBR carriage is in the service of the Engineering Department and in use as a sleeping van. Its number appears to be ED97002. It is attached to several open wagons and a closed van. Note the large chimney projecting from the roof. The occasion is not recorded but it may have been in 1948 or 1949 at the time of rebuilding of the Linthill viaduct after the August 1948 storm.

Neil Mackichan

Two contemporary engravings of the accident at Marshall Meadows, just to the south of Burnmouth, when an Edinburgh to London express left the rails, the accident being ascribed to the poor state of the track.
(Both) Author's Collection

Chapter Thirteen

Accidents at Burnmouth and Eyemouth

Various accidents occurred during the construction of the Eyemouth branch. Their details were described in the chapter on the construction of the line. However at Eyemouth, and in the vicinity of Burnmouth station, a number of other accidents and incidents have taken place, some involving branch trains and others involving trains on the main line. Some were large enough to have been subject to official enquiries or reported in the press, whilst the memories of others have been passed down by word of mouth. No doubt the details of other minor incidents were 'brushed under the carpet'! Whereas snow is known to have been a contributory factor to a number of rail accidents some railwaymen, towards the end of the line's existence, commented that only once in their knowledge had the line been blocked by snow. The date has gone unrecorded but may have been in the very hard winter of 1947 when other local lines suffered blockages.

As mentioned earlier the stretch of railway line between Berwick and Reston stations was the location of about 15 substantial accidents between the mid-1850s and the mid-1880s. These had resulted from a variety of causes including track and coupling defects, collisions, boiler explosions, falls and persons being hit by moving trains.

One such accident took place on 10th August 1880 and received wide publicity. It was pictured in the *Illustrated London News* of 21st August, 1881. The morning express train from Edinburgh to London passed through Burnmouth but left the rails at the curve approaching Marshall Meadows cutting. The train consisted of a tender engine, two guard's vans and nine coaches. The engine and tender parted and the latter was thrown onto the trackside bank. The engine was thrown across the line and the carriages were all more or less destroyed. The driver was killed instantly, a guard travelling in the first carriage also died and the fireman died after having been admitted to Berwick Infirmary. The Board of Trade enquiry focussed on the state of the track, the rails, chairs and sleepers, which appeared to have been inadequately spiked together according to the *Illustrated London News* reporter.

An accident took place on Thursday 24th October, 1889 at Burnmouth which potentially could have had disastrous consequences. It took place adjacent to the works for the Eyemouth Railway and was reported in the *Berwickshire News and General Advertiser* on the following Tuesday:

ACCIDENT ON THE RAILWAY – On Thursday morning, the 'Flying Scotsman', which leaves Edinburgh for Berwick at 10 o'clock, met with an alarming accident near Burnmouth Station. It appears that blasting operations were being conducted on the new Eyemouth Railway, where it converges on the North British system, and that a blast occurred just as the 'Scotsman' approached. It was too late to put the signal against her, and she came in contact with the material thrown up on to the line by the blast. The engine was considerably damaged, but, fortunately, it and the remainder of the train kept on the rails. At Berwick, which was reached about half-an-hour late, the engine had to be changed.

The identity of the locomotive was not recorded but after its replacement the train was able to carry on to Kings Cross. The train, its passengers and crew had a very fortunate escape, there being no fatalities or injuries.

A further accident, in the form of a collision occurred at Burnmouth station on Saturday 25th January, 1890. This was widely reported in the press as were the subsequent enquiries and legal actions.

The 5.30 pm up passenger train left Berwick heading towards Edinburgh. It overran the signals and platform at Burnmouth and collided with the engine of the 7.00 am goods train from Sighthill (Edinburgh) to Tweedmouth which was shunting some wagons. In the accident 10 passengers were injured, including one who was riding upon the engine, an unauthorized action. This passenger was so badly injured that he died shortly after the accident. Both the driver and fireman of the 5.30 pm train were burned and scalded and they died a few days later. The guard of the passenger train was also seriously injured as was the fireman of the goods train who hurt his leg when jumping from the footplate of the engine.

The Inspecting Officer for the Board of Trade was Major Marindin who would return to the area soon afterwards to inspect the Eyemouth branch before its opening. Marindin concluded that the driver of the passenger train was responsible for the accident. He had apparently missed seeing the Burnmouth distant signal and was quite unaware of the exact position of his train. Marindin accepted that as it was a very wild and windy night and that might have accounted, in part, for the driver's mistake but he attributed the driver's error principally to the presence of an unauthorized person on the footplate who had prevented the driver from paying proper attention to his duties. After the collision and before he died the driver had admitted that he had made a 'terrible mistake' and that he had 'missed the signal'. However, the deaths of others involved made some of the evidence circumstantial. The Major made some recommendations as to train operations in the area. He recommended that station arrangements at Berwick be improved, that the NBR should alter the position of the home signal at Burnmouth so as to protect the platform and be more easily seen from an approaching train. He also called attention to the way that the block system was being operated on that portion of the main line.

Later in the same year the *Edinburgh Evening News* reported an action in the Court of Session by a certain Thomas Cairns who was travelling on this passenger train from Berwick as far as Drem station. Mr Cairns was thrown violently from his seat in his carriage and suffered concussion to his spinal cord and severe shock. At the time of the court hearing (19th November, 1890) he was not yet sufficiently recovered as to be able to carry out his normal business. In a subsequent trial at the Justiciary Court Room in Edinburgh (on 22nd December) the NBR, against whom the action was brought, admitted liability in that the train had overshot Burnmouth platform despite the Westinghouse brake being applied, thus causing the accident. However, they disputed that Cairns should be paid the damages of £1,500 that he was claiming on grounds that he had suffered no permanent injury and that he had, in fact, been going about his business as usual!

One item which had appeared in Major Marindin's report was that, at the time of the accident, the driver had been on duty for 10¾ hours already (out of his daily total of 13 hours). This detail was referred to in a mass meeting of railway servants held at the Albion Halls in Glasgow about a month later. The Society secretary referred to both the Burnmouth accident and others at Gartsherrie and Maryhill and pointed out that the railwaymen involved had all been on duty for about 11 hours and that it was not unfair to infer that this fact had had something to do with the accidents. The meeting passed a resolution asking the Directors of the railway companies to meet with them to produce a satisfactory resolution to this vexing matter.

A very similar accident to the last one took place early in 1891 and was first reported in a February edition of the *Whitstable Times and Herne Bay Herald*. Again it was the 5.30 pm slow train from Berwick which was involved, when it collided with a locomotive and two wagons. Both engines were much damaged and there were several casualties. The driver of the passenger train, Cunningham, and the fireman, Thompson, both received scalds and Dedins, the guard, received cuts from broken glass as well as hip and leg injuries. Doctor Jeffery of Ayton who was travelling on the train received a cut on his forehead and was severely shaken and a Mr Charles Fenwick of Templehall had his nose broken. Other passengers complained of bruises and shock. A special train took the injured to Berwick Infirmary.

Just a few months later, in April 1891, Burnmouth station was the scene of yet another gruesome accident, this time not attributable to any failure on the part of railway personnel or equipment. According to the *Edinburgh Evening News* the last slow train of the day from Edinburgh to Berwick had just passed Burnmouth's platform at about 8.45 pm when the guard noticed an open door and saw a young boy fall from the train, immediately followed by a woman. He applied the train brake and the train was stopped. It was discovered that the boy had been killed by his fall and that the woman, who turned out to be his mother, was severely injured, sustaining a broken collar bone, broken shoulder blade, broken leg and a severe scalp wound. She was taken to Berwick Infirmary in a critical condition. She was identified as Mrs Robertson the wife of Adam Robertson, a goods guard, of Berwick. It was surmised that she and her son had been travelling to Burnmouth and that when the train failed to stop the boy had turned the door handle and fallen out, his mother following afterwards to try to save him.

The outcome of another accident which took place between Burnmouth and Reston in the early morning of Saturday 23rd May, 1891 was much happier in that no-one was injured though there were severe delays to several trains. It was reported in the *York Herald* newspaper. An express goods train had left Berwick for the north, when, just after the train had passed Ayton station to the north of Burnmouth, a coupling broke and some 16 wagons and vans left the rails, some falling down the embankment. Some of the rails were torn up and twisted. The Berwick breakdown gang was dispatched to the scene and by nine o'clock on the following day they managed to clear one line for traffic. Southbound trains were held at Reston. Saturday is market day in Berwick and several farmers and other country people had difficulty in reaching the town. Northbound trains held at Berwick included two trains from Kings Cross to Edinburgh and the early morning mail train from Newcastle to the north. These trains were on the point of being diverted via Kelso and St Boswells when the word arrived that one line had been cleared past the accident site and they were able to head northwards via their usual route. It is not known if the newly-introduced Eyemouth branch trains were extended to and from Berwick to allow Burnmouth inhabitants to attend the market.

The seemingly ill-fated Burnmouth station area was the site of yet another accident on the night of 1st June, 1891, barely a week after the previous incident! A locomotive was shunting a cattle train at Burnmouth station sidings opposite the junction for the Eyemouth branch. A special fish train from Perth to Berwick approached Burnmouth at a speed estimated to be between 25 and 30 mph. The locomotive of the fish train collided with the locomotive of the cattle train but because of the relatively low impact speed only a small amount of damage was done. The cattle train train received a broken buffer and the fish train engine also received slight damage; one cattle truck was damaged. The driver of the fish train received an injured knee and the guard of the same train received arm injuries and suffered from shock. The report of the accident appeared in the *Sheffield Evening Telegraph* illustrating the widespread interest in railway accidents at the time.

The first railway incident on the Eyemouth branch itself was written up in the *Southern Reporter* (printed in Selkirk) dated 13th August, 1891. Apparently during the previous week there had been a considerable quantity of fish traffic being loaded at the station platform at Eyemouth and the constant 'passing and repassing' of vehicles caused the edge of the platform to collapse and fall onto the adjacent line. Fortunately no-one was injured but severe disruption was caused to both passenger and fish traffic whilst the line was cleared. As a result of the platform collapse the Eyemouth Railway announced that the platform would be entirely renewed and enlarged at a cost estimated as £1,000. A new entrance from the toll road was to be made, at the foot of which there would be a new booking office. It must be remembered that Major Marindin had not been entirely happy with the platform arrangements when he sanctioned the opening of the line just a few months earlier!

The second accident on the Eyemouth branch could have had far worse consequences. It took place on Wednesday 9th December, 1891 and was first reported in the *Edinburgh Evening News* of the same date. The 6.00 am passenger train from Eyemouth, the first of the day, was scheduled to arrive at Burnmouth (referred to in the report as *'Burnmouth Junction'*) at 6.07 am. For some unexplained reason the train continued into the bay platform at full speed. Its progress was not stopped by the buffers at the end of the line and the locomotive and its carriage mounted onto the platform and ran along this until coming to a stand just before the road overbridge. Remarkably the newspaper report recorded the damage to the rolling stock as 'small'! The driver and the fireman were unhurt but Mr Scott, the guard, received a cut on his forehead. Fortunately the train was not carrying any passengers. There was an amusing sequel to this incident. A reporter of the *Portsmouth Evening News* described the incident as having taken place at Bournemouth, rather than Burnmouth, so that an article on the incident appeared in that paper on Thursday 10th December. Devon's *Western Times* also reported the incident.

One reported item, of an incident at Burnmouth, did not directly affect the Eyemouth branch. It was in 1898 that the NER instigated new patterns of train working between Newcastle and Edinburgh. In March of that year (as recorded in the *Berwickshire News* dated exactly 50 years later, on 2nd March, 1948) the first train on the new schedule was to run from Edinburgh to Newcastle in a planned time of 143 minutes. It was hauled by a pair of the relatively new

Worsdell-designed class 'D17' 4-4-0s, Nos. 1909 and 1930. Whilst passing Burnmouth a strap on No. 1930 gave way, disabling this locomotive and leaving No. 1909 to haul the extra 95 tons single-handedly onwards to Newcastle. It must have performed with credit as only two minutes were dropped against the demanding schedule.

The press recorded no further accidents at Eyemouth or Burnmouth in Eyemouth Railway days. However, several happenings appeared in the newspapers in the first decade of the 20th century. Two were recorded in 1903.

The first of these concerned a railway surfaceman, Thomas Robertson, and appeared in the *Berwickshire News* of 23rd October. The accident took place near to Burnmouth station as Robertson was on duty. He was knocked down by a passing train, sustaining very severe injuries including a serious compound fracture of his left arm. He was rushed to Berwick Infirmary where it was feared that his arm might have to be amputated.

The second, the report of an extremely sad and distressing incident, appeared in the *Berwick Advertiser* of 22nd December, 1903. At about 10 o'clock on the evening of 19th December a body of a respectably dressed man was found on the down side of the main line just to the north of Burnmouth station. The head was very much injured and it appeared that he had been struck by a passing train. He was wearing a morning coat and striped trousers and a silk tie and rolled umbrella were found nearby. His pockets contained 11s. $8^1/_2d.$ plus a watch and some reading glasses. He was recognised as a man called Johnson who had left a kit bag containing personal items such as a razor, comb and washing materials. Close to the body was found an overcoat, in the pocket of which was an envelope containing a suicide note which read: 'Anything found upon me may be given to those who find me as there will be no claimant. I owe nobody a penny and have no money and any means of getting any honestly. Bury me at once. I pray God to receive my spirit.' The same incident was reported by the *Edinburgh Evening News* on the same date under the headline 'A Pathetic Message'. It was a very sad incident, indeed.

A similarly sad incident was reported in the same two newspapers on the 2nd October, 1906 when the body of a man was found on the railway between Burnmouth and Ayton having been run down by an express train. It was reported in the following week's *Berwickshire News* that he was a certain James Dodds, a widower, mason and former soldier who was about to get married again. His body was conveyed to Swinton, his home town, for burial.

It was another four years before another incident was reported, this time occurring at Eyemouth station. On this occasion some railway workmen were moving some sleepers on a bogie wagon into Eyemouth station. One of the sleepers fell off the wagon and a Berwick surfaceman, Mr Weatherburn, received a fracture to his left leg. An 'Examiner' who was at the scene, a Mr Mace, gave immediate first aid and Dr Hermon immediately set the fractured limb. Weatherburn was then taken to Berwick Infirmary for observation. The date of the accident was Saturday 12th May, 1910 and the incident was reported in the *Berwick Advertiser* six days later.

The next reported accident appearing in the press was in the *Berwickshire News* dated 21st July, 1919. Some lorries owned by the fish curer, John Burgon, were being driven by his employees with materials from Eyemouth station on Tuesday 15th July. Some of the kippering girls tried to mount one of the vehicles whilst it was in motion. One of them, Alice Crombie, aged 15, over-balanced and fell between the wheels of the lorry, fracturing one of her legs very badly. Doctors Hermon and McLagan were soon in attendance assisted by the local nurse. A week later the girl was said to be progressing favourably! This was the last of the accidents reported in NBR days.

Perhaps a little surprisingly in view of the time of year the *Berwickshire News* reported that a spark from a passing train had ignited the contents of a potato pit at Eyemouth Hill Farm on Wednesday 1st February, 1922. About two tons of potatoes were destroyed in the conflagration.

It was on Monday 23rd July, 1923 that Archibald Spence, one of the station staff at Eyemouth, suffered an accident. He was riding his motorcycle along the Ayton Road near Hillburn, when he was thrown off his bike as a result of a tyre burst; according to the press reports he suffered head and face injuries from coming into contact with gravel on the road.

Just a month later, on 23rd August, 1923 at harvest-time, a serious accident was narrowly averted on the Eyemouth branch. A train was coming at full speed down the gradient from Burnmouth with the engine running tender first. The vigilant engine driver spotted horses struggling with an agricultural reaper which was across the rails in front of his train. The reaper was the property of farmer Mr Wood who had the right to use the crossing. It was being taken from one field to another in the vicinity of the Flemington bridge but had become stuck between the rails. According to the reports in the *Southern Reporter* and the *Berwickshire News* the driver, 'with commendable promptitude' applied his Westinghouse brake, and, at the risk of blowing out the cylinder heads of his engine, he reversed with full steam on and managed to draw his train to a stand, with a jolt, just six yards from the crossing. The warning shriek of the engine's whistle scared the horses pulling the reaper and they plunged away from the metals and into the adjoining field. The whole incident was over within a minute and the train was able to proceed on its way with most of its full complement of passengers being unaware that anything untoward had happened!

A mysterious happening took place on 2nd June, 1932. The local press reported that afternoon train from Eyemouth to Berwick met with a 'mishap' just after it left Burnmouth. The nature of the mishap was not reported but the return train, at 4.00 pm from Berwick, was cancelled.

A body was found by a platelayer (or surfaceman), to the south of Burnmouth station, as reported in the *Dundee Evening Telegraph* of 25th April, 1935. It was identified as that of Miss Ellen Laidlaw, aged 25 or 26, who had been a teacher at Burnmouth School for some 16 months. The cause of death was stated to be a mystery. Ellen had been in quite normal spirits when socializing on the previous evening.

Almost two years later, on 5th February, 1937, it was once again the gruesome task of a platelayer to discover and report another body at the side of the railway line adjacent to the top of 'The Brae', the road leading up from Burnmouth harbour. It was identified as that of Paul Johnstone, a local fisherman, of Blue House,

Burnmouth. He had gone to sea that morning, and, as reported in the *Berwickshire News*, he had 'disappeared' and his wife and other fishermen had been searching for him on the cliff sides above the village. Once again, a mystery surrounded his death.

On 23rd April, 1940 the same newspaper reported an incident on the Eyemouth branch. Works were taking place in the cutting near Biglawburn. John Gibson was a waggon [*sic*] driver who was about to tip his horse-drawn wagon when his horse started at a brisk pace causing Gibson to fall. One of the wagon wheels ran over his right arm and fractured it very badly. For specialist treatment he was taken to the Royal Infirmary in Edinburgh.

The trying conditions of maintaining a train service under the wartime conditions of blackout must have been difficult for the local railwaymen. Despite this the LNER were able to present several safe driving awards to local railwaymen for periods of several years without accidents. Amongst the recipients, listed in the *Berwick Advertiser* in 1941, were local men Joseph Duncan of Eyemouth and George Jeffrey of Ayton.

An express train for Edinburgh broke down at Burnmouth on 'Victory Day' 1946 and was held up for three hours. The passengers were clearly advised that they would not be travelling onwards for some time as many of them, according to the *News*, took the opportunity of strolling down 'The Brae' to Lower Burnmouth!

The *Berwickshire News* of 18th March, 1947 reported that the main line had been blocked near Burnmouth on the previous Friday, though the cause was not specified. No trains were run past the site of the 'blockage' and the London expresses from Edinburgh were diverted.

On the evening of Wednesday 21st May, 1947 there was an accident at Burnmouth station when an Eyemouth train, due into the station at 6.17 pm, failed to pull up on entering the platform. A van was standing at the buffers at the end of the bay platform. The engine crashed into the van causing it to telescope and fall onto the platform causing some damage to the passenger stairway but fortunately missing the station building by a matter of inches! The driver, William Waite, realised that his train was not going to stop in time and called out a warning. Fortunately he escaped injury in the collision. The fireman managed to jump from the train before the moment of impact. He was also uninjured as were the two women passengers on the train. The front of the locomotive was embedded in the remains of the van but at 9.30 pm, after several attempts, the engine extricated itself under its own steam. According to the *Berwickshire News*, whose reporter attended the scene, there was no dislocation of services on the main line. The accident was ascribed to the failure of the engine's brakes.

One further accident was reported later in 1947, on Wednesday 5th November. It referred to a shunting accident at Burnmouth on the 'Eyemouth shunting road' when a brake van was derailed with some damage occurring to a buffer stop at the end of the line. The Tweedmouth breakdown crane had to be called out and its crew speedily re-railed the van. The *Berwickshire News* of the following Tuesday referred to this as being the third time that the breakdown van had been called out in three weeks though the other incidents were not detailed in the press. A catalogue listing photographs donated to Eyemouth Museum around this time refers to one print illustrating '*an overturned carriage in the station*' though, unfortunately, the print appears to be missing.

The death of a railway workman on the Eyemouth branch was reported in the press in October 1949. Hugh Clelland Johnstone, a resident of Countess Road, Dunbar, was a railway signalling linesman based at Burnmouth station. He was at the station to repair a signal defect at the end of the branch. The accident occurred when Mr Johnstone was walking from the station towards Fairnieside along the ends of the sleepers of the Burnmouth-Eyemouth track. The high wind and the noise of a passing Edinburgh goods train on the nearby main line clearly masked the departure of the 1.10 pm Eyemouth branch train from the bay platform. The train was making a three minute late departure and had reached a speed of about 20 mph. Johnstone started to cross over the track and he walked into the path of the train some 200 yards from the station and 85 yards from the signal box. The shouts of the Burnmouth signalman, John B. Wilson, resident at the Flemington Inn, Burnmouth, who had been observing Johnstone, failed to prevent his instantaneous death. Wilson believed that the high wind and the sound of a passing Edinburgh-bound goods train prevented Johnstone from hearing his warning. The driver of the Eyemouth train, Victor Ashman, and his guard, Leslie Taylor, were initially unaware of the tragedy. Ashman said that locomotive was running tender-first and his view of the line was somewhat restricted. Even if he had been looking out of the cab window he would never have seen the deceased. However, the guard, John Hunter Purves, had heard the shouts of the signalman and immediately rushed to apply the brakes bringing the train to a stand. The fitter, having completed his work on the signal, would have known that the line was reopened and that the train was running. Had he turned he would have had a clear view of the train. The accident was reported in the *Berwickshire News* a day after the accident and also in the next edition of the *Berwick Advertiser*. An enquiry into Johnstone's death was heard at the Duns Sheriff Courtroom in front of Sheriff Murray and a jury of four men and three women. A representative of British Railways, Mr Gibb, attended the Inquest and expressed his sympathy to the relatives of the dead man.

The same newspaper reported a shunting incident at Burnmouth station which took place on Friday 15th January, 1954. A local driver, Jack Mace of Castlegate, Berwick, was shunting some wagons in the loops at the end of the Eyemouth branch. Four trucks which were being hauled towards the station became derailed. Little damage was done to the rails and traffic on the main line was not interfered with. The Berwick breakdown gang attended and normal working resumed later the same day. It may be nothing more than coincidence but Mr Mace had been involved in another shunting accident on Monday of the same week! Whilst shunting some wagons at Berwick station one had become derailed and crashed against an iron pillar at Berwick station.

A collision, occurring at Eyemouth station on 11th October, 1955, resulted in local passenger guard, James Purves, of Eyemouth, being given an official warning, though no endorsement was attached to his railway service history record. Purves was supervising a shunting movement into the coal siding at Eyemouth station at 9.30 am on the stated date. He was found guilty of contravening Rule 112(a) of the railway rulebook. This rule required Purves to be vigilant and to inform any relevant personnel that the engine was about to shunt wagons into a siding. In fact one of the road tankers of Messrs Weatherhead & Sons, of Port Seton, was fouling part of the line and its driver was not informed of the impending shunting movement. As a result the oil tanker received some damage when it was hit by the leading wagon of the propelling movement. By this time Purves had been in railway service for some 16 years. The memorandum from the Operating Department in Edinburgh to Purves, regarding the accident, is preserved in the Eyemouth Museum.

Around the same time an accident occurred at Burnmouth which almost repeated the accidents which had taken place there in December 1891 and in May 1947. This time the accident could be traced to the carelessness of one of the train crew at Eyemouth station. As mentioned elsewhere there was no run-round loop at Eyemouth. As a result, after passengers had left a train, the engine had to propel its carriages a short distance back up the line. The locomotive would then be uncoupled, the brake pipes separated and the cord pulled to allow the carriage to descend carefully, by gravity and under supervision, into the platform. The train engine would then emerge from the sidings, into which it had retreated before the carriage descended, and be attached to the Burnmouth end of the carriage. On this occasion the member of the train crew coupled the engine and carriage but failed to reconnect the train's brake pipe! The guard clearly failed to notice on the gauge in his van that the correct brake pressure was not being shown! The train, when given the right-of-way, stormed up the gradient towards Burnmouth. It was customary, if the signals were clear, for the locomotive to be given plenty of steam to allow it to climb the gradient towards the start of the Burnmouth platform. At this point the brakes would be applied and the train would come safely to a stop in the bay platform. On this

---

BRITISH
RAILWAYS (Form No. 2)   E.R.O. 5431

D.O.S.O.

........Operating.... Department Edinburgh...... Station ..7.12.. .....19 55.

MEMORANDUM To Passenger Guard J. Purves, Eyemouth.

It is reported to me that you have committed the following irregularity :—

Before carrying out shunting operations, viz. in making a propelling movement into the Coal Siding, Eyemouth, at 9.30am. on 13th October, 1955, you failed to comply fully with the provisions of Rule No. 112(a) with the result that the driver of a road tank vehicle belonging to Mess. W. Weatherhead and Sons, Port Seton, was not warned by you to move his lorry which was fouling the line, and in consequence, the lorry sustained damage when the leading wagon of the propelling movement hit it.

I have decided that in consequence

you be given a Warning, but no endorsement will be made

on your service history record.

occasion the carriage brakes were not functioning, brake power thus being confined to the locomotive. Although the engine brakes slowed the train considerably the train collided noisily with the buffers at the end of the bay platform causing them some damage. Fortunately the locomotive and carriage stayed on the track, unlike in the 1891 accident. This incident was observed by several of the Burnmouth station staff (one of whom recalls the accident clearly) and by passengers waiting on the Edinburgh platform. The Tweedmouth breakdown gang were called. Fortunately there were no injuries.

It was in January 1961, on the morning of Saturday 14th to be precise, that there was a 'runaway train' into Eyemouth. An account appeared in the *Berwick Advertiser* and the event was subsequently referred to in various articles including one in *Steam Days* magazine. A copy of guard Purves' accident report survives also.

It is well known that frost can make it difficult for braked wheels to grip on steel rails. When the rails were covered with thick rime caused by fish juices leaking from wagons, as on the Eyemouth branch, then the problem could be exacerbated! On this occasion guard James Hunter Purves was in charge of the 7.35 am class 'B' passenger train from Burnmouth to Eyemouth. It had left Burnmouth about four minutes late (five minutes in Purves' report) due to waiting for a connecting train, the 7.20 am from Berwick. Despite this the driver, Mr Borthwick, travelled at a normal speed, applying his brakes several times on the sharply descending line.

As the train passed Eyemouth (Netherbyres) Mill the guard, Purves, felt that the train was running a little faster than usual. He noticed that the vacuum gauge had gone down to nil as the driver made a full brake application. Purves decided to provide some assistance using his own hand brake as the train passed Eyemouth Mill, but noticed that the wheels were already locked and skidding along the track. The points were, of course, set for the platform road, at the far end of which were several wagons close to the line-end buffers. On entering the Eyemouth platform, described as Platform 1 in the accident report, the guard decided to jump from his van. The same decision had been made by the only passenger on the train, a railway lengthman named Johnston (reported as Johnson in the newspapers). The train continued along the platform and the locomotive collided with the wagons, thus coming to a stop. The driver, Borthwick, suffered no physical damage in the accident but both Johnson and Purves received slight injuries. 'Johnson' was taken to Berwick Infirmary for treatment after first aid treatment by a nursing sister, Sister Gallagher, who was at the station awaiting the next train, the 8.00 am, to Burnmouth. Purves was treated by his own doctor for a gravel rash on his hands and arms for which he was given a tetanus injection. He also had a muscle strain in his right arm and his right knee was swollen for some time after the accident. Purves walked the length of the platform to see how the driver had fared. He told Purves that he was alright.

Undoubtedly, as the guard stated in his report, it was the accumulated rime on the track which had been the prime cause of the accident, which was not the first of its type on the line. The earlier light rain and the severe overnight frosts in the area in the first half of January also contributed to the greasiness of the rails and no blame was ascribed to the train crew at the subsequent enquiry.

Strangely the *Berwickshire News* of 17th January, 1961 contained a report of an accident which occurred on the same Saturday, 14th January. This accident was reported as having occurred at *Burnmouth*, rather than Eyemouth, but some of the names in the article bear more than a slight resemblance to those mentioned above. The accident itself appears to have been a case of history repeating itself for the accident bears many similarities to those of 1891, 1947 and 1955 at Burnmouth!

The *News* account reported that a two-coach Eyemouth to Burnmouth train crashed into some goods wagons at Burnmouth station. The account implies that these wagons were positioned in the Eyemouth bay platform. The train had skidded on icy rails as it entered the platform, smashing into the first wagon and sending two others through the buffers and onto Burnmouth's main line platform. The only passenger on the train was a railwayman by the name of William Johnston of Cowdrait, Burnmouth. He sustained a dislocated shoulder. The other injured party was William Purvis, the train guard of Wellbraes, Eyemouth, who received a cut to his hand. The driver of the train was reported as William Borthwick of Church Street, Berwick, who escaped unhurt.

The guards concerned in the two accidents are named as James Purves and William Purvis respectively, the drivers were both named Borthwick (first name William in the second accident) and the other injured parties, though with different injuries, were a Mr Johnson or William Johnston, both railwaymen. Some remarkable similarities!

It is quite possible that there were, in fact, two accidents occurring on the line on the same day, though this would seem highly unusual for such a short line. The accidents, though, were reported as taking place at opposite ends of the line, one at Eyemouth, one at Burnmouth, and the accounts (in different newspapers and journals) appear to contain details of a precise or specific nature, such as the named persons, the nature of injuries received and the details of the accidents themselves. The other possibility, remote or strange though it may sound, was that there was only one accident. The author of the *Berwickshire News* article may have received the accident information second- or third-hand and that the 'Chinese whispers effect' resulted in a very different story. However, neither newspaper contained any follow-up items or retractions. Hence the accident accounts, in the apparent absence of any BR official reports, must be accepted. Whatever the truth of the matter the Tweedmouth breakdown gang must have been busy that weekend!

Later in the spring of 1961 there was another mishap on the branch which was investigated by a Scottish Region Accident Inspector. A train had taken a raft of empty wagons from Eyemouth up to the loop siding at Burnmouth. The driver gave a small push to a wagon expecting his guard, Bob Hay, to apply the handbrake and bring it to a stand. The driver must have mistaken the force of the shunt for the wagon sped past Hay without his being able to apply the brake. The wagon entered onto the Eyemouth line and made a rapid, gravity assisted, run down to Eyemouth, finally coming to a stand when it crashed into a line of goods wagons. Fortunately there were no men working on the track on that day as they would have received little or no warning of the arrival of the speeding wagon. Once again no blame was apportioned after the enquiry.

This was to be the last of the reported accidents that took place at Eyemouth and Burnmouth before British Railways closed the branch, less than a year later, on Monday 5th February, 1962, the last trains having run on the previous Saturday (there being no Sunday service).

THE FLOOD, EYEMOUTH HARBOUR, 12·8·48

These two commercial postcards illustrate the consequences of the Great Flood on the Eyemouth station area. The upper picture, dated 12th August, 1948, shows the Eyewater 'in spate' having burst from its normal course, flowing down the Harbour Road. In this view the station sidings are just above the level of the water but movement of fish from the harbour to load the vans would have been impossible. In the lower photograph, taken a day later on 13th August, some of the consequences of the flood are shown: a vessel has been washed up and tree trunks are hard against the harbour wall. However, the water level has subsided a little and the vans on the rails in the sidings are now some way above the water level.   *(Both) Author's Collection*

AFTER THE FLOOD, EYEMOUTH. 13·8·48.

Chapter Fourteen

The devastating flood of 1948

The devastation caused by the floods that severely affected the Eyemouth line in 1948 can be attributed to several factors. Firstly the total amount of rainwater that fell in the catchment area of the Eyewater and its tributaries, secondly the brief time in which this heavy rain fell onto the land and thirdly the nature and profiles of the catchment area itself. One mitigating factor was the presence of the main Berwick to Edinburgh 'East Coast' railway, whose long embankments held back much water and prevented the devastation becoming even greater.

The average precipitation for the Eyemouth area is around 683 mm per year, slightly below the average for Scotland as a whole. August is amongst the wettest of months of the year in the area, around 55 mm of rain being expected in a typical year. In August 1948 about one third of the total annual rainfall fell in just six days.

The Eyewater (or Eye Water) has a catchment area of some 120 square kilometres. It arises on the eastern side of the Lammermuir Hills with its principal source being on Wester Dod Hill some 300 m above ordnance datum. It flows in a south-easterly direction for around 10 km before turning north-eastwards and reaching the southern outskirts of the hamlet of Grantshouse. It regains its south-easterly route and runs in the valley between Dalks Law and Horsely Hill. It passes through the villages of Reston and Ayton where the valley widens out for some distance. It then enters a narrower valley on the Ayton Castle estate and curves almost north-easterly for the last five kilometres towards the estuary at Eyemouth. The final kilometres are through a gorge, often with steep sides. At Eyemouth the river flows to the east of the harbour, from which it is separated by a stone quay. The Eyewater has various tributaries including the major one, the Ale Water, which joins the Eye near to Linthill between Ayton and Eyemouth. Other small tributaries include the Drakemire, Brockholes, Horn and Peelwalls burns. By far the greatest part, well over 95 per cent, of the catchment area is agricultural land of various types.

The A1 trunk road and the East Coast railway both follow the Eye Water valley between Grantshouse and Reston. The A1 road remains to the north-east of the river but the railway crosses the river on several occasions. For a good part of its route between Reston and Ayton the railway is carried on an embankment to the south-west of the river whilst the main road follows an alignment to the north-east. On its old alignment the A1 crossed the Eyewater on a bridge at the south-east corner of Ayton village whilst the present route, the Ayton by-pass, takes it over the Eye on a large bridge near to Hillburn and the junction with the 'new' A1107 Burnmouth Road.

In the days leading up to 12th August a large depression, with associated strong winds producing driving rain, passed over the Borders region. Over 200 mm of water fell on the region. The floods that this caused created a huge natural disaster. All of the local rivers, including the Eyewater overflowed their banks. Ballast was washed from the railway line and the bridge carrying the

The three pictures shown here were taken in August 1948 by a local amateur photographer who recorded some of the damage to local roads and railways: subsidence on the East Coast main line arising from the washing out of ballast, tracks suspended in mid-air in several places following the complete disappearance of embankments and bridges and the destruction of local road bridges which hampered communications and repair efforts.

(All) Jock Sanderson via Eyemouth Golf Club

Horn Burn under the railway collapsed causing a build-up of water. The low-lying land near to Ayton, to the north of Prendergast Farm, was turned into a large inland lake, which, at its maximum, was estimated to contain 400 million gallons (1,820 million litres) of water! It was nearly two kilometres in length and over 8½ metres deep. The only feature which prevented this water from cascading down the Eye valley towards Eyemouth was the 18 metre high embankment on the main railway line, which, effectively, became a dam wall. If this embankment had collapsed under the pressure of water the water would have swamped Eyemouth. An immediate round-the-clock watch was placed on the embankment with coastguards having warning rockets on standby to warn the 2,000 or so local residents to evacuate their homes. Fortunately the embankments held. After the storm had passed, there was the immense problem of safely restoring the main line. The pressure of water was released by creating a sluice in the embankment whilst, the Royal Engineers built temporary bridges to replace those washed away or damaged. In present-day terms the costs of restoration and repairs, necessitated by the flood, amount to around £40m.

The full story of the flood and its aftermath is told in Lawson Wood's excellent book *The Great Borders Flood of 1948*. It also contains numerous photographs of the effect of the storm on the people, the homes, the businesses and transport in the area. Some idea of the extent of local devastation, and Eyemouth in particular, can be seen in the Pathé Newsreel clip entitled *'Berwick – Floods Sweep North, Wrecked Homes (1948)'* which can be viewed on 'Youtube'.

The damage to the branch and its viaduct

Normally the water flowing below the Eyewater viaduct is confined to the area below span No. 5. The water from the mill lade (or leat) flows between piers 1 and 2. However, following this storm there was rapid water flowing beneath each of the spans. The water was also carrying debris, such as branches and timber, which it had accumulated during its rapid flow down the narrow valley.

The scouring action of the water washed away the gravel underlying the central pier, No. 3. This resulted in its collapse. However, the steel girder superstructure held firm and was left, suspended, in mid-air high above the river. Much scouring had also occurred by the swollen river flowing along the route of the mill lade. The gravel on the river bed was removed and further scouring occurred extending some distance beneath the foundations of pier No. 2. After the river returned to its normal level much debris was piled up against the remaining piers.

The ends of the suspended girders were temporarily secured by engineers placing ties and wedges in position, pending the start of full restoration of the viaduct.

Apart from the viaduct damage there were several places on the branch where there was some damage to ballast and track, also small landslips in cuttings.

Two views of the Linthill (Eyemouth) viaduct taken in the weeks after the Great Flood destroyed the third pier.The first view is taken from the west and the second from the eastern side. Branches and other vegetation has piled up against the other, surviving, piers.

(Both) Eyemouth Museum Collection

The rebuilding of the viaduct

Clearly the priority for British Railways was the reopening of the main East Coast route and the major effort was diverted to this. The repairs to embankments and rebuilding and reconstruction of the seven bridges that had been swept away, plus the realignment and reballasting, allowed the main line to be reopened within 12 weeks of the disaster. The expertise of military engineers as well as contractors was involved and considerable use was made of military type bridges, many of which type had been used in the World War just a few years previously. The work on repairing and refurbishing branch lines took second place. In the case of the Eyemouth line it may be fortunate that it was a socialist government at Westminster for the costs of restoration were far in excess of the commercial revenue that might have been expected to accrue from the reinstatement of the line!

Fortunately the details of the rebuilding work, both on the main line and the Eyemouth branch, were well reported in the *Railway Pictorial*, the *Railway Magazine*, the *Railway Observer* and the local press. The contractors appointed for the work were Sir Robert McAlpine (Scotland) Ltd.

The rebuilding of the viaduct commenced with the total reconstruction of the third pier. To start with steel-sheet piling was driven into the remaining gravel on the river bed to a depth of 30 ft. This formed a cofferdam into which concrete was poured to a depth of 12 ft below river bed level. This formed the base for the new pier. The pier was then constructed to its original height using a concrete core within brick facings.

A second cofferdam was constructed around pier No. 2. This was also constructed from steel-sheet piling, this time driven down to solid rock 25 ft below bed level. Concrete was then packed into the scoured portion under the foundation and into the space between the foundation and the sides of the cofferdam. Attention was now switched to the vicinity of the mill lade. A 'training wall' of sheet-steel piling was driven 25 ft downwards and then capped with concrete to form a new side for the mill lade. Material from the collapsed pier was then used to bring the bed of the lade up to within one foot of the bed level. On this was laid a concrete mat, about a foot thick. The work at the mill lade, including the laying of the concrete mat, was carried out in the dry. A liaison with the Eyemouth Milling Co. allowed the work to proceed at their convenience.

Other material from the collapsed pier was used to strengthen the banks of the lade near pier No. 2. Pier No. 4 was founded on gravel overlying solid rock. Permanent piling, driven to a depth of 12 ft, created a cofferdam around this pier into which concrete was poured between the dam walls and the pier base. A new cutwater was formed on the upside of the pier. Pier No. 5 was founded on rock. A concrete wall was created down to the rock on the river side of the pier and round one end as a protective measure. This pier was also provided with a cutwater on the upstream side.

To facilitate all of the work on piers 4 and 5 it was necessary to divert the river through a new channel created near to pier No. 3. This channel was allowed to remain when the other work was completed so that it will provide an additional channel in the event that the river floods again.

Apart from the rebuilding of the viaduct the remainder of the remedial work on the branch was carried out by British Railways' own track engineers. After testing of the structure was complete, a 'J21' locomotive hauled the first passenger train over the rebuilt viaduct. The line had been closed to all public services between 13th August, 1948 and 29th June, 1949.

Some consequences of the period of closure

After the closure of the line caused by the failure of the viaduct it became necessary to create an alternative transport link to ferry passengers between Eyemouth and Burnmouth, and to allow fish to reach its English and Scottish markets. The Scottish Motor Traction Co. (SMT) provided road coaches which linked Eyemouth with Burnmouth, but the service was extended to Berwick, providing passengers with a comfortable and improved Eyemouth-Berwick service, not requiring a change of vehicle at Burnmouth. Some passengers were lost to rail forever, preferring the facility of the bus travel and subsequent to the restoration of trains many ran almost empty. In the early 1950s, British Railways recognised this and the rail service on the branch was dramatically curtailed, making it impossible, for example, for a person to use rail travel to make a return journey to and from their place of work in Berwick. Shopping trips to Berwick by rail became impossible also.

In the case of the outward fish traffic (also other traffic such as inward coal, oil or shop supplies) a replacement road motor service was instituted. Some of the fish was taken to the short loading bay platform (then referred to as the 'fish dock') at the south end of Berwick station for trans-shipment into awaiting fish vans and onward movement by rail. Other fish was taken to its destination by road in refrigerated lorries, a traffic destined not to return to rail after the line was reinstated.

The accident to the viaduct can thus be seen as a critical point in the history of the Eyemouth branch, precipitating an irreversible downturn in its fortunes leading to the line's closure in the early 1960s. The *Railway Observer* journal commented in March 1962 just after the line had succumbed: 'The most remarkable feature of the Eyemouth Branch is probably the fact that it has survived until now.'

Top left: The appointed contractors who were given the contract for the rebuilding of the pier were Sir Robert McAlpine (Scotland) Ltd. This picture shows the construction of the coffer dam for the reconstruction of the pier. Some of the contractors plant can be seen on the left and scaffolding is being erected around one of the surviving piers.   *David Anderson Collection*

Left: On one of the buildings adjacent to the harbour is a marker indicating the maximum height reached by the water on 12th August, 1948. The heights reached in other floods are also marked but none approach the 1948 flood level!   *Author*

Chapter Fifteen

'Hie-Moo' humour

Whilst researching the newspaper archives for references to the history of the Eyemouth Railway two items were discovered which both threw some light on the nature of the Eyemouth branch and its operations, and included some 'local humour'. Rather than simply quoting selectively from them, or losing much of the flavour, pathos and content through paraphrasing, it was decided to reproduce both of the items as a separate chapter. Hopefully the reader will see the reason for their choice!

For those who haven't deduced it already, 'Hie-moo' was a former dialect pronunciation of Eyemouth.

The first article was published in the *Northern Echo* and was then reproduced in the *Berwickshire News* dated 18th May, 1909, in a regularly-appearing column entitled 'In and about Eyemouth'. The second item appeared in the *Berwickshire Advertiser* of 1st September, 1916 under a sub-heading 'Non-stop travelling', as part of a longer article about the area. (The original text, spellings and punctuation have been retained throughout.)

In and About Eyemouth

It may have been, (says "An Irresponsible Critic" in "The Northern Echo") that geographically my education was sadly neglected in earlier years, or that pressure of space in my memory department had crowded out all recollection of its exact situation, but I must confess that when suddenly commissioned by the Editor to visit Eyemouth I wondered whether it was nearer John O' Groats than Land's End, and, if so, how much. I learnt later that it was "the end of a railway".

Eyemouth is a fishing village eight miles beyond Berwick. I travelled by express to Berwick, by a slow train to Burnmouth, and then on to Eyemouth. There seems to be a sort of shunting arrangement between Burnmouth and Eyemouth and a locomotive snorts backwards and forwards at irregular intervals, and pushes or pulls, straight-backed carriages between the two.

In my compartment there were no fewer than three notices warning travellers that the penalty for improperly pulling the communication chain and stopping the train was £5. Surely it is a slander upon the good conduct of Burnmouth and Eyemouth people to suggest that they need to be thrice reminded on every journey not to stop the train.

At the first stop past Burnmouth, I dropped my carriage window, read on the arm of a platform gas-lamp the words "Melrose Station", and returned once more to my paper. A railway porter came and gazed within my compartment; then the guard came and looked suggestively through the open door, although no one wanted to enter. Two ticket collectors peered at me until I began to imagine that the whole population had surely never before scanned a thunder-and-lightning check fancy waistcoat. When the porter returned, and, after a lengthy look at the other side of my paper, leisurely lifted up the window, and still lingered longer, I looked up and waited.

"This is the end of the railway", he remarked awkwardly. If he had said that it was the end of the world, I should hardly have been more astonished. I replied that I had booked for Eyemouth whereupon he retorted, "This is Eyemouth"

"Is it the terminus?" I asked again.

"I dinna ken aboot that, but the rails dinna gae nae further", he answered doggedly.

And so it was. I detrained and going up to that gas lamp, carefully scrutinised it. It had "Melrose Station" cast in raised characters on the arm, right enough.

The next gas lamp further along the platform was stranger still, If not quite so misleading. Cast in similar characteristics on its arm it said simply the date "1863". There must be a story behind those lamp-posts.

Eyemouth is a one-time very prosperous fishing village, at present under a cloud. Its population in 1901 was 2,487 and that figure still represents the strength of the village. There has been a decline, for there were 200 more people in the place in 1891, whilst in 1881 the census returns showed a population of 2,935.

A walk along the harbour edge brings you into contact with many men. Wise men they are, despite the fact that some would write their name with difficulty, if, indeed, they could accomplish the feat at all. Their knowledge of tomorrow's weather, gained from seagulls, glass, the heavens, and other portents, is profound and reliable, albeit somewhat uncanny.

I inquired about public-houses and chapels – or should the order be chapels and public houses. "It's wan to wan," my informant replied. "There's six of each of them – a fair stand-up fight it is."

Time was – and not many years ago either – when there were at least 20 licensed houses in the village, but with the growth of travelling facilities custom dropped off and some of these licenses quietly dropped out of the running.

The 14th October of 1881 is remembered as "Black Friday" for on that date a sudden storm enveloped the fishing fleet and broke up many of the boats. Altogether 189 fishermen were drowned.

House accommodation is cheap enough, for a two-roomed house may be rented for £7-10s per annum. But trade is bad. There seems to be little fish in the sea. Some fear that warships and naval manoeuvring has killed the little fishes; others are afraid that the trawling has denuded the German Ocean. It may be thought that the educated fishes of modern times now know that trawling less than three miles out is illegal, and thus keep out of peril!

It was whispered that Mr. H. J. Tennant, M.P., who represents the constituency, is agitating for an extension of the three mile limit, but not being an old salt myself, I cannot say whether any benefit would accrue or not. As a holiday resort the village grows in favour, but I do not think that the villagers quite relish these friendly invasions.

Non-stop Travelling

The Eyemouth express has been the but [sic] of every alleged wit in the neighbourhood for the last half century, but when the natives of the salubrious seaside resort observed a brand new engine and newly painted carriages appear on the system, they resolved that here at last "Hie-moo" would confound its critics. Alas! Vain dreams, phantoms of this transitory life, the glorious picture of municipal mug-wumps being drawn at lightning speed up the steep declivity to Burnmouth, has vanished into naught. On Friday at 3.30pm., and four fifths of a second to be precise, the train started from the platform amid the usual din of whistles and thumps. Everything went well until the Eye was crossed, when the engine developed an action like the cakewalk of our childhood days. Again and again it advanced, but being unable to consolidate its position, was perforce obliged to retreat, for reasons of strategy. A gentleman with a business-like hammer endeavoured to encourage the sandbox to perform its necessary functions, while another was observed to be engaged in laying minute pieces of engine ash upon the metals. Continuing the advance under difficulty, each inch of the ground being contested, Burnmouth was reached at 4.15pm., - exactly three quarters of an hour after starting. Some blame the rain for having moistened the rails and causing the stoppage, - but personally we are under the impression that the many wagons of "kippered steaks" which made up the train were largely responsible.

The site of the former Burnmouth station in 2018 as an East Coast 125 set heads towards Edinburgh. The tracks have been slightly realigned at this point to permit faster running through the curve. The former Eyemouth bay is occupied by a large box of electronics. *Author*

Chapter Sixteen

Remains of the branch
at the start of the 21st century

It is always necessary to be prudent when describing the remains of any railway route or buildings or relics. The present author experienced some considerable embarrassment following the publication of two of his earlier works. In one volume the continued existence of some 150-year-old sleeper blocks, incorporated into a wall, was described. Subsequent to the book's publication these blocks were partly vandalized and the wooden 'plugs' used for fixing the rail spikes were removed. In another volume the author described the remains of some track from a narrow gauge industrial line which existed on private property to which, kindly, he had been given access by the owners. Despite this being stated in the text and with cautionary comments about gaining access, some individuals seemed to regard the possession of the volume as a 'passport' to access the site, causing some annoyance to the landowner. Private property should only be accessed with permission.

At Burnmouth the former station site is best observed from the overbridge on the Eyemouth to Burnmouth road which takes traffic over the East Coast main line. The two tracks of this line were slewed towards the east after the branch rails were removed to reduce track curvature at this point. This new alignment now occupies part of the site of the former Eyemouth branch platform and track. The signal box was also removed as the signalling was centralized (Marshall Meadows is the boundary of signalling control between Edinburgh signalling centre and Tweedmouth signal box).

To the left, or west, side of the main line the station building survives, albeit modified, and is now a private house. The former access to Burnmouth station yard and goods shed forms the entrance to this property and to another adjacent house. The area between the station building and the trackbed now forms part of the owner's garden though at one point to the north of the property a small section of the former platform can be seen. The former goods shed and weighhouse survive. The derelict remains of the former wooden staircase leading from the station to the main road exist on the property but are overgrown and can only be viewed with permission. The view from the bridge includes modern railway equipment, including overhead wiring and colour-light signals on both up and down lines. A lay-by on the A1 to the west of Burnmouth provides an alternative view towards Burnmouth station though the buildings are largely obscured by vegetation.

At the west end of this lay-by is the junction of the lane which links the A1 with Fairnieside and its farm. The lane passes under the main line via a concrete and stone bridge. Just beyond the main line bridge are the abutments of the bridge which formerly carried the Eyemouth line over the lane.

In the direction of Edinburgh the A1 highway passes beneath the main line on a large modern bridge, shortly after which its new route forms the Ayton by-pass. For a short distance this road encroaches upon the former curved alignment of the Eyemouth branch. The main road crosses the steep-sided

The steps, leading down from the Eyemouth Road at Burnmouth formerly led to the down platform and the Eyemouth bay. Now they provide, via a locked gate, access to the trackbed for Network Rail workers.   *Author*

The former station building at Burnmouth is now converted to a private house though it still shows signs of its former purpose. The station clock, albeit non-working, adorns the exterior wall on the right and on a lintel above a door is the legend 'Booking Office'. *Author*

The garden of the station house at Burnmouth retains several of the buildings which were in operation when the station still functioned. The former goods shed is shown here. A small part of the edge of the former up platform can be seen a few yards away. *Author*

Access to the footpath along part of the old trackbed can only be made with permission from the Ayton Estate. A former occupation bridge can still be seen crossing the trackbed about halfway between Fairnieside and the former viaduct. In winter the trackbed is very boggy in places, especially in the cuttings.   *Barrie Forrest*

Gilsland bridge can be viewed by descending the steps from the Ayton Road near to the new bridge over the Eyewater. The ground level on the north side of the bridge has been raised by filling the cutting and the parapet has been removed. This is the view from the side of the Eyewater on the south side showing the bridge's skew nature.   *Barrie Forrest*

valley of the Eye Water by means of a new bridge shortly after its junction with the direct new road, the A1107, built to link Eyemouth with the A1. The works associated with building this road junction and the recent growth of trees make the tracing of some of the alignment of the former branch line quite difficult even with the aid of aerial photographs! However, a short distance along the A1107 Eyemouth road a track leads off to the left (or north-west); this was the alignment of the railway and some of the original post-and-wire fencing can still be spotted. Viewed from the A1107 the line of the former trackbed lay just to the west of the present-day fields and can be identified on present-day aerial photographs which are viewable 'on-line'. From the road the curved boundaries visible on the far side of these fields run parallel to the line's former route! However all of this section of the line lies on the Ayton Estate and access to the casual visitor via the fields is not possible without express permission. Trees are rapidly hiding the curved section of line before the site of the former viaduct which took the line over the Eye, though evidence of the former drainage work on the cutting sides is still visible. A pedestrian overbridge to the east of Balabraes (on the opposite bank of the Eyewater) survives. This crosses the former line which is in a cutting at this point. However, this can only be accessed from the A1107 via the edges of some of the fields of Redhall Farm and there is no right of public access without express permission.

It is now necessary to cross to the other side of the river as the remains of the Eyewater viaduct can best be seen from the B6355 Ayton to Eyemouth road close to Old Linthill. By car this necessitates a journey towards Eyemouth, a left turn at the crossroads after the new River Eye bridge then following directions for Ayton (B6335). After about a kilometre along this road, and just before a sharp right-hand bend, it is possible look through the gaps in the roadside hedge on the left and the viaduct pillars will be seen, especially in winter months when the trees have shed their leaves. In summer, only a couple of the brick-built pillars are clearly visible. Direction should now be reversed towards Eyemouth. (Care is needed. This road has some blind bends.)

Trees also hide much of the high embankment which led the line from the viaduct towards Biglawburn siding but they clearly indicate its route. Once again, permission is needed to cross the farmland between the B6335 road and the viaduct remains so as to gain a closer view.

Returning towards Eyemouth, on the right-hand side just after the 30 mph speed restriction sign, is a bungalow with garden which lies at the south end of the former Biglawburn siding yard and siding site. Beyond this is some undeveloped, rather rough ground which was formerly part of the Biglawburn yard. A very short metalled driveway marks the former gated entrance to this yard. Continuing towards Eyemouth the road raises slightly to the Biglawburn bridge with its stone parapets. The trackbed under the bridge itself survives but the view of it from the roadside is partly obscured by the new bungalow and the buildings in its garden. Approaching the north side of the bridge from the adjacent field requires the permission of the farmer. Looking southwards the general position of the former trackbed can be seen as it led towards Biglawburn siding, embankment and viaduct. Looking to the north the former track alignment can just be identified as it leads behind the houses on the right.

The piers of the former Linthill viaduct still stand proud over the Eyewater though they are somewhat hidden by foliage. Approaching them requires permission as it is necessary to cross private land which may contain livestock. The bases of the piers retain the concrete strengthening which was constructed following the rebuilding of the viaduct after the 1948 'Great Storm'.

Author

Near to the former Eyemouth terminus the trackbed has been converted into a short riverside pathway approached via steps from both the Ayton Road and Victoria Road. It passes beneath the new concrete replacement for the former Toll Bridge. Seats are provided and the path is popular with dog-walkers.   *Author*

Seen from Brown's Bank on the south side of the river, the former Eyemouth station site is now overgrown by trees and shrubs. However the spire of the parish church and the buildings at the side of the river help identify the location. This was a favourite vantage point for railway photographers in the 20th century.   *Author*

The location of the end of the former third and fourth rail lines, close to their buffer stops, can be reached using the riverside path. This view, looking downstream towards the harbour, is taken from that point. On the right is the boatyard, in the distance is Guns Green House museum and the harbour commences a short distance beyond the footbridge across the Eye.   *Author*

This steep driveway was originally the Eyemouth station approach road for both passengers and carts carrying goods. It was perpetually rough and muddy in North British Railway days. Later, access for passengers could be gained via the flight of steps leading down from Victoria Road directly onto the platform.   *Author*

Further on towards Eyemouth lies Eyemouth or Netherbyres Mill on the right of the road. From the roadside pavement the Eyewater can be seen in the valley below the mill and the mill leat. Then, just after the side road known as Gilsland, a bridge parapet comes into view on the right-hand side of the road only. The parapet on the left was removed some time ago as the railway cutting beneath was filled in. This skewed bridge led the road over the railway as it curved towards the Eye at the approach to Eyemouth station. A little further on, and opposite the Eyemouth town sign, is a bus shelter to the side of which is a sign-posted stepped path leading down to the bank of the river. From the lower end of this path there is a view of the abutments and parapet of the road bridge.

It is then possible to walk along the side of the river, in the main along the former trackbed, passing under the modern replacement of the former Toll Bridge. The path, in part laid on the old rail ballast, continues under the trees towards the former station site though all of the former rails and buildings have long-since disappeared. The former position of the siding immediately next to the river can be noted. A stepped path leads back up towards Victoria Road by the car park. Another view of the former station site can be obtained from the other side of the river at Browns Bank which can be approached via The Avenue, the first left turn after having crossed the new bridge on the Burnmouth road.

Further along the Victoria Road towards Eyemouth the parish church dominates the skyline to the left. This appeared in many old photographs of Eyemouth station. On the opposite side of the road, a few yards beyond the parish church gate, is Eyemouth Roman Catholic church, a pebble-dashed building with a tiled roof. The roadway in front of this leads down the bank towards the old station site. The usual warnings apply as to approaching, and photographing, what is now private property and land.

The car park on the left of Harbour Road provides a good base from which to explore the lower reaches of the river, and the parts of the harbour with public access. On one building a marker indicates the level to which the water level rose in the 1948 floods. The footbridge over the river allows pedestrians an alternative access to Browns Bank from which so many photographs of Eyemouth station were taken.

A walk along Harbour Road reveals the buildings associated with the present-day fishing industry and a short diversion can be made to the Eyemouth Museum which houses a model of the former station. On making an appointment it is possible to examine various photographs and documents associated with the local railway and fishing industries, in addition to those on public display.

Fortunately a number of relics of the Eyemouth branch have been preserved, some *in situ* and some removed for safekeeping. These include buildings, signs, railway lamps, a clock, photographs plus items of ephemera such as documents, timetables and railway tickets. Some are in public ownership such as the maps and plans in safekeeping at the House of Commons Library, the National Archive, the Scottish Archive in Edinburgh and the local record offices and museum. Some, such as the remains of the platform edge, the goods shed and other railway buildings, survive at the former Burnmouth station, plus the remains of the quay wall between Eyemouth sidings and the River Eye and the former ramp leading down to the station from Victoria Road.

Various photographic archives and collections contain images of the line, its stations, buildings and its trains, sometimes in the form of commercially published postcards. Often internet websites sell reproductions of these or, at greater expense, original items. Often copyright is retained with the vendors. Railway tickets or other printed material items relating to the line rarely appear on such sites but a variety of tickets lies in the hands of collectors of such ephemera.

Relics of the line, often with a high sale value, such as enamel signs or hand-lamps, have generally been removed for safekeeping into both private and public collections though some are integrated into remaining buildings such as the painted Booking Office sign on a stone lintel at Burnmouth station.

The present author has been delighted to gain access to, and photograph, some such items, though for obvious security reasons their precise locations are not advertised!

A railway paraffin lamp, salvaged from Burnmouth station after closure, is now in safe hands in a private collection. It forms an impressive ornament!   *Author*

Epilogue

Last train to Burnmouth
by Jim Sedgwick

This article was written by Jim Sedgwick who travelled on the last train from Eyemouth to Burnmouth and it appeared in the edition of Branch Line News *for March 1962. It is reproduced here with permission.*

On Monday, 5th February, the axe fell on yet another branch line, this time the ex-North British single track branch from Burnmouth to Eyemouth.

Due to the closure of the Peebles loop on the same date the one man expedition from Northallerton had only swelled to a four man party by the time the 10.00 am York-Edinburgh reached Berwick. The five and a half miles to Burnmouth were covered by 'bus and the writer commenced to walk to Eyemouth, taking photographs at various points along the line.

The branch commences in a bay at Burnmouth with suitable connections to the main line, and falls at 1 in 50 for about a mile before a deep rock cutting is reached where the gradient eases. Once out of the cutting the Eye Water is crossed on an iron viaduct supported by brick piers. Biglawburn Siding situated just beyond the viaduct was the unloading point of diesel fuel for fishing boats and a small storage tank is situated here. The final mile falls gently towards Eyemouth with a short section at 1 in 50 just before the small one platform is reached. In addition to the platform road there are three sidings and a small cattle dock situated, rather awkwardly, at the platform end.

Photography was difficult due to a torrential downpour as the 3.22 left for Burnmouth, consisting of a 'J39' with one ex-LNER brake compo. Better conditions prevailed, however, for the capture on film on the 3.55 pm arrival, which, strangely to relate, carried a coffin, destined to be the last 'parcel' to reach Eyemouth by rail. By this time, about ten serious enthusiasts had arrived and taken shelter in the waiting room from the biting wind. However, they were almost immediately asked to stand up by a porter who solemnly picked up the only bench, put it on his shoulder, and was last seen carrying it down Eyemouth's main street! One enterprising enthusiast thought that the last train should have a clean engine, so after purloining some paraffin and rags set about organising an engine cleaning party with such success that when the final departure came, the 'J39' fairly shone, all the grime and most of the paraffin was on the amateur engine cleaners. Indeed the station master had to remove several paraffiny handmarks from the first-class doors with newspaper and the 'North Briton' had a very peculiar smell in some compartments, as far as Newcastle.

The final run to Burnmouth and back was accompanied by the usual volleys of detonators and the solitary coach was well filled with local people. After arrival at Eyemouth for the last time, the 'J39' shunted around its coach and ambled off to Tweedmouth, so ending the career of a little line which ended as it began – with steam.

Acknowledgements

I would like to acknowledge with much gratitude the assistance provided by the following organizations and individuals that have been generous in providing assistance with my research.

The Berwick-upon-Tweed Record Office
Berwick Public Library
National Library of Scotland
National Archives of Scotland
National Records of Scotland
The Scottish Fisheries Museum, Anstruther
The National Archives, Kew
The Eyemouth Museum
Eyemouth Public Library
Eyemouth Maritime Centre
Lincolnshire Archives
Heritage Hub, Hawick (Scottish Borders Archive and Local History Centre)
Search Engine (National Railway Museum, York)
Parliamentary Archives, House of Commons Library
Birmingham: Archive, History and Photographic Service
Wolfson Centre, Library of Birmingham
National Mining Museum of Scotland (Newtongrange)
Messrs W.S. Scott, Birmingham (fish merchants)
Doughty's, W.S., Ayton, solicitors and estate agents
Ordnance Survey
Meteorological Office, London
BBC Weather Centre

Neil and Alan Craig, Ed Chester, David Dougal, Malcolm Snowball, Mel Lockett, Roger Darsley, Alex Weatherhead, Jim Sedgwick, John Burgon, David Tyreman, John Kay, the late Neil MacKichan, Kim Creamer, Gordon Hall, David Anderson, Barrie Forrest, Gareth Patterson, Barry Prater, David Dunn, Ian Moffatt, Alan Thompson, Richard Stenlake, Paul Stewart, Bill Lynn.

Members of the Railway Correspondence and Travel Society
Aln Valley Railway Archive

Officers and members of the North British Railway Study Group. In particular I must single out for very special thanks Donald Cattanach of the NBRSG who kindly made available his own notes on G.B. Wieland and the early history of the Eyemouth Railway.

Various websites have helped confirm dates and provide useful information including Wikipedia, LNER Encyclopaedia, Railscot, Scottish Archives for Schools, History Shelf, *The Scotsman*, Digmore and Canmore.

Bibliography

The following books, journals and websites, contain further reading or photographs related to the Eyemouth Railway; all of these have been consulted.

The Eight Minute Link: The Lost Eyemouth Branch Line (Lawson Wood)
  Ocean Eye/Fantasy Prints Publication
Black Friday – the Eyemouth Fishing Disaster of 1881 (Peter Aitchison) Birlinn Ltd
Main Lines Across the Border (O.S. Nock & Derek Cross) Ian Allan
British Locomotive Catalogue 1825-1923, Volume 6 (Bertram Baxter, David Baxter and Peter
  Mitchell) Kestrel Railway Books
The North British Railway Volumes 1 & 2, (John Thomas) David & Charles
North Eastern Locomotive Sheds (Ken Hoole) David & Charles
Locomotives at the Grouping: London & North Eastern Railway
  (H.C. Casserley & S.W. Johnston) Ian Allan
The North British Railway (Hamilton Ellis) Ian Allan
The North British Railway – A History (David Ross) Stenlake Publishing
LNER Carriages (Michael Harris) Atlantic Transport Publishers
Locomotives of the North British Railway 1846-1882 (The Stephenson Locomotive Society)
Berwick to Drem (Roger Darsley and Dennis Lovett) Middleton Press
St. Boswells to Berwick via Duns (Roger Darsley and Dennis Lovett) Middleton Press
BR Steam Motive Power Depots: North Eastern Region (Paul Bolger) Booklaw Publications
Railway Passenger Stations in Great Britain: A Chronology (Michael Quick)
  Railway and Canal Historical Society
Random Reflections of a Roving Railwayman (J.M. Bennett) J & G. Innes, Cupar, Fife.
The Eyemouth Branch (Brian Flatman)
  A duplicated publication published for Eyemouth Museum
The Great Borders Flood of 1948 (Lawson Wood) The History Press
Bradshaw's Handbook 1863 Old House Books (Reprint)
A Picture of Scotland (Robert Chambers) William Tait
Slaters Directory of Scotland (various editions)
Post Office Directory (various editions)

Minutes, record books and letters of the Eyemouth Railway and Eyemouth Town Council
Bradshaw's and railway company timetables: various editions
The North British Railway Study Group Journal: various editions

Various editions of *Steam Days, Railway Modeller, Railway Bylines, Locomotives Illustrated, The Engineer, Illustrated London News, Branch Line News, Railway Observer* and *Country Life*

Various editions of the following newspapers: *Berwick Advertiser, Berwickshire News, Southern Reporter, The Scotsman, Dundee Courier, Sunderland Daily Echo, Shipping Gazette, Yorkshire Post, Windsor Magazine, Hawick News, Border Chronicle, Lanarkshire Daily Record, Whitstable Times, Herne Bay Herald, York Herald, Western Times* (Devon), *Sheffield Evening Telegrap*h and the *Portsmouth Evening News*. (Copies of these were consulted on their own websites or those of the National Newspaper Library. Editions dated after 1956, which have not been microfilmed, and those which are illegible or are missing from the websites were consulted in hard copy.)

Various public passenger timetables, also goods and working timetables, both in private ownership, in the North British Railway Study Group Collection and at the National Railway Museum.

Scottish Census Records: 1891 and 1901.

Index